NO UNIVERSITY

IS AN ISLAND

CULTURAL FRONT

General Editor: Michael Bérubé

Manifesto of a Tenured Radical
Cary Nelson

Bad Subjects: Political Education for Everyday Life
Edited by the Bad Subjects Production Team

Claiming Disability: Knowledge and Identity
Simi Linton

The Employment of English: Theory, Jobs, and the Future of Literary Studies
Michael Bérubé

Feeling Global: Internationalism in Distress
Bruce Robbins

Doing Time: Feminist Theory and Postmodern Culture
Rita Felski

Modernism, Inc.: Body, Memory, Capital
Edited by Jani Scandura and Michael Thurston

Bending Over Backwards:
Disability, Dismodernism, and Other Difficult Positions
Lennard J. Davis

After Whiteness: Unmaking an American Majority
Mike Hill

Critics at Work: Interviews 1993–2003
Edited by Jeffrey J. Williams

Crip Theory: Cultural Signs of Queerness and Disability
Robert McRuer

How the University Works: Higher Education and the Low-Wage Nation
Marc Bousquet
Foreword by Cary Nelson

Deaf Subjects: Between Identities and Places
Brenda Jo Brueggemann

The Left at War
Michael Bérubé

No University Is an Island: Saving Academic Freedom
Cary Nelson

NO UNIVERSITY IS AN ISLAND

Saving Academic Freedom

Cary Nelson

 NEW YORK UNIVERSITY PRESS
New York and London

NEW YORK UNIVERSITY PRESS
New York and London
www.nyupress.org

Library of Congress Cataloging-in-Publication Data

Nelson, Cary.
No university is an island : saving academic freedom / Cary Nelson.
p. cm.
Includes bibliographical references and index.
ISBN-13: 978–0–8147–5859–5 (cl : alk. paper)
ISBN-10: 0–8147–5859–2 (cl : alk. paper)
1. Education, Higher—Philosophy. 2. Education, Higher—Political
aspects. 3. Universities and colleges—Political aspects. 4. Academic
freedom. 5. Teaching, Freedom of. 6. Intellectual freedom. 7. Political
correctness. 8. American Association of University Professors. Committee on Academic Freedom. I. Title.
 LB2322.2.N45   2010
 378.1'213—dc22   2009030682

New York University Press books are printed on acid-free paper,
and their binding materials are chosen for strength and durability.
We strive to use environmentally responsible suppliers and materials
to the greatest extent possible in publishing our books.

Manufactured in the United States of America

10 9 8 7 6 5 4 3 2 1

CONTENTS

ACKNOWLEDGMENTS

No University Is an Island is a book that in many ways wrote itself, at least in the sense that I did not have to choose relevant topics. The issues I take up represent my effort to synthesize and theorize what I learned on scores of trips to campuses across the United States and at meetings here and in Australia, Canada, and Britain. The chapters reflect the concerns faculty members raise when I talk with them. Condensed versions of almost all the chapters have been read aloud before multiple audiences, and they now embody the topics covered in discussion. Then at meals and receptions people told me anecdotes that found their way into the book as well. All of this, of course, came with more focus and urgency because of my role as president of the American Association of University Professors. Especially intense have been several conferences sponsored by COCAL (Coalition of Contingent Academic Labor), where I gave presentations and talked at length with activists from Canada, Mexico, and the United States. Then I was lucky enough to speak at several conferences devoted entirely to academic freedom, at Cornell University, Indiana University of Pennsylvania, and New York University. I talked with less sympathetic audiences when I debated Peter Wood of the National Association of Scholars and David Horowitz of Students for Academic Freedom at their annual conferences. I visited with AAUP chapters and state conferences throughout the country, in North and South Carolina, New Jersey, Connecticut, New Hampshire, Maryland, Vermont, Michigan, Ohio, Indiana, Illinois, Iowa, Oklahoma, Kansas, Oregon, California, and Washington. AAUP Summer Institutes in Nevada, Rhode Island, Oregon, and Minnesota provided further opportunities for formal and informal interaction. Twice the California Faculty Association provided unforgettable experiences. A series of presentations on academic freedom—and occasions to embody its principles as a member of the Delegate Assembly—arose at annual meetings of the Modern Language Association. And I read portions of the manuscript and took questions before audiences at McGill University, Connecticut College, the University of Florida, Pacific Lutheran University, Indiana State University, Illinois State University, the University of Illinois at Chicago, the University of Connecticut, the University of Michigan, the University of Vermont, the University of Rochester, the University of New Hampshire, the University of Washington, Ohio State University, Harvard University, Kansas Sate University, the University of Alberta in Canada, the University of Birmingham in England, the University of Illinois YMCA, the annual meeting of the Canadian Association of University Teachers (CAUT) in Ottawa, the annual meeting of the Society for the Humanities in Canberra, Australia, the annual conference on collective bargaining at Hunter College, the Nonstop Liberal Arts Institute in Yellow Springs, Ohio, and a GESO rally at Yale University.

More people than I can easily remember offered advice along the way, but some merit special mention. First, NYU Press found three careful and thoughtful readers whose detailed suggestions significantly improved the manuscript. My editor, Eric Zinner, was helpful with good suggestions at every stage of the process. My series editor, Michael Bérubé, maintained a running dialogue with me about the manuscript. My colleague Bill Maxwell was kind enough to read chapter 4, "Barefoot in New Zealand," confirming the accuracy of my memory of events during a department hiring process and correcting my chronology at one point. Andrew Ross, co-president of the NYU AAUP chapter and a member of the national AAUP's Committee A, reviewed my account of the graduate employee strike at NYU in chapter 6, based on his own active participation in those events, and discussed it with me in detail. Jeff Butts (AAUP vice president), Jane Buck (previous AAUP president), Michael Bérubé (AAUP Executive Committee member), and Martin Snyder (AAUP associate general secretary) generously gave the same help with chapters 8 and 9, while also offering advice about what events I might most usefully relate. Jeff Halpern (AAUP Executive Committee member, chair of the AAUP's Collective Bargaining Congress, and long-term Committee A member) and I had repeated conversations about the issues I discuss. Gary

Rhoades (AAUP general secretary) provided helpful suggestions about an early version of the introduction. Though he may not be happy with all of my conclusions, I should also say that the book benefited from years of conversation with (and a few scenes of instruction from) Ernst Benjamin, former AAUP general secretary and longtime Committee A activist. The Executive Committee as a whole held detailed discussions about the future of the AAUP from which I learned a great deal. My ongoing conversations with Committee A members have been equally useful. Several members of the AAUP's national staff, including John Curtis, Mike Ferguson, Bob Kreiser, Jordan Kurland, and Greg Scholtz, helped with references, statistical information, and suggestions for reading. Finally, my sternest critic for the past four decades, my partner, Paula A. Treichler, had a number of observations about what follows.

There are a number of key documents that I refer to several times. They include two AAUP statements, the classic 1915 "Declaration of Principles on Academic Freedom and Academic Tenure," and the 2007 "Freedom in the Classroom," as well as the detailed interlinear critique of the latter document issued by Peter Wood and Stephen Balch on behalf of the National Association of Scholars. They are all listed in the bibliography and all available online. The testimonials by Stanley Katz (Princeton) and Kate Bronfenbrenner (Cornell) that serve as epigraphs to chapters 8 and 9 were written for AAUP brochures. A series of those testimonials to the AAUP are reproduced on my website (www.cary-nelson.org), which also includes detailed information about my publishing history.

Finally, let me identify a double purpose for one section of the book, Chapter 8. Intended as a narrative warning to the AAUP of the danger of backsliding and abandoning the elected leadership's hard-won oversight capacity, it is also designed to give notice to other nonprofits with weak oversight. They would do well, for example, to adopt the careful financial practices the AAUP put in place in 2008. The AAUP now gives its elected treasurer real time electronic access to its ongoing financial transactions, not just periodic reports. The AAUP learned that necessity the hard way, but the financial reporting at nonprofits and throughout much of higher education is also inadequate.

Introduction

What Is Academic Freedom?

The history of academic freedom in some respects predates the use of the term. The need for the concept grew out of the long history of universities and their struggle for freedom from church and state. The medieval university had sought a degree of independence from the church, but that did not entail doctrinal independence for the faculty. Nor was the chance that faculty might spread uncertainty among the general populace tolerated. It took later cultural changes—from developments in science and philosophy, to increased exposure to national differences, to wider commercial contacts—to prepare the ground for the modern university and its essential freedoms. Academic freedom thus embodies Enlightenment commitments to the pursuit of knowledge and their adaptation to different social and political realities. The term *akademische Freiheit* was in use in Germany by the early nineteenth century and gradually gained acceptance there over the following fifty years.

Transplanting the concept to the United States, however, required significant adjustment. Although German professors were effectively state employees, German universities were essentially self-governing. But it would be an error to assume that nineteenth-century German faculty members had full academic freedom as we understand it today. American universities on the other hand were governed not by faculty but by nineteenth-century versions of boards of trustees. As denominational institutions in the United States began to be replaced by secular ones, religious boards became less common. Secular institutions had governing boards often composed of members of the business community. By the late nine-teenth and early twentieth centuries some of the conflicts between faculty and commercial interests that we know today were already in place in the United States. American universities faced interventions in their affairs quite unlike anything the German prototypes had experienced. When conflicts with their masters arose, American faculty discovered they were employees who could be dismissed at will.

In response to arbitrary dismissals and the threat they posed to the faculty's capacity to teach and pursue research in an unhindered fashion and to serve the broader needs of society, the founders of the American Association of University Professors (AAUP) articulated guarantees of academic freedom and job security. The 1915 "Declaration of Principles on Academic Freedom and Academic Tenure" includes passages whose eloquence can still serve us well, albeit with some qualification. At the time, before faculty collective bargaining had arrived on the scene, there was no risk in rejecting the notion that faculty were employees. A more nuanced model is now required. Yet the 1915 Declaration's insistence on the fundamental autonomy of the faculty in its key areas of responsibil-ity still stands, even if its qualified analogy between faculty members and judicial appointees seems at best hypothetical. The sense of urgency in the text will no doubt strike some readers as distinctly mandarin, though, as Bruce Robbins has warned, professionalism is always at risk of appearing elitist and undemocratic: "Indeed, it is hard *not* to present—as an offense against democracy. To repose interpretive authority in a community of professionals is to put it where it is not accessible to everyone" (Robbins 339). Jeffrey Nealon has suggested that the AAUP's analogy between fac-ulty members and judicial appointees may in part have been designed to make faculty professional elitism seem familiar and acceptable. But the elitist element in the claim nonetheless makes it vulnerable not only to American anti-intellectualism but also to loss of public faith that what people want from higher education depends on faculty privilege. The argument that academic freedom is a social good thus needs to be made personal, to be supplemented by an appeal to the public's self-interest. Parents must, for example, be persuaded that their children cannot get the full benefit of higher education unless faculty have academic freedom and job security. People are also, of course, less tolerant of special privileges when they are themselves confronted with employment insecurity or income loss. Here is a key passage from the AAUP's 1915 Declaration:

> The freedom which is the subject of this report is the freedom of the teacher. Academic freedom in this sense comprises three elements: freedom of inquiry and research; freedom of teaching within the university or college; and freedom of extramural utterance and action. . . . These considerations make still more clear the nature of the relationship between university trustees and members of university faculties. The latter are the appointees, but not in any proper sense the employees of the former. For, once appointed, the scholar has professional functions to perform in which the appointing authorities have neither competency nor moral right to intervene. The responsibility of the university teacher is primarily to the public itself, and to the judgment of his own profession. . . . So far as the university teacher's independence of thought and utterance is concerned— though not in other regards—the relationship of professor to trustees may be compared to that between judges of the federal courts and the executive who appoints them. University teachers should be understood to be, with respect to the conclusions reached and expressed by them, no more subject to the control of the trustees than are the judges subject to the control of the president with respect to their decisions. (292, 295)

At the immediate functional level, academic freedom serves as my assurance that I can do as I choose in my teaching and research. No doubt that arrogant definition will light vengeful fires in the hearts of conservative adversaries. Yet it is marked by cultural, professional, disciplinary, legal, administrative, departmental, and psychological constraints that could take more than a lifetime to unravel. Even my desires do not arise independently. Most of what I want to do in the classroom grows out of decades of disciplinary and institutional involvement. I spend the overwhelming majority of class time analyzing texts. The course schedule is shaped by the syllabus I write, a syllabus that mirrors disciplinary protocols and amounts to a public commitment. Perhaps I could better challenge my students if I could dream more wildly and unpredictably, but for better or worse I am, like other faculty, a product of my times and my experience.

Academic freedom thus maximizes my flexibility within the bounds of the traditions that have shaped me and the professional responsibilities I have accepted. I cannot devote my class on African American poetry to the study of bird migration. But the discipline admits wide latitude on what a course in African American poetry might emphasize. Or what you might learn from African American poetry and apply to other subjects. In a 2007 online response to the AAUP's statement on "Freedom in the Classroom"—a notable moment in the current debates reshaping the meaning of academic freedom—Peter Wood and Steven Balch of the National Association of Scholars (NAS) expressed strong skepticism about the AAUP's assertion that a course on British Romanticism might devote some time to Harlem Renaissance poets. Yet I often conclude a course on a particular historical period by exploring its legacy, just as I often begin one by looking at its predecessors. I do not *have* to do so. But I can, whether or not the catalog description of the course covers such details. That right is covered by academic freedom. To be sure, the influence of the Romantic lyric is wide and deep, but there are many good reasons to unsettle student assumptions about the racialized character of literary influence by including, say, Harlem Renaissance poet Countee Cullen's poems about John Keats, including "To John Keats, Poet, at Spring Time," among the examples of the legacy of Romanticism. The NAS's bluster on this point represents an argument conducted in ignorance and bad faith. So long as we maintain the shared governance practices that promote academic freedom, I am, happily, protected from those who would police my teaching in ignorance of the historical record.

Unlike the NAS, conservative critic David Horowitz does not specialize in skepticism. He specializes in manufactured outrage, manufactured outrage about women's studies, manufactured outrage about the excesses of leftist professors. When I last debated him—at the University of Oregon in February 2008—students testified on a film shown before the debate that they had noted one clear example of faculty bias: disrespect for Fox News. Horowitz allowed that this was "the single worst example of political bias in the academy he had ever encountered." Obviously I am missing something. Disrespect for Fox News for me represents the exercise of the minimal intellectual and cultural judgment required of someone willing to stand before a classroom. So long as those who share his unwarranted outrage have no power over me, I can continue to express such views in the classroom or in print. I am protected by academic freedom.

These functional examples, however, do not in themselves exhaust the complexity or flexibility of the concept of academic freedom. The concept of academic freedom exists in differential relationship with a series of other concepts, discourses, and cultural domains. It is of necessity frequently rearticulated to new challenges, technologies, and historical conditions. It has legal, professional, institutional, and symbolic meanings that cannot easily be encapsulated by a simple definition. When the AAUP a few years ago sought to adopt a slogan to promote itself, a couple of us independently came up with the same suggestion: "Academic freedom for a free society." We were not alluding to the legal status of academic freedom. We were invoking its cultural and political meaning. The slogan recognized that the concept of academic freedom has links with other aspirational elements of American history and culture. It suggests that academic freedom has a fundamental relationship with the Declaration of Independence and with the Bill of Rights. It asks us to reflect on how academic freedom helps preserve our other freedoms, however imperfectly they may be realized. Indeed the U.S. Supreme Court in *Keyishan v. Board of Regents* in 1967 ruled that academic freedom is a "special concern" of the First Amendment, though the Court never really clarified what that meant. Did the Court mean to elevate academic freedom to a fundamental constitutional principle or merely to assign it to a subcategory to be limited by the character of college and university employment? As Stacy Smith notes, "federal courts often use, but do not explain, the term 'academic freedom'" (300). Nonetheless, Justice Brennan's language in the majority opinion is worth quoting more fully: "Academic freedom," he wrote, "is of transcendent value to all of us and not merely to the teachers concerned. That freedom is therefore a special concern of the First Amendment, which does not tolerate laws that cast a pall of orthodoxy over the classroom."

Brennan's comment suggests that academic freedom is an individual right, since the individual teacher makes most pedagogical decisions. Yet, as Philippa Strum demonstrates, the Court has really never differentiated individual from institutional academic freedom: "As defined in the courts of the United States it frequently appears as an institutional right—one that presumably can be exercised against the individual faculty member" (152). Though the courts have in other contexts treated academic freedom as an individual right, it is clear that in the end the AAUP will have to step in to define the distinction between institutional authority and individual faculty rights, recognizing that the latter, like free speech rights, are not absolute.

In *There's No Such Thing as Free Speech and It's a Good Thing, Too*, Stanley Fish argues that true freedom of speech does not exist and thus that the concept is useless, thereby ignoring the productive cultural and political work the concept does. The mixed psychological and legal force it bears gives the society a goal and a counter in the constant struggle over individual rights. Absolute academic freedom, similarly, cannot exist; it is not even clear we could imagine what it might be, given the kind of restraints on professional identity I outlined earlier. Nonetheless, academic freedom has a history in case law and legally enforceable status in some contexts, such as collective bargaining contracts. But it is also something less tangible—a value that can be promoted both within and without the higher education community, a concept we can debate, define, and redefine in the process of seeking to establish who we are as academics. Discussions of and reflections on academic freedom can be part of a process of self-discovery and self-definition.

Yet academic freedom is partly simply a guild privilege, benefit, and responsibility. In *For the Common Good,* Matthew Finkin and Robert Post define it as "the freedom of mind, inquiry, and expression necessary for proper performance of professional obligations" (38) or "the freedom to pursue the scholarly profession according to the standards of that profession" (7). Finkin and Post have a fairly broad view of what those professional obligations can be. Fish, as is discussed in chapter 7, has a much narrower view, one that severely limits academic freedom. Academic freedom nonetheless reflects a rough, if contested, social consensus that higher education and the society it serves benefit from a high degree of protection for both the professional and the extracurricular speech of faculty members. We have come some distance since a January 21, 1916, *New York Times* editorial offered a counterdefinition of academic freedom: "'Academic freedom,' that is the inalienable right of every college instructor to make a fool of himself and his college by . . . intemperate, sensational prattle about every subject under heaven, to his classes and to the public, and still keep on the payroll or be rift therefrom only by elaborate process, is cried to the winds by the organized dons."

Many of the responsibilities and protections academic freedom entails reflect a consensus across the professoriate as a whole. But so long as faculty members receive disciplinary training and are appointed to disciplinary slots, and so long as colleges and universities are organized by departments that inherit disciplinary traditions, academic freedom will also embody unique discipline-specific expectations. But the right to resist or reject disciplinary paradigms is also fundamental to academic freedom. Moreover, as Judith Butler reminds us, disciplinary norms are always being contested; they are fundamentally in flux and in dispute. They are inevitably applied in differential, interested, and inconsistent ways. They do not represent stable, serene consensus. "Norms have origins other than the well-meaning and well-educated judgments of professionals. Academic norms are wrought not only from cognitive judgments but also from a confluence of historically evolved and changeable institutional and discursive practices" (Butler 129). And interdisciplinarity and multidisciplinarity, to say nothing of paradigm conflicts within disciplines, considerably complicate disciplinary norms.

In the end, academic freedom is worth little unless it is vested in the individual faculty member's right to negotiate these overlapping and conflicted intellectual and professional commitments and decide for himself or herself how to proceed. Although I agree that academic freedom cannot simply be construed as an individual right, it is fundamentally exercised by individuals within professional and institutional traditions. Faculty need to argue for that position despite some federal court decisions, such as *Urofsky v. Gilmore*, decided by the Fourth Circuit in 2000, which held that academic freedom "inheres in the University, not in individual professors." Academic freedom is both a right and a burden for individual faculty members. It recognizes that many of the choices and decisions faculty members make are context specific—specific to an individual's research goals, specific to the dynamic that develops in individual classrooms. Academic freedom means that institutions should be very reluctant to intervene in an individual faculty member's teaching and research.

But interventions are sometimes warranted, as when a faculty member is inclined to do corporate research on campus on the condition that the results not be published. Thus, Berkeley's Chancellor Robert Birgeneau was ill advised to claim that it was a violation of academic freedom to argue that British Petroleum should not be able to operate its own commercial research lab on campus in such a way as to be largely exempt from academic regulation, even if Berkeley faculty members wanted to collaborate in the research (Brenneman).

Although academic freedom historically originates from the need to protect research independence, recent experience also suggests not only that controversial research can threaten a faculty member's career but also that teachers are at least as vulnerable in the classroom. The massive shift to contingent labor in the academy, addressed in detail in chapter 3—with so many college-level teachers subject to casual dismissal or nonrenewal—means that protecting the academic freedom of those off the tenure track has become a critical priority. The AAUP also specifies that for some professionals academic freedom is a task-specific right. Thus, graduate students and academic professionals employed to teach classes must have full academic freedom in their teaching roles. It does not matter whether they are lecturing to five hundred students or leading a thirty-student discussion section. In teaching a discussion section of a lecture course offered by a faculty member, a graduate student or academic professional is guaranteed the right, after fairly representing the views of the week's lecture, to offer an independent perspective. Teachers cannot do their jobs adequately—displaying the frankness and intellectual courage essential to inspiring students and winning their respect—without the support and protection of academic freedom. Once again, the AAUP's 1915 Declaration, despite its gendered blindness, is clear on this point:

> No man can be a successful teacher unless he enjoys the respect of his students, and their confidence in his intellectual integrity. It is clear, however, that this confidence will be impaired if there is suspicion on the part of the student that the teacher is not expressing himself fully or frankly, or that college or university teachers in general are a repressed and intimidated class who dare not speak with that candor and courage which youth always demands in those whom it is to esteem. The average student is a discern-

ing observer, who soon takes the measure of his instructor. It is not only the character of the instruction but also the character of the instructor that counts; and if the student has reason to believe that the instructor is not true to himself, the virtue of the instruction as an educative force is incalculably diminished. There must be in the mind of the teacher no mental reservation. He must give the student the best of what he has and what he is. (296)

In our own time, of course, the nature of those standing at the front of the classroom has radically changed. In response to increased use of graduate employees and academic professionals to teach—even to teach large lecture courses—the AAUP has had to clarify who merits academic freedom in the classroom. In "Statement on Graduate Students" (1999) and "College and University Academic and Professional Appointments" (2002), documents I helped to write that are published in the AAUP's *Policy Documents and Reports*, popularly known as the *Redbook*, the organization states that nonprofessorial employees performing roles traditionally assigned to the faculty, especially teaching, require full academic freedom in that capacity. As "Statement on Graduate Students" makes clear, all graduate students also have the same academic freedom as faculty members have in their extramural statements and in their statements on institutional and departmental governance. But we need to distinguish between, say, the full academic freedom that a graduate student has in teaching a class or commenting on departmental governance versus the intellectual freedom, or qualified academic freedom, he or she has in fulfilling an assignment in a degree program.

All students, graduate and undergraduate, have intellectual freedom—including both freedom of thought and freedom of expression, along with the right to choose their own course of study, to hold their own beliefs, and to be protected from "prejudiced evaluation"—but they do not in my view have full academic freedom in every context, despite efforts from the Right to muddy the waters by arguing that they do. In the original German context, two parallel terms—*Lehrfreiheit* and *Lernfreiheit*—differentiated research and teaching freedoms, with the second term encompassing the student's right to freedom from administrative coercion in the learning situation (Metzger 112–13). The use of differentiated, parallel terms never quite caught on in the United States, perhaps in part because our heritage of religiously affiliated institutions of higher education and of small liberal arts colleges with highly organized programs left us less inclined to guarantee students freedom from curricular requirements and other interventions. Andrew West's 1885 essay "What Is Academic Freedom?" notably does not even mention faculty academic freedom; it devotes itself entirely to warning that the American college student is not prepared to "choose his studies and govern himself" (432). Working collaboratively with several other higher education organizations, the AAUP defined student rights in detail in the important 1967 "Joint Statement on Rights and Freedoms of Students." It remains perhaps the single best policy document about student rights ever written. Although one could simply differentiate between faculty and student academic freedom, as the AAUP's 1940 "Statement of Principles on Academic Freedom and Tenure" does ("Academic freedom in its teaching aspect is fundamental for the protection of the rights of the teacher in teaching and of the student to freedom in learning"), I believe using different terms in the classroom and student context is the clearer route. The academic freedom that faculty have is based on professional training, expertise, and specific responsibilities. Students do not have the same professional status, but they have the freedom to explore ideas and the freedom to express themselves. Like faculty, students also merit personal respect, but that does not protect their ideas from severe critique. Not all ideas merit respect. Inevitably, as Matthew Finkin and Robert Post point out, some students will find critiques of their ideas embarrassing and experience them as personal assaults (105). Academic freedom must protect instructors from reprisals for challenging their students. That is one protection conservatives seek to undermine.

The intellectual freedom that both graduate and undergraduate students have gives them, among other things, the right to pursue their own research interests and publish whatever they wish, subject to any relevant review process. But that freedom does not protect them from professional consequences. A faculty member, for example, in my view has every right to refuse to write a letter of recommendation for a student who has, say, published an anti-Catholic, anti-Muslim, or anti-Semitic essay or an essay advocating genocide. A graduate program cannot discipline a student for such statements, but it has a right to refuse a student's advancement in a degree program if the faculty members believe prejudices or convictions like these mean that no one in the program will ever be willing to write a recommendation on behalf of the student because everyone is convinced the student can never be an effective professional. A graduate student can do whatever research he or she wishes, but that freedom does not mandate that a dissertation committee agree that it fulfills the degree's requirements. Supervised research is not as free as the research one can do after earning the PhD; the awarding of the terminal degree signals the acquisition of full academic freedom. Yet assistant professors' academic freedom does not guarantee that their tenured colleagues will be enthusiastic about their work and recommend tenure. Nor does academic freedom mean that a senior faculty member's research will guarantee approval of a grant. The Right's attempts to claim full academic freedom for both students and faculty have muddied these waters by failing to draw such distinctions.

As I discuss in chapter 2, the assaults on classroom academic freedom from the Right are but one of the continuing and emerging threats to academic freedom. These begin with religious intolerance, with its insistence on doctrinal conformity, and extend to increasing corporatization, with its emphasis on disciplines that can produce income, to neoliberal ideology and the managerial administrative techniques that accompany it, and to the growing emphasis on higher education as job training. All these trends threaten both pedagogy and research. Academic freedom is also faced with serious legal challenges, mostly over the fundamental faculty right and responsibility to be engaged with and critique administrative policy without being punished for doing so.

Constitutional protections for employee speech on institutional policy at private corporations have never been sufficient. Now court cases are challenging employee speech regarding institutional policy at public institutions. These developments may represent far more serious threats than anything David Horowitz, Anne Neal, or the organizations they represent can muster. It is also a clear example of the difference between constitutional free speech, which guards against retaliation by the state, and academic freedom, which protects faculty from institutional repression. Only a strict adherence to principles of academic freedom can protect the essential role faculty must have in setting policy regarding their fundamental responsibilities, among them shaping the curriculum and hiring other faculty.

Much the same conditions affect extramural speech outside a teacher's official areas of academic expertise. Constitutional guarantees protect your right to speak but do not prevent an employer from deciding that your extramural speech impairs your fitness for the job. Once again, institutional reprisals for faculty members' political speech in the public arena have to be prohibited by academic freedom, save instances when extramural speech demonstrates faculty ignorance about areas of professional expertise and thus demonstrates an inability to do their job adequately. Thus, a history professor, unlike an engineer, who asserts that the Holocaust did not happen in a speech off-campus may well raise doubts about his or her professional competence. Robert O'Neil addresses this issue— and the case of Northwestern University's notorious Holocaust-denying engineer Arthur Butz—in *Academic Freedom in the Wired World* (1–11). One can, howeyer, also easily imagine some instances of external speech that would violate university rules and justify internal discipline, such as reading another faculty member's confidential tenure file aloud in a public square against the faculty member's wishes, though it is very difficult to craft reliable language listing prohibitions absent the details of specific cases.

A far more problematic area is public morality, where once again the benefit of the doubt must be given to faculty members making public statements. A faculty member should be able to advocate for nonviolent civil disobedience, but not for murder. A faculty member in a state that prohibited miscegenation should have been able to endorse it without penalty from his or her institution. Colleges and universities must resist mass sentiment. The AAUP censured the University of Illinois in 1963 after the institution fired a faculty member for speaking out on the issue of free love. In areas such as politics and sexuality, public certainty is often judged harshly by history.

In September 2007, the AAUP issued "Freedom in the Classroom," which detailed a series of pedagogical rights and responsibilities, responded to several arguments raised by critics of the academy, and mounted a strong defense of the faculty right to political speech within the classroom. Most political speech in the classroom, we recognized, and as I explain further in chapter 7, grows out of comments on, analogies to, and contrasts with assigned subject matter. Such evaluative and comparative work represents nothing less than the life of the mind. The AAUP also supports occasional intrusions of commentary not directly relevant to the course subject, so long as they are not persistent enough to derail the class.

There were several rejoinders from the Right, all focused on the issue of political speech. Some faculty make a point of expressing their hope that students who take their courses leave more committed to social justice, more committed to minority rights. That is largely what Norma Cantu of the University of Texas meant when she remarked, at a December 2008 Modern Language Association panel on academic freedom, that she hopes her students are radicalized by her courses and trusts that other faculty share the same aim. David Horowitz, also on the panel, delivered a talk titled "Teach the Conflicts, Don't Preach Them," thereby endorsing Gerald Graff's twenty-year mantra. Horowitz responded to Cantu with a phrase, "Weed them out," despite his assertion a few minutes earlier that he has never urged the elimination of leftists from the faculty. The NAS resorts to the same horticultural metaphor in its analysis: "Those unable to modulate their behavior into valid pedagogical norms, should probably be weeded from the professoriate" (Wood and Balch 28). Given that our mechanisms and standards for evaluating pedagogical performance can change—and given that new mechanisms and standards are regularly advocated—perhaps I can be excused for not being altogether reassured by NAS's invocation of "the normal procedures of the university" to do the weeding. Having in the course of my career conducted numerous interviews of people who lived through the 1950s, I have some awareness of how weeding is done. "No one," the NAS assures us, "is attempting to purge the political Left from today's campuses" (ibid. 34). Perhaps not, but they are surely trying to discredit them, cow them, restrict their academic freedom, selectively root out those committed to progressive pedagogies, and reduce the likelihood that more progressive faculty will be hired. Meanwhile, in areas such as Middle East studies, as I point out in chapter 4, we have seen organized efforts to deny tenure to leftist faculty.

Horowitz alternates claims that he is simply appealing to our better natures with implicit threats of chemical warfare: weed killer for the professoriate. He is essentially running a bait-and-switch operation, with protestations of reasonableness aimed at luring us into sanctioning a system to carry out official reprisals. Some of the same mix of conflicted impulses runs through the NAS manifesto by Wood and Balch. Thus, the assertion "We have called primarily for good institutional self-governance" is followed by the qualification that "the state, however, has a legitimate role to play at least with respect to public institutions of higher learning" (33). And the NAS then praises legislative hearings into possible political bias in the classroom. Perhaps one may be forgiven for suspecting that the NAS's declared aims are shaped by what is politically possible.

I do not myself share Norma Cantu's radicalizing goals, because forty years of teaching persuades me that they are unrealistic. I find that most undergraduates arrive on campus with fairly well formed political beliefs. I am, however, very much interested in putting progressive, radical, and conservative views before them, but the students drawn to my views are always those who already share them. Beyond that, I could not care less whether my classes convert or persuade them. I put ideas out for consideration. They can take them or leave them. Then we each get on with our lives.

At the same time, my classes are pervasively political. I ask you to give some attention to why that is the case. It is because of what I teach. My primary field is modern American poetry. I teach a course on the poetry of Langston Hughes and Claude McKay, two African American poets who spent much of their careers portraying, analyzing, and indicting American racism. I teach their poems sympathetically. We discuss the social and historical topics they address. And certainly we ask whether what they argued beginning in the second and third decades of the last century remains true. I also teach a survey course in modern American poetry. It includes a large number of poems about cultural attitudes toward gender, some progressive and others conservative. In the week I spend on the 1930s, we read a series of poems by Communist Party members. In the week on the 1950s, poems about nuclear war and poems describing and attacking McCarthyism, including several by Edwin Rolfe, are among those featured. The 1960s and 1970s weeks cover poems about the Vietnam War. Politics has a place in my classroom because the poems we read are often thoroughly political. When the historical record includes poems of quality from a variety of political viewpoints, I represent the record fairly, though not with any aim of giving equal time. But it would falsify the record to suggest, for example, that poems, unlike a few popular songs, supporting the Vietnam War had much cultural presence or represent poetry of high quality.

Like most literature teachers, I try to teach texts sympathetically, and my syllabus emphasizes poems I consider of high quality. The one exception is my course on Holocaust poetry, in which I regularly expose the students to what I consider failed Holocaust poems. I also share a few Nazi anti-Semitic poems with my classes. I guess that counts as "balance," though I do not disguise my own attitudes in class. I let my students know where I stand with regard to the historical events and social issues raised by the poems I teach, but I encourage them to agree or disagree as they will. This fits the AAUP's model of showing them an instructor taking a strong position and modeling informed advocacy. That is part of what they should be able to do as intellectuals and citizens.

I make every effort to make students feel at ease expressing their own opinions. One way I do that is with humor. No doubt that makes me guilty of what Wood and Balch call "flippant analogy," so they can if they choose accuse me of being "an instructor who is pedagogically self-indulgent and strews his class with irrelevancies" (29), who "strays from the topic of a course" (25). No doubt some of my humor is "gratuitous, politically motivated" (28) and employs the "tools of irony, sarcasm, and innuendo" (10). And in the absolutist rhetoric of the NAS, I am guilty of the ultimate heresy: "taking classroom time" (25), typically as much as fifteen seconds per class hour. I can, however, offer an evidentiary defense of the benefits of my pedagogy: my students have played a major role in reshaping the scholarly field of modern poetry (Rothberg and Garrett). Meanwhile, readers of this book will find similar strategies at work, because humor can also drive a point home. And, in the darkening groves of academe, we need humor to help us endure the moment when we see the forest, not just the trees.

Following AAUP principles, I have learned not to mock my students' beliefs or their confusions. In "Freedom in the Classroom," the AAUP maintains that students should not, for example, be held up to ridicule "for advancing an idea grounded in religion, whether it is creationism or the geocentric theory of the solar system." The first example, creationism, is of course one of the most common fundamentalist beliefs that teachers confront. It can include the conviction that the Earth and all its species really were created in seven days and that the fossil record was placed on Earth by God to test our faith. The second example, heliocentrism, is chosen to be implausible, to signal that, no matter how absurd and unscientific students' convictions are, we should not humiliate students for them. Last year I was presented with the following question: "My minister says every August the university administration turns the campus over to be run by witches' covens. Is that true?" In truth, I may have been too astonished to laugh. In any case, I answered that I have been on campus for nearly forty years and would surely have heard if that were the case. More prosaically, when a class was discussing a Langston Hughes poem about race discrimination, a student launched into a diatribe against "welfare cheats." I asked if he knew whether there was an established welfare program in the 1920s, when the poem was written, and thus whether such a contemporary complaint could be relevant. Having restrained myself in the face of challenges such as these, it is pretty easy to avoid criticizing students for their political beliefs.

I have begun by relating some elements of my personal story because there are thousands of such faculty stories out there. The NAS has a much easier task ignoring our individual stories and demonizing hordes of anonymous progressive faculty by imagining we are misusing the classroom. Classroom practice is not only context specific and a function of each faculty member's aims and beliefs but also a function of the relationship between a faculty member and students that develops over the course of a semester. If we want to engage in a serious, well-informed, and fully professional conversation about the role and status of political observations in the classroom, we need to credit and deal with the specific character of individual faculty practices. That requires input from the faculty members themselves, not simply the scorched-earth slander and error-ridden documentation that David Horowitz employs in *The Professors* and *One-Party Classroom* or the exceptionally crude and dishonorable yellow journalism of "How Many Ward Churchills?" a report by the

American Council of Trustees and Alumni (ACTA), which I discuss further in chapter 7.

The garden-variety red-baiting that Horowitz resorts to in *One-Party Classroom*—he finds a communist hiding in every humanities syllabus—marks a new low in cultural debate. He would cast out the loyal opposition by castigating them as the enemy. They are, he declares at the opening of his book, determined "to instill ideologies that are hostile to American society and its values" (Horowitz and Laksin 1). Horowitz cannot understand that the long progressive tradition of pressing the country to live up to its founding ideals may be the single best American political tradition we have.

Nonetheless, I regard ACTA's publication of its "How Many" pamphlet as the watershed moment of indicative irresponsibility in more than a decade of university-oriented culture wars, since so much of Churchill's recent professional history makes him an exceptional, not representative, figure—not only because his "little Eichmanns" remark was so ill considered and over the top but also because he has been the subject of a vast national debate, with his professional integrity being seriously questioned by faculty review committees and a limited number of plausible press reports on other of his activities, while others have defended him at length. But I do not find some of the NAS's tactics inspiring either. Its response to "Freedom in the Classroom" lambastes the AAUP for failing to thoroughly investigate the prevalence of classroom political remarks, even though its own body of evidence is limited to a handful of anecdotes from among millions of students. In what is surely one of the most hollow rhetorical gestures in this whole cultural struggle, NAS trumpets, "The absence of evidence is not evidence of absence." The AAUP has no interest in wasting its resources on a wild-goose chase. The organization has more important things to do.

The most widely criticized passage in "Freedom in the Classroom" is the one that asserts that an instructor teaching Melville's 1851 novel *Moby-Dick* might compare its ship's captain, Ahab, with George W. Bush. Given that the captain of a ship might well be a figure for the head of the ship of state, the analogy is not surprising. Indeed the comparison between Ahab and Bush already exists in Melville scholarship. Does the NAS believe classroom faculty should be prohibited from commenting on published scholarship in the field? Presumably it is once again acting in ignorance of the scholarly record. The possibility that such a comparison might generate a very rich discussion has meanwhile been demonstrated by over one hundred comments provoked by a critical Stanley Fish column on the same subject in the online version of the *New York Times* ("George W. Bush and Melville's Ahab: Discuss!"). This online dialogue, which I discuss in detail in chapter 7, creates a wonderful cyberspace classroom.

There are also some genuine cheap shots in the NAS report. Among these is the repeated feigned distress about the AAUP's purported failure to provide a full account of the goals of higher education in "Freedom in the Classroom," given that the statement primarily cites the importance of students acquiring "the desire and capacity for independent thinking." But the AAUP statement was not intended to lay out all of higher education's aims. That would have to be a long document of its own, not one focused on faculty rights and responsibilities in the classroom. And, in any case, the AAUP has produced a great many policy statements and reports engaged with a whole range of educational values and goals.

Elsewhere, the NAS joins forces with ACTA and Horowitz's Students for Academic Freedom in betraying real ignorance about recent disciplinary and interdisciplinary work. By marketing false characterizations of academic disciplines, these groups are able to claim that academic freedom is being misused. The NAS's crude view of postcolonialism—as claiming that all the ills of the developing world are due to their colonial history—bears no relation to the field as I know it. "Postcolonialism" is first of all a neutral historical category, referring to the decline of colonial empires over the past century and the reconstitution of nations and cultures under those conditions. The field acknowledges the varied mixture of affinity and resistance toward these countries' colonial past that still shapes some of them. It has developed a sophisticated vocabulary and set of theoretical frameworks to help us understand these complex societies. That it includes anger at the legacies of colonialism is certainly true, but to reduce the field to that—its lowest common denominator—is both ill informed and irresponsible. What is more, attacks on "postcolonialism," in the aftermath of 9/11, now stand in for conservative rage at any sympathy for Muslim societies.

The NAS's understanding of postmodern or poststructuralist relativism is no better. Postmodernism does not announce that there are no values; it argues instead that values are contingent, not transcendent. Thus, the struggle to sustain the values we believe in is even more important. Nor is all this reducible to power relations, unless you count persuasion and nonviolent witness as exercises of power. The work of sustaining the values we believe in is unending, because nothing is guaranteed. If the twentieth century taught us anything, it is that anything is possible within human behavior, that societies can endorse values that are genuinely monstrous. Relativism reminds us that only continuing education and advocacy can sustain human decency.

That said, I think the NAS does raise some real and substantive issues for discussion. That they are framed as attacks on the AAUP is regrettable, but they nonetheless represent the potential basis for a productive dialogue. The AAUP has, for example, long recognized that classroom freedoms are constrained in various ways. As Judith Areen writes, "Individual faculty have somewhat less freedom with respect to their teaching, as the authority to decide such institutional academic matters as what courses will be taught and what grading standards are to be followed is vested in the faculty as a body" (957). All faculty members have to conform to broad professional norms and expectations. Individual departments can set course requirements in a variety of ways, from mandating a minimum number of pages of writing in composition courses to mandating that introductory chemistry include some hands-on laboratory experience. Catalog descriptions set general parameters for coverage, though they typically allow very wide latitude in designing a syllabus and raising collateral topics. But academic freedom does not permit a faculty member to refuse to teach the course he or she is assigned.

Yet clear guidelines for differentiating between institutional or departmental authority and an individual teacher's professional independence really do not exist. Should that chemistry teacher be prohibited from teaching some experimental methods by way of computer simulation? Should composition teachers, no matter how many years of experience they have, be compelled to use a prescribed text book or, even worse, be told in what subject areas their paper assignments must fall? My answer to both questions is no. Even in multisection courses, academic freedom requires that these power relations need to be negotiated in the context of respect for the individual teacher's pedagogical philosophy and goals. Compromises that honor both individual and institutional rights and interests need to be reached. As Robert O'Neil very helpfully points out in the eighth chapter ("Whose Academic Freedom") of his *Academic Freedom in the Wired World,* however, case law on such conflicts is sparse and far from encouraging, two of the worst cases (*Edwards v. California University of Pennsylvania* and *Brown v. Armenti*) having been decided in the Third Circuit in 1998 and 2001, the first by Supreme Court justice Samuel Alito when he was serving there (219–20). It is thus imperative that the AAUP establish its own values and precedents. To that end, I established an ad hoc committee in 2009 to report on this issue and make recommendations (Nelson, "Whose Academic Freedom?").

When professional norms may have been violated, it is the job of one's faculty peers to review conduct. The 1915 AAUP Declaration implicitly denies administrators the key role in deciding whether faculty members have exceeded the bounds of academic freedom; this power, it states, should never "be vested in bodies not composed of members of the academic profession" (298). Formal hearing bodies, however, are typically not disciplinary. Administrators may have responsibility for administering elections to faculty committees and for carrying out such penalties as a committee may assign. They can also bring charges to committees. Boards of trustees have final authority for dismissals. The 1915 Declaration also makes the powerful observation that "classroom utterances ought always to be considered privileged communications. Discussion in the classroom ought not to be supposed to be utterances for the public at large" (299). Thus, public monitoring of classrooms was deemed unacceptable. So much for conservative groups that claim to endorse the 1915 Declaration while encouraging legislative review of classroom presentations.

But for conservative groups the key problem area in establishing norms is disciplinarity. Most departments instantiate some version of an international academic discipline, however selective they may be in emphasizing particular subdisciplines or choosing among competing disciplinary paradigms. As Joan Scott has written, "academic freedom protects those whose thinking challenges orthodoxy; at the same time the legitimacy of the challenge—the proof that the critic is not a madman or a crank—is secured by membership in a disciplinary community based upon shared commitments to certain methods, standards, and beliefs" ("Academic Freedom" 166). Almost all permanent faculty members at four-year colleges and universities have undergone specialized disciplinary training. For better or worse, an academic discipline provides the primary context and intellectual horizon for the work most faculty members do. Although "Freedom in the Classroom" emphasizes that academic freedom mandates that faculty have the right to reflect on and critique their disciplines—and some of us have spent our careers partly doing so—the reality is that many faculty are ill equipped to think outside their disciplinary box. Indeed, many faculty members believe deeply in their discipline's aims and areas of intellectual consensus. The most serious recruiting that most faculty do is not for their political beliefs but for their disciplinary values.

What fairly troubles the NAS is that academic disciplines or subdisciplines can pass through periods of relatively unreflective, even dogmatic, conviction and advocacy. Can this involve the discrediting of alternative points of view in the classroom and their implacable suppression in print? Yes. Although these practices may often eventually be corrected—both by internal disciplinary debate and by interaction with faculty from other areas—their real-time effects can be unwholesome. It has been difficult for many faculty to admit this in the midst of a sustained assault from the Right, but higher education advocates need to be more reflective and forthcoming about the complexity of disciplinary history and practice. The NAS adds that the standards for what counts as true within disciplines vary widely, especially when the humanities and social sciences are compared with hard-science disciplines.

As I suggested earlier, many of the disciplinary critiques leveled by conservatives have—in my view—been either poorly informed or based in ideological bias. As I detail in chapter 7, Horowitz regularly attacks women's studies programs for teaching the theory that gender is socially constructed as a fact, an obsession that is one of the central arguments in *One-Party Classroom*. He seems unable or unwilling to distinguish between physical differences and the *cultural meaning and understanding* of them. In my view and the view of many others, all human understanding is culturally and historically constructed. We have no unmediated access to any facts. Consequently, I teach the cultural construction of gender as true, though my students are free to disagree. I advocate for this view, as the AAUP allows, not only because it is what I believe but also because my students should see how I arrive at and account for my intellectual commitments.

The NAS observes, in its own version of disciplinary confusion, that "it is indeed indoctrination to teach women's studies students that women are universally oppressed by patriarchy" (Wood and Balch 5), a monolithic view that helped create women's studies as a field in the 1970s but that has not dominated the field for at least twenty years. The change in the field was highlighted by a historic conference on pornography at Barnard in 1983, which helped free women's studies from fundamentally conservative views of sexuality and introduced productive debates into the discipline. In some cases this new emphasis was signaled at the departmental level by programs adding "gender" to their title. Some gender studies programs are now headed by men, something that would have been virtually impossible in the 1970s. Disciplines thus can be self-healing; they can evolve past periods of ideological restraint. Yet a period of inflexible (and oppositional) conviction may be necessary to a field's development.

But academic disciplines can be coercive enterprises. Contrary to the NAS's train of thought, however, they enforce paradigms mostly by rewarding, rather than punishing, their members and their students. Under normal circumstances, rewarding conformity to disciplinary norms and expectations, as Michel Foucault has helped show us, is the most effective cultural strategy. Affirmation, not ridicule, is the weapon of choice. While the AAUP, in turn, can work to curtail ridicule and to protect the freedom to disagree, there is precious little it can do to relieve the power of affirmation. Disciplinary training opens intellectual opportunities for students and faculty alike; it generates intellectual excitement and agency. It also closes off options and curtails dissent. That is its core paradox. Politics—in the narrow sense of supporting attitudes conventionally categorized as political—is often a very small part of this pattern, though in a much broader sense the politics of disciplinarity is pervasive.

Of course, rewards for conformity are also balanced by potential punishment, and the culture wars, campus speech codes, and political reprisals against controversial speech have all contributed to a climate in which compliance, with its rewards, looks better than resistance, with its penalties. Certainly the threat of charges and hearings is a sufficient reason to choose behavior likely to be rewarded (Sniderman). The more high-profile assaults on academic freedom have also reinforced a tendency to isolate overt political speech and suppress reflection on the pervasive politics of knowledge.

The NAS has chosen to ignore this more fundamentally political character of disciplinarity because its altogether selective critique of academic disciplines and their use of academic freedom is itself a thoroughly political construct. What about the philosophy departments that teach only Anglo-American philosophy and disparage those students who develop an interest in Continental philosophy? What about the psychology departments so embedded in a positivist ideology that their faculty members have effectively disavowed belief in human consciousness? What about the political science departments whose constricted view of modernization led them for decades to endorse only USAID models for development? What about the sociology departments so committed to quantitative research that they suppress students' curiosity about qualitative sociology? I sometimes feel that dealing with the NAS and its few thousand members is like confronting a claque of Iranian mullahs who are paradoxically resentful of modernity but committed to bowing five times a day toward Wall Street. Indeed, disciplinary bias can become political in the narrower sense. How many business schools give balanced treatment to the benefits of unionization? How many economics departments offer introductory courses with a healthy (and, may one say, timely) skepticism toward free-market principles, instead of effectively exporting a supply-and-demand gospel worldwide? Despite all this, Horowitz and the NAS think women's studies is the great risk to intellectual openness.

Pressure on academic disciplines to reform themselves and critique their own paradigms is appropriate and necessary, but the NAS's roster of problem disciplines is both inadequate and dishonorable. Horowitz expands his list of defective academic specializations in *One-Party Classroom* to include "Women's Studies, African-American Studies, Peace Studies, Cultural Studies, Chicano Studies, Gay Lesbian Studies, Post-Colonial Studies, Whiteness Studies, Community Studies, and recently politicized disciplines such as Cultural Anthropology and Sociology" (283), but it is still an ideologically biased list. Despite the Right's efforts to hold the hard sciences blameless, the cultural effect of these assaults is arguably broader: to discredit disciplinarity itself. Academia presently operates with what amounts to a Darwinian theory of the survival of ideas: those ideas that find their disciplinary niche survive and prosper, reproducing themselves and evolving. The Right seeks to undermine disciplinary credibility so that the new niche that provides the only test for academic thought is the market-dominated environment of public political debate.

Yet disciplines are for the foreseeable future the only rational models for organizing faculty we have. Thus, "Freedom in the Classroom" relies on disciplinary consensus as a guide to what faculty can require their students to master, what faculty can insist that students be able to comprehend and apply. Disciplinarity is also a guide to what many faculty members may well believe about their subject matter and their preferred objects of study. Although one might endorse greater ongoing skepticism and reflexivity about disciplinary consensus, it is highly unrealistic to mandate it. These dour attitudes toward disciplinarity and its effects on colleagues, I should add, may not reflect the views of my AAUP colleagues, but they help explain why I am willing to endorse the cold realism of "Freedom in the Classroom" on this count. I agree with the NAS that "'accepted as true within a relevant discipline' is not the same as true" (Wood and Balch 5). The AAUP has in response deleted the words "as true" from the phrase in its revised version of "Freedom in the Classroom." It is also worth considering what it means to claim, as the NAS does, that "some disciplines have much stronger epistemological warrant than others" (ibid.). Epistemological warrant, alas, is also culturally constructed and managed, not an absolute ontological condition.

The AAUP's 1915 Declaration relies on the scientific method as a model for the ideal exercise of academic freedom. In a broad, multidisciplinary context, that means rationality, willingness to test hypotheses against evidence, openness to counterclaims by peers, and so forth. The NAS wants to cast this as a choice between scientific method and the blind willfulness of disciplinary conviction. But different disciplines and subdisciplines focus on different kinds of evidence, deal with them differently, and negotiate scholarly debate differently. The humanities fields I know best—literature, history, and art criticism—all have textual and historical evidence at stake, but the textual evidence is open to variable interpretation, and the historical record changes continually.

In my field, poetry, the primary evidence is the incredibly compressed and ambiguous language of the poem itself. Next comes the language of all the other poems by the same author, then all the other potentially relevant texts and discourses of the historical period. An author's intentions may be relevant, if we can discern them, but authors are often not in full control of the meanings and effects of their discourse. It is the job of the discipline to help establish the nature of evidence—how it should be handled, what the field's interpretive protocols are.

Given that academic freedom is grounded in professional training and expertise, reliance on disciplinary consensus to judge faculty appointments, tenure decisions, curricular design, and much of classroom advocacy may simply be unavoidable. The AAUP is not arguing for "disciplinary infallibility," to cite the NAS's clever but overheated phrase; it has simply recognized how academic knowledge is organized and administered. Meanwhile, both the AAUP and the NAS urge tolerance of and encouragement of dissent. Yet administrative judgments and decisions made outside disciplinary norms are far more likely to be arbitrary. Nonetheless, a certain price is paid by all for the highly departmentalized organization of the modern university. Despite these reservations, I endorse many of my discipline's values. The only really relentless recruitment I do is not for leftist politics but for the love of poetry.

One would hardly think that the commitment to teaching and writing about poetry would be at the crux of one recent effort to eviscerate academic freedom, but it is, as is detailed in my discussion of Stanley Fish's *Save the World on Your Own Time* (2008) in chapter 7. The book is important because its determined assault on academic freedom comes not from the Right but rather from a faculty member who once possessed moderately progressive credentials. It will thus be cited by many people who would never use Horowitz or other far-Right cultural critics to support constraints on classroom freedom.

As Fish's work and the critiques by the NAS make clear, nothing less than faculty members' very jobs and their intellectual integrity, as well as the integrity of higher education and its capacity to challenge and inspire our students, is at stake in the current struggles over academic freedom. Much as we might like to imagine that academic freedom is a stable, unchanging value, a kind of Platonic form, in truth it is under constant pressure to redefine its nature, its scope, and its application. The need to clarify academic freedom anew, to elaborate on its implications, and to respond to its critics is never ending. It is important to remember in this context that both the AAUP itself and its classic statements of principle developed in specific historical contexts and reflect specific cultural and political struggles: "Professional academic freedom grew out of collective faculty resistance to university administrators and trustees in the early 1900s, at the height of capitalist industrialization . . . in a social movement at the turn of the twentieth century, when faculty made collective demands for autonomy over their research, teaching, and professional self-governance" (Lieberwitz 267–68).

In the introduction to a 1990 bibliography on academic freedom, Janet Sinder observed that academic freedom, as a result of its history, is "a subject with many facets: academic freedom of public and private school teachers, of university professors, of universities themselves, and of students" (383). William Van Alstyne warns us in the same volume that "the AAUP's own notions of the varieties of academic freedom, like the notions of the Supreme Court, have become more complex over time" (83), a statement that is even more true now. Developments since then would lead us to warn that a distinction between the rights of teachers at public and private institutions would have to be applied to university professors as well. Indeed, academic freedom in the United States—as a reality and as a concept—has evolved over a century and more in response to changing social and political conditions, changing forms of university governance, developing case law in the courts, and AAUP investigations and policy statements, as David Rabban suggests: "Threats to professors from university trustees loomed behind the seminal professional definition produced in 1915. . . . Threats to universities from the state, arising out of general concerns during the late 1940s and 1950s about the dangers of communism to American society and institutions prompted the cases that led the Supreme Court to identify academic freedom as a first amendment right" (229).

With so many different registers and contexts for defining academic freedom, it must clearly continue to be discussed and debated. Yet most faculty members are not well versed in the relevant history or issues. Stanley Fish, as I discuss in chapter 7, argues that for some faculty academic freedom is no more than a "magical" term they invoke to justify unacceptable practices. In 1996, Richard Rorty worried that faculty understanding of academic freedom has so declined that for some it does little more than name "some complicated local folkways" (21). *No University Is an Island* is designed to help remedy that situation. But the remedy cannot be limited to a philosophical and historical review of the development of academic freedom in the United States. That has been ably done by others, notably at first by Richard Hofstadter and Walter Metzger. Academic freedom now confronts challenges powerful enough to ask not what its future will be but whether it will have a future at all. The uncertain answer to that question lies in the politics of struggle, which is my main focus in what follows.

Since the American Association of University Professors first investigated institutional violations of academic freedom and issued its historic 1915 "Declaration of Principles on Academic Freedom and Academic Tenure," it has been the major force in the effort to define and protect this fundamental value. This book is first of all an effort to evaluate the state of academic freedom in the emerging neoliberal university and then an effort to judge what role the AAUP can play in preserving it. This introduction defines academic freedom and reviews some of the challenges it now faces, because it is in response to current challenges, as the quotation from David Rabban suggests, that academic freedom is historically clarified, defended, and sometimes put at risk.

No University Is an Island aims to track the effects of these political forces and to suggest how both the AAUP and faculty nationwide can better resist them. Chapter 1 outlines the relationship between academic freedom and shared governance, the latter concept being critical to sustaining academic freedom but arguably even less well understood. Chapter 2 identifies sixteen specific threats to academic freedom, a number of them still emerging. Chapter 3 takes on the pervasive threat to academic freedom built into our increasing reliance on contingent faculty with no job security. Chapter 4 joins the effort to break the Left's relative silence on the issue of political correctness and assesses its impact on academic freedom and the faculty. In chapters 5 and 6, I argue that collective bargaining can play a major role in preserving faculty responsibilities and rights, resisting neoliberal ideology, and reforming the professoriate but that the character of unionization will have to be transformed if it is to play a more progressive role in the future. As the reader will discover, a number of events are treated more than once in what follows, receiving, for example, a shared governance evaluation in chapter 1 and an academic freedom analysis in chapter 2. My debates with other scholars are comparably contextualized and are thus sometimes staged in more than one chapter. And in order to give each chapter some capacity to stand on its own, I repeat some arguments briefly, while pointing the reader to the chapter where they receive more detailed coverage.

In describing the current state of higher education, especially in chapters 2 and 4, I draw detailed examples from the institution I know best, the University of Illinois at Urbana-Champaign. In evaluating the AAUP's role, especially in chapters 7 through 9, I draw on fifteen years in its national leadership. Although I was elected the forty-ninth president of the AAUP in 2006 and reelected in 2008, I cannot pretend to speak officially for the organization in everything that follows. For one thing, on some of the finer points of academic freedom—such as whether it covers the disclosure of political beliefs in the classroom in acts or comments not related to class assignments—not everyone in the AAUP leadership agrees. More fundamentally, however, I have decided to reveal more of how the AAUP functions and has responded to recent challenges than others in the leadership or on the staff have done before. Some of my colleagues have urged me to do so. Others have urged me to remain silent. I am convinced, however, that the organization cannot thrive unless faculty members generally have a greater stake in its operation. I do not believe that to be possible unless there is more knowledge, both of what is at stake and of how the AAUP has struggled to balance its competing constituencies and competing visions. People also must understand how the AAUP has suffered from the way it has negotiated these challenges. Although all organizations pay a price for the very bureaucratic structures that enable them to function, and all organizations fall prey to the vagaries of human character, when the organization's effectiveness and very existence is threatened thereby, broader revelation and discussion is necessary. That said, there is no question that, save for two periods—when it succumbed to repressive national law and public hysteria during World War I and when it retreated into silence in the face of McCarthyism—the AAUP's record of putting the principles of academic freedom into writing and defending them has been unequaled in the higher education community. It was the organization's general secretary, Ralph Hinstead, who prevented the AAUP from doing investigations in the 1950s; members who wanted investigations staged a revolt and ordered him ousted in 1955. He died at his desk before he could leave, and the AAUP again began to defend academic freedom. Thus, in the early 1950s there were effectively two AAUPs: one represented by the national office and one represented by the members.

That kind of broad interest in and commitment to the AAUP's efforts is one this book aims to help restore. Although faculty members in a wide variety of disciplines continue to contribute to discussions of academic freedom—from law to history to education to literature—their number is far fewer than it should be. Everyone in higher education should follow the debates about academic freedom and express their own views in their venues of choice. This book is designed to promote that engagement. Chapter 1 addresses the fundamental governance structures that sustain academic freedom, structures also in need of repair.

1

The Three-Legged Stool

Academic Freedom, Shared Governance, and Tenure

[C]ontrary to common understanding, academic freedom is about much more than faculty speech. . . . Rather, academic freedom is central to the functioning and governance of colleges and universities. . . . It is not only about faculty research and teaching; it is also about the freedom of faculties to govern their institutions in a way that accords with academic values whether they are approving the curriculum, hiring faculty, or establishing graduation requirements for students.

—Judith Areen, "Government as Educator" (947)

The American Association of University Professors has long maintained that academic freedom is really only one leg of a three-legged stool. Academic freedom, shared governance, and tenure together support the higher education system we have had in place for over half a century. As Robert Birnbaum puts it in an unpublished 1993 paper, "'Governance' is the term we give to the structures and processes that academic institutions invent to achieve an effective balance between the claims of two different, but equally valid, systems for organizational control and influence. One system, based on legal authority, is the basis for the role of trustees and administration; the other system, based on professional authority, justifies the role of the faculty." Shared governance establishes the mechanisms through which faculty professional expertise becomes functional; it moves that expertise from a concept to an operative reality.

Effective governance and job security are interdependent. You cannot really have either professional authority or academic freedom if you can easily be fired or nonrenewed, the latter being the fate so many part-time faculty face. But you do not have functioning academic freedom unless the faculty is in charge of the curriculum and the hiring process and can thus control who does the teaching and what they can teach. Shared governance agreements also shape and guarantee peer review, from grievance procedures to the tenure process. Academic freedom is an empty concept, or at least an effectively diminished one, if the faculty does not control its enforcement through shared governance.

It is not just a question of who exercises the final decision-making authority. It is a question of who manages the process and assures appropriate input along the way. Thus, for example, administrators responsible for overseeing numerous departments lack the disciplinary expertise to distinguish between genuinely innovative dissertations that suggest a job candidate will be an inspiring teacher and an influential scholar and unimaginative dissertations that suggest exactly the opposite. But administrative oversight is necessary to make certain that those are indeed the values in play. At the same time, left to their own devices to make hiring decisions, administrators dealing with multiple disciplines may settle for uninspired graduates of prestige institutions. Similarly, an upper-level administrator who confronts a parent or a legislator offended by course content should be able to offer a basic academic freedom defense but cannot be expected to offer a response based on disciplinary knowledge. This mix and balance of responsibilities is part of what has to be negotiated for shared governance to succeed.

The relationship between the three components that sustain the role faculty play in higher education is clearly under increasing threat from numerous forces: (1) the managerial model that now dominates the corporate university; (2) the massive reliance on contingent faculty, doubled over the last thirty years, which (as discussed in chapter 3) leaves most faculty nationwide with no structural role in shared governance; (3) the loss of faculty vigilance over and understanding of the relationship between shared governance and academic freedom, exacerbated by the presence of two generations of tenured faculty focused on their careers and disciplinary commitments to the exclusion of their community responsibilities; (4) the renewed culture wars waged by the Right to deprive faculty of both academic freedom and the key elements of shared governance, most noticeable in the effort to restrict and surveil faculty speech in the classroom but also in attacks on academic disciplines and in occasional argumentative efforts to divest shared governance of its basic meaning; (5) the rampant laissez-faire commercialism that is increasingly denying faculty senates any say in how campus commercial relationships are to be structured (Washburn); (6) real or fabricated financial crises that are leading administrators to impose furloughs, salary cuts, or program eliminations without proper consultation with the faculty.

In the introduction, I wrote in detail about the fourth item in this list, the very selective conservative assault on academic disciplines, most notably women's studies, but the Right's attacks on postmodernism and on critiques of American empire are designed to put a whole series of humanities and social science disciplines under erasure. This whole effort mounts a fundamental assault on academic departments and on their authority to hire, fire, design a curriculum, and conduct peer review of teaching and scholarship. The Right's arguments imply that the authority ceded to departments and the disciplines they represent should be withdrawn and relocated elsewhere. They eliminate confidence in the discipline-based peer-review process conducted by academic journals and publishers. The Right is thus engaged in an assault on both academic freedom and shared governance.

The public demand by politicians to dismiss Ward Churchill from his tenured position at the University of Colorado was also simultaneously an assault on academic freedom and a transgression against shared governance. It both triggered and compromised his subsequent evaluation by faculty committees. That remains the case whether or not one considers the later faculty reports to include serious violations of professional conduct. David Horowitz's efforts to legislate restrictions on classroom speech and to produce ideologically "balanced" faculties are similarly two-pronged projects: they threaten both individual faculty freedoms and the shared governance processes by which faculty are appointed and curricula approved. Protests against actions such as these may not be effective if they cite only the principle of academic freedom, while ignoring the shared governance structures that sustain it.

Just what it means for faculty to have no academic freedom, or to grasp how deficiencies in shared governance and academic freedom can dovetail, can be difficult to imagine for tenured faculty in relative comfort at major institutions. Consider this: at Antioch University McGregor in Yellow Springs, Ohio, where no one has tenure, faculty were asked to vote on a major construction project in 2006. The president gathered them in an auditorium, asked those who supported her proposal to stand, then wrote down the names of those still seated. Proper shared governance would require a secret ballot for such a vote. The following year she informed the faculty that talking to the press about the university was grounds for dismissal. Academic freedom would hold faculty harmless for such extramural speech. At Bacone College in Oklahoma, the president has no problem unilaterally eliminating from the curriculum all the courses taught by faculty members he wants to fire, thereby circumventing both peer review and senate approval; the faculty member has no work to do and no place to exercise his or her academic freedom. At DePaul University, the president had no problem unilaterally denying Norman Finkelstein his appeal rights for his tenure case, a violation of governance agreements that certified the end of Finkelstein's job.

Fully functioning shared governance is also a protection against outside interference in university affairs. Those individuals outside DePaul who attempted to intervene in Finkelstein's tenure case, or in the cases of Middle East scholars at Barnard and Columbia, were essentially exercising their First Amendment rights. Whether or not we endorse what they did, including scandalously misrepresenting people's scholarship, is a separate issue. Good shared governance procedures make it considerably easier for both faculty committees and senior administrators to exclude all unsolicited communications from a tenure file and make certain that tenure cases are decided on the basis of the file alone, not by rumor, character assassination, undocumented allegation, and unsolicited opinion.

A shared governance crisis often has a single triggering event, but a review of AAUP reports about shared governance suggests there is typically also a history of problems at issue. A representative series of investigative reports published in *Academe* (the AAUP's official journal of record)—about Elmira College in New York (1993), Lindenwood College in Missouri (1994), Francis Marion University in South Carolina (1997), Miami-Dade Community College in Florida (2000), and Antioch College and Antioch University (2009)—give a convincing and troubling portrait of the pattern, meanwhile demonstrating that no part of the country is immune. Reading accounts of pure violations of academic freedom can provoke a sense of near incredulity, as you realize how idiosyncratic some administrative behavior can be, or how diverse our colleges and universities are. Shared governance abuses, on the other hand, offer unsettling moments of recognition, as we remember similar incidents at our own institutions. The five AAUP reports are each fairly long and quite detailed, but a few representative excerpts from two of them will illustrate what I mean.

At Elmira, the AAUP's investigating team noted, "aggrieved faculty members report having filed appeals with the Faculty Grievance Committee (FGC) which were sustained by that body only to have the FGC's positive findings and recommendations overridden by the dean and the president" (48). Faculty authority over appointments was compromised: "the administration refused to invite for an interview one of the candidates proposed by the search committee, allowed administrators who were not members of the search committee to review applicant files and rank the candidates, and ended up appointing someone whom the members of the search committee had expressly declined to recommend" (48). Meanwhile the board chair suggested faculty members could face disciplinary sanctions if they made public "statements disparaging the college as a place for students to attend or for alumni or donors to support" (50).

At Lindenwood, 1989 began with a declaration of financial exigency. A new president, however, soon brought the school financial stability. Nonetheless, he announced a "freeze on tenure" the following year. He then notified faculty that their governance documents, the *Faculty Constitution* and *Faculty Bylaws,* were voided. He unilaterally revised the *Faculty Handbook* to state that Lindenwood operated by annual contracts and did not grant tenure (61). Graduation requirements, plans for creating new majors and degree programs, and decisions to eliminate courses or add new ones were made without faculty input (64). Reappointments and promotions were approved or denied against faculty advice. Then he began granting faculty status and professorial rank to full-time administrators. "Among the full-time administrators granted such status and rank are the president's daughter and son-in-law" (66). A comparable decision to ignore faculty authority took place at West Virginia University in 2007, when administrators awarded the state governor's daughter an unearned degree (Redden, "Failures").

The risks universities face when shared governance is undermined are often unanticipated: they become fundamentally weakened institutions. Would administrators at Elmira or Lindenwood be able to use shared governance to resist external political pressures? The norms established by the AAUP are designed to put in place systems that will help prevent or resist such abuses if the norms are maintained. The AAUP issued a statement about shared governance in 1920 and revised it in 1938, but the organization's thinking on the subject continued to evolve and deepen until it published its "Statement on Government of Colleges and Universities" in 1966 and its "On the Relationship of Faculty Governance to Academic Freedom" in 1994. Developed in conjunction with the American Council on Education and the Association of Governing Boards, the 1966 statement was later supplemented by other policy documents, among them "The Role of the Faculty in Budgetary and Salary Matters" (1972) and "Faculty Participation in the Selection, Evaluation, and Retention of Administrators" (1974).

Although governance practices inevitably vary from campus to campus and with different types of institutions, there is a clear need for generally accepted norms. Too often shared governance now amounts to an opportunity for faculty to express their views, and then, as Greg Scholtz puts it, "once people have talked things over, those in charge make the final decision." But the AAUP's 1966 statement "does not conceive of the college or university in starkly hierarchical terms—as a power pyramid." Rather, Scholtz goes on to say, "it portrays the well-run institution as one in which board and president delegate decision-making power to the faculty." Indeed the AAUP's 1994 "On the Relationship of Faculty Governance to Academic Freedom," building on the AAUP's original 1915 Declaration on academic freedom, makes it clear that faculty have fundamental autonomy in their areas of expertise.

In *Save the World on Your Own Time,* Stanley Fish inaccurately suggests that some arguments on behalf of shared governance, including that of AAUP activist Larry Gerber, are grounded in a mistaken belief that democracy is a supreme value in all institutions within a democratic country. Since "democratic imperatives are not central to academic purposes," Fish writes, "the rationale for shared governance pretty much collapses" (111). It is true that faculty members occasionally reference the value of democracy in conversations endorsing shared governance, but the AAUP has never done so. Indeed, neither I nor the AAUP staff and leaders I have consulted can remember any scholarly essays on the subject that do.

Shared governance cannot install full democracy in a university. It is a negotiated strategy for sharing and adjudicating power and its application and effects. Shared governance exists when boards of trustees agree to cede authority over areas—such as curriculum development and faculty hiring—where the faculty have greater expertise. It has nothing to do with democracy. Rather, it recognizes that governing boards do not have the requisite competence to make these decisions. Shared governance can also differentiate among responsibilities and assign them to specific groups. As Gerber points out in a rejoinder to Fish, the faculty is "not one undifferentiated mass":

A college or university is composed of many overlapping communities of expertise. Shared governance represents a means of effectively tapping into that expertise by giving primary responsibility for different academic issues to the appropriate community of expertise. Shared governance does not mean establishing "democracy" on campus so that all members of the campus community—from custodians to football coaches—participate equally in decisions affecting academic matters. Nor does shared governance mean giving all Physics faculty an equal vote with English faculty in judging the qualifications of professors of literature; nor does it mean allowing the History faculty to participate as a group in determining what classes should be required of a Chemistry major. There are, however, academic issues, such as general education requirements or establishing a campus-wide grade forgiveness policy, that do cut across disciplinary boundaries, and on these issues all faculty should have an equal voice.

Many issues also arise in a college or university that are nonacademic, for which faculty have no particular expertise. Such issues as building construction, financial investments, or parking are largely matters of administration, but insofar as they might impinge on carrying out the educational mission of the institution, administrators who hold primary decision-making responsibility should at least seek faculty input. Thus faculty might not be equipped to decide on what contractor ought to be hired to construct a new Biology building, but it would be foolish not to consult faculty about what facilities needed to be included in that building. ("Defending" 6)

The negotiated campus standards for shared governance may lay out (and differentiate between) areas for fully collaborative decision making, for full autonomy, and for consultation followed by final decisions. All this, unfortunately, has become increasingly unclear to faculty over the past generation. Many faculty members no longer have any idea what the norms for shared governance should be. As shown by a 2003 survey report titled *Challenges for Governance,* faculty disagree about how campuses are or should be governed. Few could readily offer a satisfactory definition of shared governance. Others are themselves skeptical about many shared governance procedures.

As the new millennium began, it was clear that the growing resistance to shared governance had become a point of pride for some university administrators. Corporatization had repeatedly provided the local flashpoint. A chancellor or university president wanted to move quickly on a contract to provide services for a business partner. The prospect of significant income loomed. Then the damned faculty intervened. A bunch of pansies in the history department saw a "problem" with putting the university's logo on land mines manufactured by slave labor. Worse still: why would faculty object to having an arms manufacturer as a co-owner of all online courses on international relations? Could they come up with a more dogged distributor?

At a 2001 conference at UCLA, I heard former University of Michigan president James Duderstadt forcefully declare that faculty had to be taken out of the loop of university decision making. Higher education had to be restructured so administrators could make decisions and get the job done without interference by faculty. Derek Bok sought to counter that view two years later:

The entrepreneurial university, it is said, must be able to move quickly. It cannot wait for windy faculty debates to run their course lest valuable opportunities be lost in the fast-moving corporate world in which we live. In fact, there is remarkably little evidence to support this view. Looking over the checkered history of commercial activity on campuses, one can much more easily point to examples of costly unilateral decisions by impatient administrators, such as ill-advised Internet ventures or grandiose athletic projects, than to valuable opportunities lost through inordinate faculty delays. (B9)

Until Duderstadt talked, it had seemed that broad-brush open contempt for faculty was limited to activists such as University of California regent Ward Connerly, who responded to a reporter's 1995 question about shared governance with the faculty by blustering with a mix of humor and ideology: "We share too damn much with them now" (quoted in Scott, "Critical State" 42). Now it seemed lip service need no longer be given to the notions of dialogue, consultation, negotiation, and community. Even those with prestige university connections could freely express more than impatience with the time-consuming character of collaborative process. If we wanted to move forward, we had to get the faculty out of the way.

It is worth noting, as Bob Kreiser of the national AAUP office pointed out to me, that the national AAUP does not get substantially more complaints about violations of governance expectations than it did a decade ago, though there is an area of significant increase. What the office now gets, as the investigative reports cited earlier may suggest, is larger numbers of academic freedom cases embedded in or overlaid with governance problems. In other words, academic freedom is now regularly curtailed or denied, or its erosion enhanced, by the failure to follow good governance practices or because the practices are absent. Shared governance, many of us now estimate, will be a focal point of higher education struggles over the next decade and more. Meanwhile, economic expediency makes many administrators resent the time and energy expended on governance processes.

An administrator who thinks he or she ought to be able to pursue or endorse commercial opportunities without subjecting such relationships and contracts to established channels for oversight may well come to feel he or she also ought to be able to discipline faculty members with a free hand. Due process then becomes the next inconvenience to be set aside or circumvented. Appointing ad hoc, rather than elected, committees to handle these matters is one common strategy. On other campuses, administrators simply ignore decisions by faculty committees. That is one of the complaints I have received from University of Washington faculty.

It is a generally reliable rule that successful administrators avoid using all the power they have, that they consult more frequently than they are required to by the charters that grant them their power. At my own campus, the University of Illinois at Urbana-Champaign, power is vested in line administrators in a fashion that imitates military chains of command. Beginning with department heads—who, unlike chairs, are not actually required to consult their colleagues about hiring, retention, curriculum, salaries, or tenure decisions—administrators typically have the authority either to overrule or not even to consult the bodies that advise them. But an administrator who routinely dismisses such advice usually does not last long.

Used judiciously, that power can be a good thing. An inexperienced or poorly informed committee can make bad decisions that damage careers unfairly. Administrators should thus focus primarily on reversing ill-considered *negative* decisions. If a faculty committee acts to compromise academic freedom or deny recognition to a deserving faculty member, it should be asked to reconsider and, if necessary, be overruled. Years ago, as a student at Antioch College, I learned to respect a dean who altered student or faculty disciplinary decisions that were too harsh. Wisdom does not reside exclusively in one group. That is one of the benefits of shared governance.

The further one gets from department life, however, the greater the risk of misjudgment when power is exercised outside systems for peer review. When arbitrary upper-level administrative power is exercised widely against the grain of shared governance and many faculty are affected, resistance and protest often follow, and the administrator may be forced to reverse course or resign. Of course, a rogue administrator who is supported by a rogue board of trustees or regents may be able to prevail despite organized faculty resistance. That is partly what happened in the notorious case of Bennington College, when it abolished de facto tenure in 1994.

It is also true, however, that few administrators can prevail against a faculty as a whole that acts in concert. Sufficient faculty solidarity is a nearly irresistible force and can be used to guarantee proper forms of shared governance. A president who, say, dissolves a faculty senate or refuses to form one in the first place can be compelled to change his or her mind. In the end, a strong vote of no confidence, followed by a strike if necessary, makes it clear how much power resides in a faculty that reaches consensus. Dissolving a faculty senate is a clear example of a governance violation that will produce academic freedom consequences, since most senates review proposals for program creation, revision, and termination.

Such broad assaults on shared governance typically abolish major elements of academic freedom. As Larry Gerber put it in a 2001 *Academe* essay, faculty "need affirmative authority to shape the environment in which they carry out their responsibilities" ("Inextricably Linked" 23). Under AAUP principles, shared governance gives faculty the authority to shape the curriculum, select who will be their colleagues, arrange teaching schedules, and so forth. When such authority is ceded to administrators who lack disciplinary expertise, academic freedom becomes meaningless.

Since there are institutions where faculty have ceded these powers—or have had them taken away—it follows that not all faculty have academic freedom. The academy can be a satisfying and mutually supportive, if contentious, community; it can also become a hostile and counterproductive environment in which to work. The collapse of shared governance readily leads to the latter, often with reprisals for the exercise of free speech. These are not petty concerns, which is why Gerber argues that

> the practice of shared governance deserves to be supported not as a means of serving the particular interests of faculty, but rather because shared governance ultimately serves the needs of society. Without shared governance, our colleges and universities would be less likely to foster the unimpeded pursuit and dissemination of knowledge that are necessary for the healthy development of society; they would also be less likely to provide students with the broad liberal education they need to become informed citizens who can participate fully in our democracy. ("Inextricably Linked" 22)

Of course, the aim of preparing students to be critical participants in a democracy—a somewhat edgier construction than Gerber offers—is exactly what both the Right and the corporate university typically seek to undermine. Faculty members' academic freedom gives them the right to shape instruction so as to enhance students' ability to be critical citizens, an increasingly central value in the post-9/11 world, but one already under assault before then. Neoliberal, corporatized universities oriented toward income generation and job training had already begun opting instead for strictly instrumental vocational instructional aims. In the end, therefore, unless shared governance includes a faculty role in defining institutional mission, everything else about the educational environment is at risk. Yet as boards of trustees become increasingly aggressive and assertive, they often become less and less tolerant of faculty input.

The flow of interchange—and the institution's shared governance traditions—needs to move in both directions, from departmental decisions upward and from trustee deliberations downward, if faculty are actually to have a hand in shaping the educational environment and its goals. When any major area of academic life is severed from shared governance, it infects and endangers everything else.

Shared governance can also be slowly undermined both by weak governance structures that are not regularly revived and tested and by an accumulation of decisions by administrative fiat that sidestep multiple forms of due process. Many recent AAUP Committee A reports deal with institutions where academic freedom and shared governance have been pervasively undermined. Its 2007 reports on the aftermath of Hurricane Katrina in the universities of New Orleans, of course, recounted the rapid and wholesale abandonment of these principles. The 2009 report on Antioch recounts a series of major faculty disenfranchisements over a period of years. But a gradual accumulation of small betrayals of due process can be equally damaging, in part because it is less likely to draw faculty attention and response.

Several of the incidents detailed in the next chapter include evidence of weak or nonexistent shared governance checks and balances. When the Institutional Review Board (IRB) at the University of Illinois (UI) decided a few years ago to penalize a faculty member without even telling him that he had a case before it, ingrained awareness of due process should have made board members aware that that was improper. When they threatened him with prior restraint on publication of an essay he had written, ingrained awareness of principles of academic freedom should have alerted them to the fact that they were in violation of long-established standards. Good governance would have provided checks and balances to build more reflection into the process.

When my provost's office decided to threaten a faculty member with reprisals unless he removed his careful research on diploma mills from a university website, they should have thought twice before doing so. They should have been willing to defend him, not chastise him, for contributing to the public good. Shared governance and due process should both have produced a different result.

When the UI president's office in September 2004 decided to announce in the local newspaper that henceforth all discussion of public policy issues was prohibited on university email, it ought to have realized that this violated constitutional rights to free speech and flew squarely in the face of the most fundamental notion of academic freedom. Shared governance should have prevented the announcement being issued before being vetted by faculty committees. The initial story appeared in a banner headline above the fold on page 1 of the *News Gazette* (Clements). The university spokesperson later retracted her statement in a rather less visible letter to the editor. Shared governance would instead probably have generated a well-publicized and widely visible repudiation.

In two of these cases, notably, faculty members were bullied and terrorized. They certainly feel that shared governance and academic freedom are endangered species in Champaign-Urbana. Most faculty members, however, took no notice of these events, despite their being publicized in either news reports or scholarly journals. Focused on their own affairs, faculty stepped nimbly around their colleagues' bodies—as on a battlefield—and got on with their own business. Shared governance should have produced a public discussion of these cases, so that the structural failures that helped produce them might have been corrected. The local and national AAUP played a role, but UI's faculty senate, long controlled by administration allies, said nothing. We recently watched a highly ranked graduate program on campus nearly be destroyed without input from the faculty affected and without oversight from the faculty senate. Shared governance is nowhere in evidence. My own preference is to work collaboratively with upper-level administrators whenever possible. Yet "my provost right or wrong" does not seem a sufficient model of professional independence.

The pattern of faculty generally not being aware of individual cases in which academic freedom is violated exists at many large institutions. On a 2008 visit to the University of California at Irvine, I found not one faculty member in the audience aware of their own administration's legal stance in a potentially critical case involving one of their colleagues, Juan Hong. At stake was whether faculty speech about governance issues in public institutions is protected. The Irvine administration was on the wrong side, advocating a major abrogation of academic freedom. The national AAUP had submitted an amicus brief in the case. Selected members of the faculty senate at Irvine had discussed the matter, but they had done so in a closed session without subsequently informing the faculty as a whole.

Where shared governance and academic freedom are most frequently imperiled—and sometimes largely absent—of course is at religiously affiliated institutions, including a number of religiously affiliated historically black colleges and universities (HBCUs), and at institutions relying heavily on contingent faculty. Practices at religiously affiliated schools vary widely by denomination, and they change over time. Faculty at those institutions may often not only willingly but joyfully cede some of the freedoms that secular faculty expect. But even at religious institutions the limits on speech should be arrived at consensually, through shared governance, not simply imposed.

That need is never more painfully evident than when religiously committed faculty are silenced or punished against their will. It is a difficult terrain for the AAUP. The organization has chosen to keep these schools within the fold and to work with them, when appropriate, to correct practices that cross over the line. So when Brigham Young University summarily fired (for heresy) a devout young faculty member who publicly announced that she prayed to both god the father and god the mother, the AAUP eventually censured it. I have been deeply touched every time faculty members from BYU tell me how much the AAUP's intervention mattered to them. But I would be even more touched if they had the courage to join the AAUP.

It should be clear to everyone that shared governance is both a structure and an ongoing process. It only works if it is renewed continually, if good people involve themselves in it. As my UI colleague Ken Anderson is fond of saying, "Don't expect shared governance to work if you don't do the work of shared governance." Neglected, shared governance atrophies. Yet the contemporary use of the term is inevitably tinged with a certain institutional sorrow. Shared governance may work best when it is so ingrained in our practices and values that the concept almost never needs to be mentioned. Looking back to a past we have left behind, we foreground the concept because it is often not honored. The term identifies what many institutions have lost and must try to restore. But the lesson now is that we can still lose more.

So how do we preserve all the legs of the stool, once we realize that the stool will topple without them? The UC Irvine story suggests one problem with relying on a faculty senate as the sole agent charged with guarding shared governance. Senates too often develop a cozy relationship with administrators, one that leaves the majority of the faculty out of the loop. My own senate recently charged a small ad hoc committee with renegotiating a major structural violation of shared governance and academic freedom—a campus institute dedicated to funding faculty appointments and research to be controlled by outside donors—while keeping the original, unacceptable Memorandum of Agreement secret. The deal was cut to provide cover for the chancellor, who negotiated the original plan.

Senates too often make their peace with power, when part of what is needed is an independent voice that will speak truth to power. As Greg Scholtz, now head of the AAUP's Department of Academic Freedom, Tenure, and Governance, points out in workshops he conducts, "the senate won't be in front of the administration building handing out fliers, but the AAUP can be." An AAUP chapter can play that role and more: it can communicate with the board of trustees as an independent organization; it can be an informational and activist resource for work in academic freedom and shared governance; it can, in effect, serve as the senate's political whip. It can do these things in order to make good policy options public and press for their adoption, which is one of the reasons why all campuses need to strengthen their chapters or create one. Faculty senates and AAUP chapters are ideally allies, not opposing forces, but the AAUP chapter possesses more flexibility and freedom of action. In the absence of strong, unionized grievance procedures, an AAUP chapter can also investigate violations of academic freedom and partner with the national office to gain relief for affected faculty. An AAUP chapter with majority or near majority membership—Fairfield University in Connecticut is a good example—can wield considerable power, but even a chapter with 10 percent faculty membership can be very effective in addressing academic freedom cases.

But university presidents have been known to close down faculty senates. And the presidents at Bacone and Antioch McGregor fired all their AAUP activists, eliminating the chapters entirely, actions that met with deplorable silence from the national AAUP office. A faculty handbook that sets out shared governance procedures and academic freedom guarantees may often be unenforceable, though the legal status of handbooks varies from state to state. In right-to-work states and on private university campuses, genuine faculty solidarity is the only meaningful alternative. Elsewhere, at least for public higher education, the answer is unequivocal: mirror all your handbook shared governance structures, tenure regulations, and academic freedom guarantees in a legally enforceable union contract. Perhaps it is not too surprising that the one realistic way to do battle with a corporation is to organize. It is not too late for many campuses to preserve the critical features of higher education as we have known it by building shared governance into binding agreements.

To do so, however, we will have to open new conversations about shared governance nationwide. That necessity has long been clear because of a generation of neglect, but its urgency increased in 2006 when the U.S. Supreme Court decided *Garcetti v. Ceballos* and asserted that a public employee's statements about official responsibilities are not shielded from disciplinary action by employers. Judith Areen, a law professor at Georgetown University, has written an up-to-date analysis of court decisions about academic freedom and shared governance:

> Faculty at public institutions may not have a constitutional right to participate in academic governance, but their speech on such matters such as student academic standards has been granted constitutional protection by the Supreme Court. Lower federal courts have extended constitutional protection to an even broader range of academic governance speech including criticism of a department's unsound teaching and administrative practices, discussion of admissions policy and size of the student body, and criticism of the administration at a meeting of the faculty senate.

The protection granted to faculty governance speech has been limited, however, by the increasing application by courts of public-employee speech doctrine to faculty claims. Both the *Pickering* balancing test and the *Connick* public concern test in particular have been used to deny constitutional protection to faculty governance speech. The *Garcetti* official-duty test now threatens to terminate all constitutional protection for it, and for academic freedom generally. (987–88)

Faculty at public universities, of course, have a fundamental right and responsibility to participate in policy debates and comment on administrative proposals and decisions at every level of the university. That is part of the broad warrant of shared governance. Justice Souter authored a dissent in *Garcetti*, warning that the Court's decision could imperil academic freedom, and Justices Ginsburg and Stevens joined him. Unfortunately, district court cases have since put faculty in *Garcetti*'s line of fire.

The most widely publicized relevant case is one decided by a federal district court in California, *Hong v. Grant* (2007), in which UC Irvine faculty member Juan Hong sued administrators for denying him a salary increase, alleging that the act was in retaliation for his criticism of hiring and promotion practices. In what at first reads like a solid defense of shared governance, the court asserted that "as an active participant in departmental governance, Mr. Hong has a professional responsibility to offer feedback, advice, and criticism about his department's administration and operation from his perspective as a tenured, experienced professor." But then the court ruled that all this is part of Hong's "official duties" and thus, following *Garcetti*, not protected. The *Hong* case has been appealed and awaits formal argument before the federal court of appeals for the Ninth Circuit. As the AAUP has warned in an as-yet-untitled report drafted and scheduled for revision before late 2009 publication, we face "a significant threat that only professorial statements of minimal benefit to society will now be able to claim protection, because only those statements fall far enough beyond the speaker's expertise to avoid the 'official duties' stigma." In June 2009, the Academic Senate's Committee on Academic Freedom and Responsibility at the University of California at Davis distributed a memo warning colleagues that "faculty participating in shared governance are in a position in which they may voice strong views and concerns that could lead to lawful but punitive reaction by the administration, including denial of merits and even dismissal." They went on to self-censorship.

Two other Supreme Court cases, both cited in Areen's comments, were meanwhile waiting in the wings to drop their shoes: *Pickering v. Board of Education* (1968) and *Connick v. Myers* (1983). As William Van Alstyne points out, *Pickering*, a case growing out of a high school teacher's criticism of the board of education in a letter published in a local newspaper, reinforced the notion that a public school employee could not be construed as accepting a job on condition that he forbear from criticizing the schools: "a rule forbidding any teacher or school employee to comment publicly on any matter affecting the local schools without administrative permission would be an unconstitutional prior restraint under the first amendment" (104). But *Pickering* also established a new balancing test for public employee speech. A public employee's free speech rights were now to be balanced against the government's interests as an employer in "promoting the efficiency of the public services it performs." *Connick* added another complication: public employee speech was to have constitutional protection only when the subject matter was of public concern. Faculty members like to think that their values benefit the country as a whole, but courts are just as likely to see many faculty interests as self-interests. Hong is a case in point. The district court ruled that Hong's speech did not rise to the level of public concern and thus failed the *Connick* test.

The mounting ironies embedded in recent court decisions are now clear. The AAUP's draft report, again, spells them out:

> What has emerged from these rulings is a negative or inverse correlation between the scope of a professor's (or a faculty's) role in shared governance and the breadth of potential protection for expressive activity. Those institutions (like the University of California) that accord their professors the deepest stake in shaping the mission and guiding the course of the university are now most clearly empowered to sanction unwelcome faculty speech—quite simply because its professors enjoy the widest range of participatory roles. Indeed the district judge in the *Hong* case seized upon that perverse correlation in citing the scope of shared governance across the UC system as a prelude for proclaiming the administration's "unfettered discretion [in restricting] statements an employee makes on the job and accord-

ing to his professional responsibilities." In brief, as the cases stand now, one could argue that the less of a stake you have in your institution's shared governance, the freer you are (as a First Amendment matter) to criticize how it is governed, and vice versa.

Areen proposes an effort to establish a body of government-as-educator jurisprudence in response to these challenges. It could recognize that the government's role in higher education at public universities differs from its role as an employer in other agencies. Speech that might count as insubordination in the traffic department could fall within necessary shared governance responsibilities at a university. Relief from such an effort, however, will not come soon enough to counter the mounting legal threat.

The AAUP's special committee reported on the implications of these cases in 2009 and will continue to intervene in future cases with amicus briefs, but faculties should also organize to protect their interests locally. The faculty senate at the University of Minnesota proposed that the board of regents revise university policy to protect the free and open debate about governance that is central to university life. The board adopted new language in June 2009:

> Academic freedom is the freedom to discuss all relevant matters in the class-room; to explore all avenues of scholarship, research, and creative expression; and to speak or write without institutional discipline or restraint *on matters of public concern as well as on matters related to professional duties and the functioning of the University.* Academic responsibility implies the faithful performance of professional duties and obligations, the recognition of the demands of the scholarly enterprise, and the candor to make it clear that, when one is speaking on matters of public interest, one is not speaking for the institution.

Comparable efforts are under way at the University of Michigan. The aim is to establish the policy that academic freedom insulates the speaker from retribution for speech addressing institutional policies or actions uttered as a member of a unit of institutional government or simply as an intramural critic. All campuses should adopt similar language and use the occasion as an educational opportunity. In the process, an effort might well be made to define the right of administrators to comment openly on policy proposals as well. Administrators are responsible for implementing policy once it is put in place, but they should be able to debate its strengths and weaknesses beforehand and then advise on the impact of its application. Our campuses need more, not less, open debate.

For shared governance to work, faculty and administrators need to communicate. Faculty members need to understand the pressures administrators now face, and administrators need to understand faculty culture and priorities. Yet the impulse to renegotiate or circumvent the procedures that put shared governance into practice is very strong among administrators. Open communication is thus essentially meaningless unless faculty operate from a position of strength.

As campus administrators began to respond to the worldwide economic recession in 2008 and 2009, we saw an instructive and sometimes inspiring mix of imperious administrative action and organized faculty resistance. Unilateral administrative announcements of pay furloughs or salary cuts were followed immediately by principled statements protesting the imposition of decisions without consultation with the faculty and full consideration of the alternatives they could propose. AAUP chapters and state conferences took the lead in organizing these interventions across the country. On March 16, 2009, the Louisiana State University AAUP chapter issued a detailed letter demanding full consultation and recommending consideration of pay deferrals redeemable upon retirement, rather than furloughs. It also urged that any such actions be progressive, with higher percentage reductions on higher incomes. On April 15, the North Carolina AAUP state conference issued a full statement of principle and concern, protesting the lack of transparency in emergency budgetary decisions and the adoption of extreme measures prematurely. It then laid out a set of recommended guidelines. It is clear that AAUP activists understand shared governance and remain committed to its full realization. To that end, AAUP members were not only insisting on shared governance but also educating their colleagues about how to apply the concept in a crisis.

2

How a Campus Loses Its Way

Sixteen Threats to Academic Freedom

Privatization and casualization represent a repeal of academic freedom. . . . In the strong sense of academic freedom as guild control, we now have relatively little control of our labor conditions and little autonomy.
—Jeffrey Williams, "Academic Bondage" (424–25)

Knowledge production driven by market forces that reflects the hierarchy of power slowly restructures institutions of higher learning by promoting certain lines of inquiry and quietly burying others. Over time, the process becomes hegemonic, in the sense that unwritten rules about what is fundable and what is not are bureaucratically internalized and modalities of self-censorship act as a filter for condoning or shunning proposed research, teaching, and extramural utterance.
—Beshara Doumani, "Between Coercion and Privatization" (38)

When the AAUP reported in 1997 on Brigham Young University's decision to fire a young faculty member for heresy—specifically for publicly admitting she prayed to both god the mother and god the father—many readers of *Academe* were reminded of how different life could be on another campus. In most campus towns, such a "confession" would have trouble finding an administrator who would care, let alone getting newspaper coverage. The unique diversity of American higher education, embracing both private and public institutions, secular and religious schools, small liberal arts colleges and megauniversities, community colleges and research universities, was once again on view. Yet there is a counternarrative increasingly available.

Early in 2008, I spent a day with faculty members at Tulsa Community College, which has a vibrant and growing AAUP chapter. My time there brought home to me with special clarity and force some relatively new things. I had of course known that people without PhDs could serve critical roles in local vocational degree programs. What was new for me was to realize what a huge contribution to faculty governance could be made by people coming to academia from nonacademic careers. One of the people I met with was a retired fire chief, now teaching in Tulsa's fire safety and staff training program. He brought to higher education years of experience in the interrelated areas of staff management, local political dynamics, administrative bureaucracy, and collective bargaining. He possessed a tactical realism that many of my own colleagues might well wish they had. I acquired a considerably enhanced respect for the kind of diversity community colleges can achieve in their faculties.

But in other key respects, it seemed as if I had not left home at all. I come from a Research One institution, the University of Illinois, often preoccupied with a sense of its own importance and prestige. Despite its land-grant heritage, it likes to focus instead on its elite status. But what struck me repeatedly was that faculty in Champaign-Urbana and Tulsa were fighting exactly the same battles.

In 2007, my Illinois colleagues fought to revise a plan announced by the system president to create a special online division of the university, with degrees designed by central administration, without faculty input or oversight, and with courses taught exclusively by part-timers whom the permanent faculty would have no role in selecting. Contrary to our statutes, the plan was not submitted to the faculty senate for approval. It was simply announced. Some months later, faced with the possibility of a vote of no confidence, the president relented and recognized the faculty's authority over curriculum and hiring, two fundamental AAUP principles now embodied in most faculty handbooks. I report more about this matter later in this chapter. Suffice it to say here that faculty at Tulsa Community College had been simultaneously struggling with an online-degree proposal that similarly cut them out of the action.

With a tiered education system serving economically differentiated constituencies, and very different institutional missions, community colleges and research universities sometimes seem to have little in common.

Yet I am repeatedly persuaded that faculty at both types of institutions are now all very much in the same boat. The neoliberal ideology and managerial administrative style that have overtaken higher education in the past decade affect all of us. Though we are not sufficiently aware of our common concerns and interests, and are even less devoted to working on them, we are in some respects all one national faculty.

The economic and cultural force of corporatization—with its neoliberal economic values, instrumental view of educational mission, and managerial model for administration—has subjected very different sorts of institutions to similar pressures for change. It has also brought permanently exclusive and proprietary contracts to campus culture, along with elaborate security regimes designed to protect corporate secrets. The lifestyle that corporatization imposes on the faculty entrepreneur— whether in the sciences or the humanities—can be very different from a traditional model based on peer review by the National Science Foundation or National Endowment for the Humanities. You may now have to spend a great deal of time cultivating individual donors. Even from the most distinguished private foundations, some grants are administered in a fickle, opportunistic fashion, with the mission changed and the budget redirected repeatedly midstream. The entrepreneur's life may no longer be primarily the life of a university intellectual. As a result, there is a mix of threats to academic freedom, some specific to institutional type, some affecting many types of institutions. After I enumerate these threats, I will document how one research university, my own, has seen them materialize. Though the current and emerging threats to academic freedom certainly overlap and interact, here is a provisional list:

1. *Instrumentalization.* The notion that higher education is first and foremost job training has blossomed into a broader instrumentalist epistemology that concentrates pedagogy and research alike on narrowly defined goals and outcomes. It has taken root in K–12 education and in many community college degree programs. It provides the raison d'être for proprietary schools, contributes to public attitudes toward higher education as a whole, and has helped fuel the movement for more testing and accountability. It poses several interrelated dangers: to faculty's freedom to teach as they believe they should, to the research that will be supported and rewarded, to definitions of institutional mission, and

to the capacity of democratic societies to promote critical citizenship. That some students may want nothing more than a career pathway from a college education does not mean that faculty and administrators should submit to that view. As Hannah Gurman puts it in a recent review essay, universities "can function as a locus for an alternative middle-class culture that does not automatically elevate the logic of markets above all else" (317). The risk in the end is that all knowledge acquisition will be judged by its vocational uses, marketability, and practical applications. As Beshara Doumani puts it in an equation against which all commercialization efforts should be tested, "as the commercialization of knowledge expands, the space accorded to academic freedom contracts" (34). Already many students are impatient with any other standard than that of market-tested knowledge, a value system that began threatening efforts to teach professional ethics years ago. Departments in the multiversity in some cases have already ceded all or most of their commitment to a broader educational model. There is an alternative way to integrate work into the curriculum: opt for multiple job experiences, as Antioch College did, rather than job training, thereby educating students about the nature of work in the United States and helping them to make career choices they might even be happy about a decade later.

2. *Contingency.* As I detail in the next chapter, higher education as a whole has doubled its reliance on contingent teachers—from graduate student employees to part-time faculty to full-time faculty hired off the tenure track—over the past thirty years. They now do more than two-thirds of all college teaching. Since most lack any real job security, they work in fear of losing their jobs. They thus have no protection from students, parents, administrators, politicians, or community members offended by what they say in the classroom or in print. Generally cut out of shared governance, they have little or no role in hiring decisions or curriculum design. Their academic freedom is at best severely curtailed, at worst largely nonexistent.

3. *Authoritarian administration.* Unlike most of the entries in this list, instances of colleges governed by administrative fiat have a long history. The problems are perhaps most notable in tenureless institutions, in proprietary schools, and in small colleges with little history of shared governance, including some religiously affiliated institutions and some HBCUs.

The investigations reported by the AAUP's Committee A on Academic Freedom and Tenure regularly document the consequences of authoritarian administration. When a single administrator is the problem, the faculty can rise up and demand his or her replacement. That is not a useful tactic when the general culture of the upper administration is at stake, as will be clear in the University of Illinois examples I describe later.

4. *Abuses of the national security state.* In the aftermath of 9/11, we have seen a whole range of very serious affronts to academic freedom justified on the basis of national security. A few faculty members have been arrested without convincing justification and held in solitary confinement. A number of distinguished foreign scholars—among them Tariq Ramadan and Adam Habib—have been prevented from attending conferences or taking up teaching positions in the United States. Efforts have been made to institute surveillance of library usage. The U.S. Customs Department has asserted its right to impound laptop computers and cell phones without explanation. Warrantless wiretaps have proliferated. Federal efforts to prevent communication with foreign scholars are a very specific violation of academic freedom, whereas in other cases academics have simply been drawn like other citizens into the extralegal ambit of the national security state. Although we have seen some improvements in this situation with the Democratic administration elected in the United States in 2008, it will take continued vigilance, organization, focused advocacy, and political access to preserve academic freedom in all these areas. Because the national security state is an international phenomenon. We were reminded of that when William Ayers, a faculty member at the University of Illinois at Chicago, was denied entry to Canada in January 2009 after being vilified by the Republican vice-presidential nominee during the U.S. presidential campaign.

5. *Administration restrictions on the use of communication technology.* As new technologies appear, the effort to secure them as appropriate terrains of academic freedom requires both policy work and political struggle. Administrators in the corporate university often assume that traditional academic freedom does not, for example, apply to email or to college and university websites. Ill-advised state regulation, as in the state of Washington (Nelson and Watt, *Academic Keywords*), can restrict faculty use of email in public institutions. Private universities may assert corporate

ownership of the systems themselves and grant administrators the right to monitor messages. Although email is certainly subject to discovery in legal proceedings and loses confidentiality if it is forwarded, it should otherwise have the same privacy as first-class mail. Faculty and graduate students should have the same freedom to publish on university websites that they have in journals and books, despite administration claims to the contrary.

6. *Unwarranted research oversight.* Set up by federal regulation and intended primarily to protect the health and rights of subjects of medical research, Institutional Review Boards (IRBs) have steadily sought to expand their mission to embrace prior approval of humanities and social science research that involves interviewing or surveying human subjects. The unworkable demands IRBs have made include requirements for consent that indigenous peoples do not have the cultural context to comprehend, absurd objections to the psychological damage survey questions can cause, and even rejection of proposed protocols for students' conversations with family members. Cumbersome and intrusive IRB review procedures have had a chilling effect and have caused faculty to delay or abandon research projects and lesson plans.

7. *Neoliberal assaults on academic disciplines.* As the corporate university increasingly adopts the belief that market forces should set academic priorities, disciplines less able to raise outside funds are regularly threatened with downsizing or local elimination. Even faculty with tenure can be vulnerable under those conditions. Humanities and interpretive social science faculty are the most frequent victims, as they lose the structural support they need to pursue their research and teaching commitments, interests they have long thought were safeguarded by academic freedom. Meanwhile the omnipresence of market logic dehumanizes all university employment.

8. *Managerial ideology.* The rise of a separate class of career administrators and the substantial increase in their sheer numbers has helped fuel the belief that faculty are not full partners in the educational enterprise but rather resources to be controlled and managed. As Marc Bousquet argues, the administrative class increasingly conceives of itself as higher education's true vanguard. As will become clear shortly, it is not only a U.S. but also an international phenomenon. It leads to efforts to circumvent faculty governance or diminish its impact. It makes some administrators less interested in hiring full-time faculty and more willing to

unbundle faculty responsibilities and hire people to serve narrow functions. It is often the logic employed to promote corporatization and the instrumentalization of higher education. Its influence in higher education is enhanced by its victories in other professional domains. Physicians employed by managed-care corporations, for example, have lost a good deal of their professional autonomy.

9. *Circumvention of shared governance.* As discussed in chapter 1, shared governance reinforces academic freedom by establishing and securing the environment that sustains it. Shared governance refers to the negotiated agreements and processes that structure the relationship between the legal authority of trustees and the professional expertise of faculty, with primary authority ceded to the faculty in such areas as hiring and curriculum. The AAUP has defined shared governance principles in a series of key documents issued since 1920. Assaults on shared governance principles intersect with many of the other categories in this list.

10. *Globalization.* Globalization is a historical, political, and economic process that not only affects higher education but also opens opportunities that can transform its character. As universities seek to market their product in other countries—and now to establish satellite campuses abroad—they may be tempted to abandon the standards and structures that support academic freedom and shared governance in their home institutions. Tenured and full-time employment with benefits appear to be unnecessary expenses, threats to the revenue stream. International capital frequently sees higher education either as an investment opportunity or as a service industry for international finance. Thus, the International Monetary Fund (IMF) has repeatedly insisted on a shift to contingent faculty as a loan condition; rapid shifts in curriculum and ease in replacing faculty can help guarantee the kind of graduates needed to facilitate international investment. These forces and the choices they entail meanwhile corrupt the institutions participating in the globalization of higher education. Higher education should not simply be treated like any other commodity.

11. *Opposition to human rights.* If health care, a living wage, vestment in retirement systems, safe working conditions, and the right for employee groups to bargain collectively are basic human rights, then those universities that deny them have ceased to be admirable or ideal institutions. Many of the values higher education has traditionally promoted—from free

inquiry to a commitment to the public good—cannot remain credible if a university adopts the employment policies of a ruthless corporation.

12. *Inadequate grievance procedures.* Many colleges and universities, including my own, have inadequate or largely nonexistent grievance procedures for faculty. Academic senates do not overall have a good record of handling individual cases of violations of academic freedom. AAUP chapters are typically more knowledgeable, and their advice may often be heeded, but they have no authority to settle a case or enforce an agreement. Too often the only appeal is to the very administrator responsible for the offense. The increasing number of part-time faculty without tenure has made it even more important to institute grievance procedures that can protect academic freedom and job security, block workplace exploitation, and ensure safe working conditions for everyone. That will most often not happen outside collective bargaining.

13. *Religious intolerance.* Both here and abroad there are colleges and universities so consumed with their sense of doctrinal certainty that they really do not honor an acceptable standard of free inquiry. Some are essentially colleges and universities in name only. That faculty and students willingly and happily accept extreme restrictions on speech does not change the expectation that higher education should challenge fundamental beliefs, and such institutions do not do so. On the other hand, many high-quality religiously affiliated schools in fact leave most academic disciplines virtually untouched by doctrinal issues. Religious fundamentalism, whether in the United States or Iran, poses a serious threat to academic freedom.

14. *Political intolerance.* Political intolerance is also an international phenomenon. In the United States, it has been promoted by the renewed culture wars of the past decade, with the right wing's well-funded special focus on classroom speech and campus life. But in specific university settings, as I point out in chapter 4—from political meetings to department meetings and hiring committees—political intolerance can come from either the Right or the Left (Bérubé, *Left at War*). Meanwhile the ground has been prepared for still more aggressive political attacks on academic freedom from outside the university, from politicians demanding that faculty be fired to donors attempting to block controversial speakers on campus. Certainly further terrorist attacks on American soil would decrease

public support for campus-based dissent (Nelson, "Higher Education"). Yet the need for the campus as a place for passionate but reasoned debate, as a home for the loyal opposition, has rarely been greater.

15. *Legal threats.* As I pointed out toward the end of chapter 1, the federal courts are threatening to curtail both academic freedom and shared governance at public institutions. Unless the courts prove willing to carve out a special status for faculty, their current tendency to reinforce the authority of the state in its role as an employer will sweep up the faculty in its wake. This trend could leave faculty speech rights massively undermined.

16. *Claims of financial crisis.* The 2008–10 recession gave administrators the opportunity to claim that their institutions were in financial crisis whether or not it was true. Their plans often demonstrated that they did not share the same values, priorities, loyalties, goals, and sense of mission as the faculty. Deciding how to deal with either real or imagined financial constraints entails fundamental moral and ethical issues. How well schools deal with them—whether they are even willing to address them—may depend on how staffing and compensation have evolved over the past two generations. An institution that pays its president and its football coach half a million dollars a year or more, an institution that has bought into huge disparities between salaries for humanities and business faculty, an institution that already pays contingent faculty subminimum wages may have lost its moral compass and thus be ill prepared to address the ethics of employment in a "crisis." Nothing is more disingenuous in the context of an amoral salary schedule than an administrative declaration that "we all have to share the pain equally." If the worldwide recession continues, many institutions will face a fundamental choice: whether to exacerbate or ameliorate pay schedules and working conditions that are wholly unfair. Should campuses now reap the fruits of gradually enhanced exploitation or take this as an opportunity to address them? In any case, the central issue is always how you spend the money you have. That requires broad campuswide consultation. Otherwise both shared governance and academic freedom will suffer.

A decade ago I might have collapsed several of these entries under the single heading of "corporatization," but the evolving culture of higher education now requires further differentiation of the forces shaping our present and our future. They are no longer narrowly economic. If there is a single heading under which we can list the forces operating on higher education, it may well be "neoliberalism." As Paul Treanor writes in a definition that has become ubiquitous, "neoliberalism is not simply an economic structure, it is a philosophy." As such, it has "answers to stereotypical philosophical questions such as 'Why are we here' and 'What should I do?'" We are here, in effect, to echo language that has thoroughly penetrated the university, to be entrepreneurs, to compete for ourselves as individuals. "An entrepreneur is a person whose profession is to respond to market forces. . . . Neoliberalism," therefore, "is a philosophy in which the existence and operation of a market are valued in themselves . . . without any attempt to justify them in terms of their effect . . . and where the operation of a market or market-like structure is seen as an ethic in itself, capable of acting as a guide for all human action, and substituting for all previously existing ethical beliefs." It is because neoliberalism is a philosophy and a value system, not just a set of economic practices, that it has provided a context in which the emerging dimensions of the new university can coalesce. As Sophia McClennen has argued, it "teaches individuals to live, to understand their place in the world, and to imagine the future" (461); it has helped "convince the public that higher education should be a privatized commodity rather than a common good" (460). Henry and Susan Searls Giroux are equally pointed: it has led faculty to become "models of moral indifference and civic spectatorship" (278). Perhaps it is not surprising that shared governance has withered in this climate or that academic freedom has been allowed to suffer from market forces.

Not all these trends can be successfully resisted, but a campus often has sufficient relative autonomy to resist some and shape others. To do so, faculty will have to see the need for more than episodic collective action, which is the best, unfortunately, that many faculties can now muster. In the absence of broader analysis, reactive, episodic action is a recipe for destructive changes to go unnoticed and for injustices to remain unaddressed. Some problems cannot be solved by belated, ad hoc organization. In some crises an unprepared faculty will simply be overwhelmed. Episodic, issue-specific responses are all that my colleagues at the University of Illinois at Urbana-Champaign have been able to offer, though a number of administrative actions suggest that there are general problems to be addressed.

My campus opened the new millennium by demonstrating repeatedly that administrators who abandon shared governance are liable to find their increased power corrupting. My provost, now UI's chancellor, in seeking to advance his career by closing a department—and thereby making his bones in administration—focused on an unlikely department in the College of Communication, the renowned and highly ranked Institute for Communications Research (ICR). The college had drawn unwelcome attention to itself when faculty in the Department of Advertising had acted badly in public and then failed to conduct proper tenure reviews. Instead of going after Advertising, however, the provost chose ICR as a target. ICR is best known for its cultural studies work. Though the provost, a mathematician by training, knew little about cultural studies, he had an impassioned informant in the person of the associate provost, formerly head of the rival Department of Speech Communication and longtime foe of cultural studies.

The associate provost convinced his boss that cultural studies was a fraudulent methodology. Rather than take the risk of going through established channels to review ICR's program, the provost then appointed a carefully selected ad hoc committee, one of the burgeoning routes around shared governance on American campuses. One committee member, no practitioner of cultural studies herself, nonetheless convinced the others that she spoke with authority. The current head of Speech Communication and another cultural studies foe, she was the ad hoc committee's chief resource, helping to draft a report replete with demonstrable falsehoods, among them a claim that ICR had a deplorable placement record for its PhDs. The dean of the Graduate College, still for a time an honorable administrator, countered by testifying that ICR's distinguished placement record was one any other campus humanities program would envy. The report stood.

Meanwhile, under prolonged stress, a longstanding ICR tradition of cooperation between cultural studies and political economy began to disintegrate. Proponents of the latter were joined by a few opportunists, and they set about to aid in the department's destruction. Almost every element of due process was ignored. When the university's faculty senate recommended procedures for program quality reviews in 1999, it specified a number of principles and conditions, including (1) that a unit being reviewed should have the opportunity to propose members of the reviewing committee; (2) that an extended period for self-study should be allowed and the resulting report be substantively considered; (3) that any review should be conducted according to a memorandum of understanding negotiated and agreed on by all parties; (4) that any recommendations for action be similarly negotiated and result in a comparable consensual document. These are all good AAUP shared governance practices.

None of these conditions were met in the review of the college. Three developments brought the process to an end: the provost became chancellor and no longer needed to prove himself, the associate provost unexpectedly died suddenly, and a new provost saw no benefit in a continuing battle. ICR survived under a new name. No lessons were learned.

In 2002—in a story related in *Academe* and in *Office Hours* (Nelson and Watt)—my university's Institutional Review Board decided for the first time to exercise prior restraint in an effort to prevent David Wright, an assistant professor of English at the time, from publishing an essay in the *Kenyon Review* that they disapproved of (Wright). Sent to them by an administrator from another department, the piece was an example of creative nonfiction, a category that neither the campus IRB nor the university lawyers seemed able to comprehend. Among the things they demanded was that he report a "crime" described in the piece to California police. In this case, the local and national AAUP combined forces with a former chancellor who believed in academic freedom to make the university back down.

Like other campuses, as I suggested earlier, Illinois has had repeated controversies over whether traditional values and principles will be extended to new technologies. We cannot rely on most current administrators to do so. Email is but one continuing site of efforts to undermine academic freedom. Some administrators do not believe faculty have the same free speech rights on university websites as they do in university-sponsored journals, despite an AAUP policy statement on the subject. It is the job of local faculty to press for adoption of such policies.

Illinois underwent a struggle on that front in 2003. Physics professor George Gollin had become interested in online diploma mills and proceeded to do some rather thorough research on their methods and on the people operating them. He found out they were often operated by individuals with a history of running other kinds of scams. In time he established a website on a university server reporting the results of his research. When a couple of the diploma mill sites threatened to sue, the university—this time in the person of the exceptionally authoritarian associate provost—demanded he delete the entire site (Foster). Be assured that his research was thorough and accurate. Be assured that the higher education community has a vested interest in exposing diploma mills. Be assured that my increasingly corporatized university could not have cared less. The physics professor was ruthlessly bullied and threatened with sanctions. Again, the AAUP was involved, arguing on the physics professor's behalf, but the case became moot. The state of Oregon, unhappy with its inability to warn its citizens in detail about diploma mills, asked the UI faculty member if it could copy all his material. He now updates the site on behalf of the state of Oregon, after deciding it was not worth the fight with his own, wholly unsympathetic institution. Then, in 2005, Singapore officials complained about a website constructed by UI chemistry graduate student Chen Jia Hao that was critical of their government (Farrell). The university was in the process of negotiating commercial agreements with Singapore. This time the vice chancellor for research intervened and bullied Jia Hao into removing the website. When the University of Illinois announced the opening of its Advanced Digital Sciences Center in Singapore in February 2009, chancellor Richard Herman took the occasion to praise Singapore for its "proactive government" (Des Garennes). In 2008, another chapter was added to the Gollin story, when complaining diploma mill operators were convicted and began to serve prison sentences (Working).

In the midst of the fall 2004 presidential campaign, the spokesperson for the University of Illinois gave an interview to the *News-Gazette*, the local newspaper. She took the occasion to remind our faculty and students that they were prohibited from "electioneering" on the university's email. Originally designed to bar individuals from campaigning for public office themselves by using state resources, the prohibition was now being extended unilaterally to any expressions of opinion about candidates for office. This could obviously pose some problems for, say, journalism or political science faculty and students studying the election process, who might want to forward news articles or editorials to their colleagues or classmates. Most people think of their email as the equivalent of personal correspondence. Though they realize it is not that private, awareness that it could be subject to surveillance or discovery recedes into the background. As it happens, I forwarded a University of Maryland study of both Bush and Kerry supporters to my department's faculty and graduate students. One of my colleagues, a fellow known for having "anger management problems," decided that I had violated the policy and asked my department's administrative secretary how he could arrange to have me fired. In the end, he settled just for bellowing at me in the hall, saying that I had neither the ethics nor the intelligence required of a faculty member.

The university spokesperson, however, had gone quite a bit further in her newspaper interview. She went on to say that henceforth discussion of any and all public policy issues was forbidden on university email. The spokesperson operates out of the office of the three-campus system's president and had previously been a newspaper reporter focused on higher education; one would have *thought* she would have been broadly familiar with the institution's research and teaching missions. As one might expect, there are numerous public policy courses taught at the university, one of them, as it happens, taught then and now by one of the university's former presidents. The students and faculty in such courses were effectively being barred from communicating with one another about their classes.

I emailed staff at the national office of the AAUP to alert them to this story, and as I expected, they acknowledged that the policy was a complete violation of academic freedom. In the end, as another administrator put it, the university decided it had "gone a little too far" and announced that it would not enforce the policy. It did so in a letter to the editor that I did not even notice at the time, hardly the public repudiation that was warranted. The original interview had been printed above the fold on page 1, where it occupied half the page. When the president's office betrays fundamental ignorance about the university's mission, it does indeed seem that something is wrong. Four years later, the university celebrated the 2008 presidential campaign by declaring that faculty, staff, and graduate employees were prohibited, among other things, from attending political rallies on university property (Jaschik, "Beware"). It was not the first time the university's restrictions on speech violated community members' constitutional rights.

These attacks on academic freedom and shared government have been followed by program initiatives built on attempts to circumvent shared governance. Silent about the earlier events, the faculty senate finally awoke from its long sleep to take action. In 2007, the university president, who oversees all three University of Illinois campuses, announced the Global Campus Initiative and set it in motion without the required senate approval. A series of online degree programs was to be created, all controlled by a new limited liability corporation. The university's faculty would have no say in the curriculum and no say in appointing the part-timers who would teach the courses. The corporation would own all the work done on its behalf. It was a dramatic coup. A whole new wing of the university—a kind of University of Phoenix within the University of Illinois—was to be established, and the existing faculty were to be nowhere to be found. These were the events that later occasioned my sense of déjà vu at Tulsa Community College. A similar story had unfolded at Cornell University in 2000, after the administration announced plans to create "eCornell," a for-profit corporation that would develop and market distance-learning courses (Lieberwitz 306–10). Cornell's faculty senate protested and won back control of the online curriculum, limiting it to noncredit courses.

In Illinois, after the local AAUP protested and the senate provoked a confrontation, UI's president, Joseph White, appeared to give his faculty back their control over curriculum and hiring as well. But the president remained unhappy with his loss of independent authority. Driven in part by his staff's characterization of the faculty as an impediment to progress, the board of trustees in the fall of 2008 approved seeking separate accreditation for the Global Campus. This time the faculty submitted. This empowered the university to go forward with a new low salary scale for those hired to teach in the program, despite widespread recognition that online teaching is tremendously time consuming. Meanwhile, the president's staff has routinely refused all faculty offers to design courses for the enterprise (including my own), insisting instead on considering only full degree programs. This foolishly ignores the growing market for students interested in supplementing a residential degree with online courses, thereby potentially reducing degree completion time. And it ignores the possibility that full online degree programs might be gradually assembled from individual courses. Meanwhile, over twenty-five million dollars has been spent "developing" a program that has enrolled fewer than four hundred students. Cloning students might be cheaper.

The faculty at all three University of Illinois campuses made yet one more joint effort to regain control in May 2009, issuing a report recommending a substantially scaled down version of the program, under faculty supervision, that would no longer hemorrhage money in the midst of a recession (Wood, "Faculty"). Amusing efforts were made to provide a modest fig leaf for a president who had basically wagered his job on a rogue initiative. "We owe Global Campus a debt," opined vice provost Richard Wheeler, perhaps unintentionally punning about a program that had run up a massive deficit: it "stirred up campus to think about online learning" (ibid.). That month the board of trustees retreated to the more modest version of Global Campus, cutting its annual budget by 80 percent.

At the same time as Global Campus was under development, UI chancellor Richard Herman was quietly conducting negotiations with donors interested in founding a new Academy on Capitalism and Limited Government. Its board of directors would include Stephen Balch, president of the highly conservative National Association of Scholars through 2008. Its advisory board was to include Anne Neal of ACTA, but her name has apparently since been removed from the list, erased like Trotsky's image in Stalinist-era dissemination of historical photos. Balch and Neal are, of course, primarily noted for their record of attacking progressive faculty members. Yet another Academy board member, Hoover Institution fellow and military historian Victor Davis Hanson, gave the keynote address at the January 2009 annual meeting of the National Association of Scholars, warning in hyperbolic terms that Western civilization was in danger from radical professors. There was thus good reason to suppose the avowed focus on capitalism was actually a cover for a focused assault on campus academic freedom.

This time a different strategy was employed to circumvent shared governance. The Academy was set up under the auspices of the University Foundation (Jaschik, "Hoover"). Yet the Academy was designed to fund courses and faculty positions, and thus the effort to cut the faculty senate out of the action was an unacceptable violation of shared governance. Although the Memorandum of Agreement approved by the chancellor has been kept confidential, the few faculty leaders who later saw it found that a disturbing level of authority over grants and appointments was ceded to the outside donors, a fundamental violation of academic freedom. The AAUP and the senate compelled the chancellor to renegotiate, a process that failed during 2008 when the donors refused any of the compromise proposals.

At about the same time, a proposal embodying the neoliberal values summarized at the outset of this chapter surfaced. The Campus Research Board met to consider eliminating all research funding for the humanities. Humanities faculty would not even receive support for an annual trip to present a paper at a conference. I informed *Inside Higher Education* about the proposal, which had apparently already been endorsed at the campus level, and it covered the story (Redden, "Threats"). Publicly embarrassed, the university had to scale back its defunding plan.

The summer of 2009 saw a major scandal break in press coverage of the University of Illinois. Investigative reporters at the *Chicago Tribune* discovered that some eight hundred students in recent years had been admitted to the University of Illinois at the request of state politicians and other powerfully connected people (Maternowski). Although legacy and other special admission programs are common at private institutions, evidence that a public university supported by state funds regarded some taxpayers as more equal than others was deeply troubling. At the center of the story, effectively managing part of the arrangement, was UI chancellor Richard Herman.

The scandal intensified in June, when a Freedom of Information Act request produced a still more dramatic series of emails between Chancellor Herman and Heidi Hurd, then dean of the law school (Wood, "Documents"). Now the notorious former Illinois governor Rod Blagojevich was part of the story. The chair of the three-campus board of trustees, Lawrence Eppley, had served as the governor's bag man, carrying lists of the governor's chosen law school candidates to Herman. These candidates were not up to the law school's admission standards, so the dean had to be pressured to accept them. In exchange, Herman funded full fellowships for other students.

The damage done to the university's reputation is obvious. Less obvious is the toll taken on admissions officers responsible for both undergraduate and graduate admissions. Always under pressure, they try to operate ethically and honorably. But they were, in effect, ordered to segment their jobs into honorable and dishonorable portions. They argued against the special admissions, but to no avail. Their principles were expendable, ready to be sacrificed to corporate-style priorities of money and political power. Faculty oversight of the admissions process could have provided enough sunlight to prevent this scandal from ever happening.

The chancellor no doubt believes he did what was politically necessary, that he acted in the best interests of the university overall. Events would seem to have proven him wrong. But this latest crisis is arguably the fruit of ideological commitments that have dominated the campus for some years. Repeatedly, money and profit have trumped all other values, and those priorities have been embodied in administrative decisions by fiat that circumvented shared governance. Richard Herman has not been alone in embodying this pattern. Yet ever since coming to Illinois as provost in 1998 and then becoming chancellor in 2005, he has been at the center of this emerging neoliberal institution still known as the University of Illinois.

When, as provost, Herman sent around a memo detailing the ways we might cash in on the new federal commitment to homeland security, he listed a number of ways existing departments could contribute to the cause. Many of our ongoing activities, he pointed out, could be enhanced with homeland security funding, and many of our research initiatives matched things for which the government was already looking. Nowhere did he suggest that departments such as Communications, History, Journalism, Sociology, and Political Science might also be well suited to reflect on and evaluate the effects and implications of increased emphasis on national security. Universities have long established themselves as places to gain an evaluative distance from public policy. But critical reflection on homeland security was not what he had in mind. He wanted funding for boosters for the national security state. Institutionalized critique might inhibit cash flow, since not all U.S. presidents are eager to see their critics funded. When money was available, the university should be ready to set aside its principles, its independent identity, and its traditional evaluative social mission. Nor did Herman want to see a broad campuswide discussion of whether we should climb giddily onto the national security bandwagon. In this as in all other things, broad debate and discussion were an inconvenience and an impediment. The direction would be set by the man at the helm.

In this particular matter Herman made his preferences clear. In many other contexts he was often described as unreadable. Endless debates took place on campus about where he stood on issue after issue. Time after time it was impossible to know. A member of his staff once testified to me that he had never known a senior administrator so willing to change his mind, so ready to reverse direction. The two tendencies seemed to me to dovetail. He simply had no convictions, no core beliefs save ambition and economic opportunism. On many issues he stood nowhere, waiting to see where influential opinion and personal opportunity would come together, but when opportunities for institutional profit arose he would often act decisively on his own. This mix of a near featureless identity—embodied in an administrator without qualities—combined with the ruthless pursuit of profit substantially defines the contemporary neoliberal administrator.

It was only a few years ago that I used to assure my colleagues that academic freedom was well protected at major, long-established research universities. It was the other, smaller, often newer places they had to worry about. They owed it to the profession and to the country to keep up their memberships in the AAUP to guarantee their colleagues elsewhere the same freedoms we had. Their graduate students, I argued, might well go on to teach where our values were not honored. That was then. Academic freedom is now in danger across the country and throughout the world.

Commercial enterprises are notoriously intolerant of employee dissent. Anything that gets in the way of maximum profits is to be crushed. When asked what undergraduate majors we should support most strongly, the man who is now my university's chancellor replied bluntly a few years ago: those most likely to graduate students who will become wealthy enough to make major donations to the university. At that point, to be sure, almost everything faculty members identify as the university's mission is gone. But in fact securing future donations is not the only priority. We are equally committed to supporting those disciplines most able to turn a profit themselves. What is good, what is excellent, is money—not truth, not witness, not the public good, but money. In 1996, Bill Readings complained in *The University in Ruins* that "excellence" was a largely empty category. That empty space has now been filled with dollar signs. In a semiliterate plan for the future, my chancellor touts "excellence" over and over again. But he does not actually mean excellence within disciplinary understanding and judged by intellectual standards. He is not talking about quality. Excellence to him means entrepreneurial skill and success. We will pursue "excellence," and we will kill off or curtail what fails the test of profitability.

Sometimes new jargon is invented to disguise what are fundamentally commercial aims. At UI, the former vice chancellor for research was fond of promoting what he called "translational" research, which some faculty members thought sounded either hopefully interdisciplinary and theoretical or aimed toward wider public communication. What he actually had in mind was work producing practical, marketable results. The call was to translate your ideas into products. In fact, the term is in wide use in the biomedical sciences, where it aims to bridge the dichotomy between basic and applied research by addressing applications that benefit patients. The UI usage degraded this humane aim to mere product development. It reflects a growing trend to conceptualize and reward science research as a search for patents and products. As of 2009, translational research is now an official route to tenure at the University of Illinois.

A certain kind of unofficial system of checks and balances against the campuswide imposition of value systems such as this has historically come from the sheer diversity of views on many campuses, not only among faculty but also among senior administrators. A given administrator, in making decisions within his or her area of authority, might simply ignore such business-oriented priorities and award support for faculty or graduate students on the basis of a more traditional notion of quality. In a large university, the relative autonomy of various divisions has historically made a sometimes healthy ideological inconsistency entirely possible.

At the University of Illinois the central administration maintained a blacklist of faculty and graduate students who supported collective bargaining throughout the 1990s. They were denied positions on committees, denied administrative appointments, and denied campus-based awards and support. The existence of the list was kept secret until a midlevel administrator refused to appoint a particular graduate student to the Women's Studies Advisory Committee. He responded to her nomination by blithely announcing, "We can't appoint her; she's a union supporter." That helped me to understand why my own campus committee appointments stopped abruptly after I became the first faculty member to testify under oath on behalf of the graduate employees organizing for collective bargaining. Yet at the same time, the College of Liberal Arts and Sciences, which supported academic freedom until the fall of 2004, when an unsympathetic dean took charge, ignored the campus-level practice. The previous dean had appointed a strong union supporter as head of the history department and another strong union supporter as director of the Illinois Program for Research in the Humanities.

Our current university president is determined to impose a uniform business-based neoliberal model on the system as a whole. He set in motion a rapid university-wide planning process and sent numerous other signals that things will change. Adding, if you will, a commonplace element of low comedy to the threat, he directed all senior administrators to read the current bible of neoliberal economic politics, Thomas L. Friedman's *The World Is Flat* (2005).

Of course, the United States has a complex mix of four thousand colleges and universities. No one can impose ideological consistency across such a diverse spectrum of institutions. Countries with a nationally organized and mostly centrally funded higher educational system are much more subject to imposed uniformity. In late 2005, there was much furor when the government minister overseeing the Australian Research Council (ARC) decided to deny some humanities grants in areas such as gay studies that the faculty peer-review committees had recommended for funding. It was a familiar pattern, since in the United States the federally funded National Endowment for the Humanities had been doing much the same thing since Ronald Reagan became president. It is what one might well expect a conservative government to do. The NEH soon realized it was easy to stack the review panels with conservatives as well.

In the end, however, federal-government funding for the humanities in the United States is only a tiny portion of the total. In Australia, most funding for humanities research comes from ARC. It underwrites not only faculty research but also graduate-student support. Far more threatening than any showboating over controversial projects, however, is ARC's increasing preference for research with practical outcomes. In 2005, the ARC staff began traveling the country announcing that the days of solitary humanities research were coming to an end. They began looking for "linkages," meaning joint research teams composed of people from university, government, or corporate sites who are focused on projects clearly designed to produce practical results. We are not talking, therefore, about the sort of collaborative work in fundamental social and political understanding that took place in the Centre for Contemporary Cultural Studies at the University of Birmingham under Richard Hoggart and Stuart Hall from the 1960s through the 1980s but, rather, about collaborative efforts to produce marketable products or plans for savings or improvements in public services. A typical ARC example of a successful research project was the effort to change the direction of water-conservation rhetoric in Sydney, shifting from castigating water wasters to praising those who save water. These policies were somewhat ameliorated when a modestly progressive government was elected in 2007, but they have not been wholly withdrawn; ARC still prefers projects with "linkages."

Although it is often argued that a system that prioritizes economic interests inevitably devalues people, it is not widely understood just how pervasively dehumanizing values can penetrate a university community. We know, to be sure, that many corporate-style higher education managers seek to extract labor from their employees at the lowest possible cost, even if that means denying them a living wage, adequate health care, and any retirement benefits. But, to give one telling and disheartening example, consider this question: why would a dean rush over to a hospital on a Sunday afternoon? Perhaps, one might suppose, to show concern for a student or faculty member who had been hospitalized. Well, concern *about* a community member was at issue in the case I have in mind, but certainly not concern *for* the person at issue.

A few years ago, my university put in place procedures for *involuntarily* withdrawing students who posed health risks and possible insurance liabilities or whose parents might acquire grounds to sue the institution. In one example, a graduate student was in the hospital for a possible suicide attempt. The student was scheduled to be released on Monday, so a university official rushed over to tell the student she was being forcibly withdrawn from school. No matter that the news would upset the student, a particularly vicious result under the circumstances. No matter that the student would consequently immediately lose health insurance coverage. Should the former student take her own life the following week the university would not be liable. In this particular case, faculty members joined forces to force the administration to back down. The student completed a PhD and became a successful faculty member.

Perhaps the first thing to note is how many of the sixteen threats to academic freedom that I listed at the outset of this chapter are entailed in these UI stories: globalization and the reliance on contingent faculty are both at stake in the Global Campus Initiative; corporatization, the instrumentalization of mission, and neoliberal assaults on academic disciplines were at issue in the proposal to defund humanities research; inappropriate restrictions on communications technology are exemplified in the email and website cases; unwarranted research oversight is central to the IRB case; violations of shared governance range from the effort to create the Internet-based Global Campus to the announcement of the Academy on Capitalism; a willingness to deny a basic human right is entailed in the effort to cancel a student's health coverage. It is also notable how many different senior administrators are involved in these events. My accounts of their motivations, I should add, are based both on long association with the principal players and on extensive interviews with Illinois faculty and administrators.

These University of Illinois stories might not be of much interest if they were unique, but similar patterns are unfolding across the world. I challenge faculty elsewhere to consider whether a comparable dossier of academic freedom and shared governance abuses can be assembled for their own institutions. The events I describe accompany the emergent dominance of the corporate university, one designed to produce docile workers for corporations while maximizing the institution's income. Set aside is any notion of educating students to be critical participants in a democracy, an aim that necessitates protecting academic freedom and strengthening, not marginalizing, key "nonprofitable" humanities and social science fields. If we rally behind the mission of preparing students to be thoughtful citizens, we may yet educate the public about the importance of academic freedom and resist the movement toward instrumentalizing higher education, but time is very short.

Time is short in part because a huge generational shift is taking place. The faculty hired in the 1960s and 1970s are being replaced by younger faculty and contingent teachers who have no memory of a time when some administrators could be counted on to defend academic freedom and occasionally to do so eloquently. The loss of institutional memory among the faculty makes for a wonderful opportunity for higher education's corporate managers: they can remake higher education without objection from a faculty that does not know the difference.

For decades, power in large universities flowed outward from the central administration toward academic departments. In the 1990s—first in Britain, then in the United States—the flow began to be reversed, with power being withdrawn from departments and reinvested in higher-level administrators. Suddenly provosts began to have ideas about in which areas departments should and should not hire new faculty. Administrators began to seek new ways to restructure and disinvest in academic programs without faculty approval.

On the international scene, these changes can be rather more direct. The International Monetary Fund regularly makes restructuring and instrumentalizing higher education a loan requirement, and the World Bank supports the same goals. Higher education is to be directed toward graduating people prepared to facilitate international investment. The humanities are to help train those students; their academic freedom to pursue their disciplinary objectives is to be set aside. The IMF is, to be sure, not involved in a conspiracy with higher education manager/administrators in the developed countries. But global capital interests have remarkably similar aims for higher education, and the commonality of practical goals and ideological commitments makes for a worldwide environment that rationalizes a spreading neoliberal ideology.

Meanwhile a series of long-term trends will continue to facilitate loss of academic freedom and the continuing dehumanization of the humanities. The trend toward increased use of contingent faculty, discussed more fully in chapter 3—or sessional employees, as they are sometimes called in Canada—will be exacerbated in those countries with increasing student populations. More students means more need for instructional services, which only intensifies the temptation to meet those needs with part-timers. Part-timers in turn are less empowered to resist administrative fiat and more vulnerable to abuses of academic freedom. It is easier to centralize power in the administration with a disposable, contingent labor force.

Some seemingly inexorable small-scale forces have additional potential to housebreak critical faculty and diminish the presence of inconvenient faculty dissent. Three or four decades ago a university press scholarly book readily sold two thousand copies and easily recouped its full publishing costs, which are several times the base cost of printing a book. Reliable sales in many disciplines are now down to roughly two hundred copies, a stunning 90 percent decline since the early 1970s. Online publication works well for journals, since you need only print out the essay or essays you need, and reading short articles online is tolerable, but the book remains the main vehicle for major arguments in many fields. Two hundred copies, however, does not make widespread impact likely. Why set aside time for humanities professors to do major research projects if they have no suitable venues for book publication? Why make book publication a requirement for tenure if it is not realistic? Why hire full-time faculty if there is no meaningful research component to their job? Why not dramatically increase teaching loads if research is irrelevant?

In Britain and Australia, the traditional major research project is already being marginalized. Britain's Research Assessment Exercise (RAE) explicitly ranks participating university departments on the basis of a quantitative, not qualitative, model for evaluating research. Australia's Research Quality Framework (RQF) will probably do much the same. Britain's five-year rankings cycle means that individual departments can repeatedly gain or lose hundreds of thousands of dollars and eventually turn themselves into targets for elimination. The peer pressure to produce the expected number of publications is intense, and many faculty members realize that modest articles not challenging prevailing assumptions are the most reliable products. Putting all your eggs in a book basket can be immensely stressful as the deadline approaches, especially since only published (not merely accepted) works can count. If you do not get your book done in time, you have failed not only yourself but also your colleagues. The whole department will pay a financial price. The emerging piecework model for academic publication discourages risky, innovative, unconventional work and encourages mediocrity. It also, to be sure, guarantees a working level of familiarity with the current state of the discipline among most faculty—a clear benefit—but at the cost of undercutting more radical intellectual ambitions. Yet some faculty like it; it makes academic life more predictable and manageable. Applying Frank Donoghue's analysis, they have internalized the very business values of productivity and efficiency that have been deployed against the humanities for over a century. In all countries with such ranking systems, the number of institutions receiving significant research support is to be kept very small. In a system radically differentiating between winners and losers, competition rules and the sense of interinstitutional community diminishes.

Even now only a small percentage of the professoriate gets meaningful research support, but the profession as a whole depends on the dissemination of that research. Only that way can historical events and texts be reinterpreted to contextualize analysis within present cultural and historical conditions. Only that way can new evidence be incorporated into historical understanding. Conservative models of humanities teaching have us dutifully transmitting unchanging truths to new generations, a model for which academic freedom is less crucial. Humanities faculty are left with two roles: teaching business majors to write memos and providing uplifting entertainment for scientists and engineers. With faculty members reduced to being clerks or clowns, there is hardly any reason to tolerate their presenting politically unpopular opinions.

In this context, a strong national AAUP or equivalent organization— the Canadian Association of University Teachers (CAUT), the Association of University Teachers (AUT) in the United Kingdom, the National Tertiary Education Union (NTEU) in Australia—is essential for raising faculty consciousness. All these organizations need to be strengthened. All the forms of a successful faculty presence on a campus, moreover, involve solidarity and collective action. Without collective action, corporatization and its attendant realignments of campus power will leave faculties with no meaningful role in defining institutional mission, no effective role in campus governance, and no way of sustaining academic freedom. We are at a tipping point both for hundreds of individual campuses and for higher education as a whole. We could be living in the last days—internationally—of what Stanley Aronowitz heralded as *The Last Good Job in America* (2001).

At the same time, there are genuinely hopeful signs. They all have one thing in common: the decision by faculty to act collectively, to combine individual agency with group solidarity. In the process, new identities or subject positions become available to faculty members used to concentrating exclusively on their own self-interest. From the decision to strike over intellectual property rights and control over online curricula in Toronto to the citywide living-wage campaign in Boston, faculty on a number of campuses have begun to realize the impact they can have when they act together.

The truth is that faculty members *have* the power they need to save higher education's key roles if they choose to exercise it collectively. A renewed and conscious commitment to the task of educating students to be critical participants in a democracy may be the linchpin of every other issue. That will require a level of faculty consensus we have not seen for decades, especially at the large multiversity. It may require building consensus on more practical workplace, income, and benefit issues first, before ideological investments in institutional mission can be tackled, because at present there is no faculty consensus about higher education's mission. And some faculty members are perfectly comfortable with divergent commitments to job training and personal research. There will need to be discussion, compromise, and mutual understanding among faculty across disciplines if academic freedom is not to be ceded to the neoliberal faith that economic forces should determine our future.

The only longstanding faculty consensus is that higher education is underfunded. That complaint plays poorly in the public sphere, in part because the public is at least vaguely aware that some higher education enterprises are very well funded, just as they are aware that some faculty and administrators are handsomely rewarded. Tenured faculty members need to focus on *how universities spend the money they have*. The moral implications of budgeting—including the ruthless exploitation of some employees—needs to be addressed if we are to have any credibility. As I suggest in chapter 5, unions can play a major role here. Higher-paid faculty and administrators need to recognize that their comforts are founded on the exploitation of other members of their community. We need to reconceive privilege in terms of its structural relationship to a wider and imperiled academy.

Of course, virtually no one in higher education thinks he or she is overpaid. Yet a sense of community responsibility requires admitting that a large, corporate-style spread in wages and benefits undercuts any sense that universities are ethical institutions committed to the common good. The flawed public image of our ethical status undermines academic freedom and diminishes every element of our mission. A university that acts like a corporation cannot expect to be viewed as anything else.

The challenges we face entail the very heart and soul of higher education. Yet the lesson of recent activism is that new faculty identities can embody both disciplinary loyalty and community responsibility. Despite decades of careerism in the academy, there remains a vital core of idealism in the professoriate. This idealism can be tapped to preserve academic freedom and to make higher education stronger, more responsible, and more influential.

[3]

Legacies of Misrule

Our Contingent Future

The core argument for tenure, the special job security of academics, has always been that they needed this protection in order to practice research and teach freely to the benefit of their students, the institutional mission of higher education and the society as a whole. . . . For most faculty now, these rights exist as nostalgic historic artifacts. . . . This casualization and collective disempowerment of the majority of faculty is by far the greatest threat to academic freedom and activism on campuses.

—Joe Berry, "Contingent Faculty and
Academic Freedom" (359–60)

Why contingency? No university administration refers to its contingent faculty as contingent. That would be to admit that there was a labor system instead of a few people earning pin money. They use lots of terms to describe those they humiliate, but not "contingent." Those activists who formed COCAL (Coalition of CONTINGENT Academic Labor) chose the term for two reasons. First, no administrators used it. It could be ours. Second, and more importantly, the term refers to the exact nature of the problem: the contingent appointment.

—John Hess, posting to Contingent Academics listserv

It was the most gradual of the changes shaping higher education. Contingent faculty members had slowly but inexorably come to dominate higher education's teaching workforce. Not that they dominate anything else, as their authority anywhere in the industry—from the classroom to administration to governing boards—could hardly be less. For half a century, tenure had been the key guarantor of academic freedom. Now

tenure is available only to a minority of faculty members. Higher education's reliance on contingent teachers has steadily increased over two generations. Although the complete current cohort of part-time faculty is far
less likely to have the PhD or an equivalent professional degree—as of
2003, 80 percent of the full-time faculty at four-year institutions had such
degrees, whereas only 35 percent of the part-time faculty did—contingent
teachers are increasingly drawn from the same pool of potential employees who fill tenure-track jobs (National Center for Education Statistics).
More recently hired contingent faculty now typically have the same or
equivalent qualifications as faculty on the tenure track. Their exploitation,
always reprehensible, is thus also professionally unjustified. In some cases,
the treatment of contingent faculty members is fundamentally sadistic, as
when a tenured faculty member gets a gigabyte of memory for an email
account, while a part-timer is limited to one hundred megabytes.

The extreme economic vulnerability of contingent faculty—and the
fundamentally corrupt nature of higher education's job system—became
dramatically evident en masse in the 2008–10 recession, as schools seeking to cut budgets paradoxically began jettisoning their least expensive teachers. This left some contingent faculty without incomes—and
in an industry where there remained plenty of work (teaching) to do.
Enough work remained in fact that some community colleges hired more
part-time faculty to cope with expanded enrollments as potential students retreated from unemployment or higher tuition at other schools.
Meanwhile, the salaries of high-paid faculty and administrators typically remained untouched. In at least one case—Weber State University
in Utah—the administration proposed cutting part-timer salaries by
7 percent, while leaving the salaries of full-time faculty and administrators untouched (Trentelman and Nelson). Other schools contemplated
across-the-board salary cuts or furloughs, with no special consideration
for employees living on the edge of poverty.

A modest level of contingency in the academy—exemplified by short-
term postdoctoral employment—can give new PhDs a chance to build
their vitas at their home institution or to gain experience in a different
kind of academic setting. It gives community members employed elsewhere a chance to contribute to higher education part-time and lends
experiential and occupational diversity to the college and university

workforce. But nothing justifies the creation of a vast army of underpaid MAs and PhDs who cobble together a frenzied, itinerant, subsistence lifestyle teaching six or eight courses a semester at multiple institutions. Nor do we benefit from increasing the number of full-time faculty off the tenure track, without job security and the full guarantees of academic freedom. Yet that, if anything, understates the problem, now that the bulk of undergraduate teaching is no longer done by tenured faculty. Of the roughly 1.4 million faculty members teaching in the United States nearly 1 million are contingent. Is this workforce overpaid? About 70 percent of those standing in front of an American college classroom earn less than sixty thousand dollars annually. Only 10 percent of U.S. faculty earn more than eighty thousand dollars a year. Those institutions that do not have major research expectations for their tenured faculty—and that means well over 90 percent of American colleges and universities, despite fatuous and hypocritical claims to the contrary—should give all their long-term contingent faculty tenure. The faculty members themselves should be able to choose between full-time and part-time tenured positions.

Part-time faculty with full-time positions in other employment sectors often do not see contingency as structurally degrading. But it would be foolish to suppose that even those engaged in fully voluntary contingency would object to being paid fairly, to enjoying better working conditions, and to having some reassurance of continuing employment. No one I know objects to confirmation that his or her labor is valued. Voluntary contingency, moreover, can easily become exploitive, as when new PhDs who take part-time employment as a bridge to a tenure-track position discover that one part-time position can follow another indefinitely, eventually amounting to permanent second-rate employment without relief. Notably, even science postdocs over the past decade have become serialized, with those who hold them turning into lifetime members of an academic underclass.

Employment insecurity is, to be sure, a widespread feature of a globalized corporate economy. Neoliberal dogma insists that all forms of job security are passé, that market forces will reshape employment continually, and that people as a result can expect to change careers many times over the course of their lives. But the jobs available in these fragmented careers are often not of comparable quality. Meanwhile, as Steven Greenhouse demonstrates, exploitation of both full- and part-time employees is spreading throughout the economy: Wal-Mart managers commonly falsify work records to reduce employee take-home pay, JPMorgan Chase terrorizes workers so they do not report overtime, and Microsoft repeatedly rehires its temporary help so as to make them essentially permanent. These radical forms of exploitation are grounded in a cultural shift that has evolved over two generations. As Mary Burgan writes,

> By the mid-1990s, just-in-time, outsourced, and short-term contract employment had become common practices in industry. The industrial unions, which had demanded assurances of security and benefits for work-ers during the years that saw the rise of the American middle classes, were cast as villains in a troubled world economy. There seemed to be a general agreement that entering the global marketplace entailed loosening tradi-tional benefits for workers. Demands for contract provisions that covered medical and retirement benefits for employees were considered a form of union blackmail, and job security was viewed as one of the last vestiges of outdated employment systems. (32)

Those who seek to take advantage of contingent labor in the academy thus have broad cultural and economic warrant for their opportunism, despite that fact that teaching and research based on professional exper-tise cannot be primarily grounded in short-term careers. A casualized commitment to a discipline hardly offers a sufficient knowledge base for either disciplinary or interdisciplinary research, and many academic dis-ciplines have no substantial nonuniversity career options.

Governing boards dominated by businesspeople nonetheless typically consider the neoliberal warrant for employee exploitation definitive. If other industries reduce costs that way, why shouldn't higher education? Why should one industry be out of step? There is little in the culture of many governing boards themselves that would lead to a defense of the special character of higher education. Certainly declaring education a basic human or civil right gets one nowhere, given that health care is already commodified and corporatized in the United States. Indeed, as

Marc Bousquet argues, universities have already adopted the corporatized health care system's delivery model.

The core argument—that job security is necessary to maintain the integrity and quality of the distinctive higher education industry— needs to be restated continually, but local higher education administrators often enough argue the opposite case. Not only community college presidents but also other administrators accustomed to running tenureless campuses can readily come to see contingency as a tremendous managerial advantage, especially if they view their mission exclusively as marketing job training and credentialing to student consumers. Their product can be quickly retooled, and their marketing can respond rapidly to corporate needs and students' wishes. The last thing they want to do is promote anything that would challenge or discomfort their consumers. A docile faculty is a tremendous benefit in this instrumental model; they deliver the product without complaint or delay. Even members of governing boards with quite different ideological commitments may well hear such perspectives in their states or local communities.

Elsewhere in the world, quite specific forces can play a role in maximizing part-time academic employment. The World Bank and the International Monetary Fund sometimes require applicant countries to increase the percentage of part-time teachers in higher education, since they view such "flexibility" as the best way to ensure that local industries will have exactly the trained employees they need (Hulbert and Mason; Jones; Kuehn). As new job categories become business priorities, a university is expected simply to release the faculty who were better able to train last year's required labor. The IMF also gives close attention to another key employee category: graduates best suited to facilitate foreign investment; there too, priorities change, and disposable faculty maximize flexibility.

American colleges and universities are likely themselves to contribute to the internationalization of the trend toward increasing use of part-time faculty. Our institutions are rapidly becoming interested in establishing satellite campuses abroad, and with profit the primary motive in these ventures, part-time, untenured faculty will be the rule. We also can expect contingent faculty in these satellite enterprises to have little or no role in shared governance, even at the most fundamental level of designing curriculum and degree programs. Peer review is likely to have no place at all.

We may look to New York University and its Abu Dhabi project as an early indication of what to expect from other schools (Krieger; Ross). Faculty at the home institution who have some share in governance, meanwhile, must force compliance with ethical workplace standards on those administrators who think they can operate rapaciously at a distance with impunity. American, Canadian, and British faculty can compel their administrators to replicate AAUP- or CAUT-style principles in the rules for foreign adventures. If they travel to the satellite campus, faculty can monitor compliance. There is no reason why we have to tolerate practices elsewhere we would not tolerate at home. In April 2009, the AAUP and CAUT issued "On Conditions of Employment at Overseas Campuses," a joint policy statement on just that issue.

The human cost of contingency spreads across all industries worldwide, and the loss of employee loyalty is universal, but the price each industry pays in its ability to function is partly context specific. A software company with too many people arbitrarily selected for expendable employment may undercut its capacity for technical innovation. A college or university addicted to contingency loses different benefits: the critical intellectual courage of its teachers, the awareness of institutional history among its employees, the wisdom and good judgment gained through experience, the cooperative relationships built over time, the knowledge of how to access local resources, the renewable relationships with students possible with long-term full-time employees. We see that happening not just in the United States but also in other countries relying heavily on part-time faculty. In North America alone, Mexico's faculty is about 70 percent part-time (Ramos), and Canada's is about 40 percent or more (Oliver). But in fact a swath of countries in Latin America from Mexico to Argentina rely on part-time faculty for 70 percent or more of their college and university teaching (Altbach). These faculty members cannot be said to have careers in any full sense of the word. In Mexico, those faculty members lucky enough to qualify rely on free food handouts.

. . .

Our current overreliance on contingent teachers can damage the academy in the following ways:

1. *It undermines academic freedom,* by breaking the link between academic freedom and job security that has been fundamental to the AAUP's stance throughout its history. You do not have academic freedom if they can fire you tomorrow or nonrenew you next semester.
2. *It destroys shared governance,* by excessive reliance on teachers who have little or no role in governance—who may even be barred from it—and who risk losing their jobs if they resist administrative fiat or criticize administration plans or proposals.
3. *It undermines teaching effectiveness,* because some contingent teachers have less time for student advising and less time to work at staying current in their fields, especially if they have to teach numerous courses at several schools to support their families. They may also be more difficult to contact for recommendations. Thousands of contingent faculty members over two generations have been unable to produce as much scholarship as they wanted. Students and faculty alike have thus lost the benefit of their underutilized and costly doctoral training. The abusive working conditions contingent faculty often face can undermine the quality of education. Thus, Dan Jacoby has reported that graduation rates are lower at community colleges that make heavy use of part-time faculty. Audrey Jaeger's research shows that attrition rates increase for students who take more courses with contingent faculty. Adjunct teachers also have less time to spend in class preparation and less time for office hours. Using 1998 data from the U.S. Department of Education's National Center for Education Statistics, Ernst Benjamin points out that 47 percent of part-time faculty—but only 7 percent of full-time faculty—hold no office hours whatsoever ("Reappraisal" 88). The problem, however, is not with the faculty themselves but rather with their terms and conditions of employment, which do not enable part-time faculty "to involve themselves adequately in promoting student learning" (ibid. 85). One piece of counterevidence comes from Cross and Goldenberg's 2009 study of ten elite universities, which shows that adjunct faculty at such institutions

receive higher teaching evaluations from students than tenure-track faculty do. Of course, some of these adjunct teachers face less brutal working conditions than adjuncts elsewhere.

4. *It maximizes vulnerability to political pressure,* because teachers without job security are increasingly subject to outside political intervention. Contingent faculty subject to summary dismissal are less likely to risk making controversial statements in the classroom. College and university independence is thus undermined. Events off campus—such as terrorist attacks—are sure to decrease public tolerance for campus-based political dissent. Contingent faculty are the most vulnerable.

5. *It decreases respect for the teaching profession and its credentials,* since pervasive use of underpaid, expendable labor devalues faculty and erodes both public and institutional respect for the professoriate and for professional qualifications such as the PhD. Faculty who are little more than minimum-wage seasonal employees cannot expect the respect accorded comparable professions.

6. *It decreases faculty control over the curriculum,* by giving administrators more power over its design and priorities, thereby removing it from the authority of those with the greatest knowledge and expertise. Faculty responsibility for the curriculum is a fundamental AAUP principle and expectation.

7. *It threatens benefits for all teachers,* because when part-time faculty are employed without a living wage, health care coverage, vestment in a retirement system, and appropriate professional working conditions, cost-conscious administrators are tempted to whittle away at benefits for full-time faculty.

8. *It encourages unfair employment practices elsewhere,* because hiring teachers at less than a living wage encourages other industries to adopt slave-labor employment practices. Inadequate pay for contingent teachers also creates pressure to reduce pay increases for tenured faculty.

9. *It decreases support for advanced research,* because a largely contingent faculty workforce has less overall support for the intensive research that benefits both academic disciplines and the entire country. Institutions have less inducement to support the careers and intellectual interests of employees they view as expendable or temporary, even when those perceptions are untrue. Excessive reliance on con-

tingent faculty also undercuts the justification for funding advanced research libraries.

10. *It destroys lives and breaks the human spirit,* as the ruthless, long-term exploitation of contingent faculty exacts a huge cost in broken lives, most dramatically for those lacking union representation. Contingent faculty in collective bargaining not only see their working conditions improve; they also gain a sense of solidarity and dignity that is both a personal and a social benefit. Those who must fend entirely for themselves may show the effects of years of unremitting stress and insecurity. Decades of frag-mented work can be a major source of personal trauma.

The thirteenth section of the AAUP's Recommended Institutional Regulations, approved in November 2006, addresses some of these issues, offering contingent faculty advanced notification of reemploy-ment, peer evaluation, due process for dismissal for cause, and expecta-tion of continuing employment, based on years of service. But that does not relieve tenured faculty of their responsibilities. They must defend part-timers' academic freedom. They must argue for better salaries and working conditions for their contingent colleagues. They must help contingent faculty organize for collective bargaining. They must do so not only because it is a moral and professional responsibility but also because part-timers especially are geographically dispersed and vulner-able to antiunion retaliation. If tenured faculty members are in collec-tive bargaining, they can negotiate a contract that limits the use of con-tingent labor on campus, generally by specifying the overall percentage of campus courses that can be taught by part-time faculty. Part-timers themselves need to build a sense of community. They should not mourn but organize, though they face daunting challenges to collective action, including their scattered professional lives and their well-grounded fear of losing their jobs.

In the meantime, it is not unreasonable to pose a blunt question: Is tenure dead? The question is less a provocation than a cliché. Certainly several groups and numerous individuals have been busy for years trying to kill it off. The Pew Foundation has long been seeking alternatives— any alternatives short of extraplanetary exile for tenured faculty. Richard Chait and Cathy Trower have been dancing an antitenure two-step for any paying audience for more than a decade. Francis Fukuyama, having failed in his notorious pronouncement about "the end of history," now settles for urging the end of tenure. Mark Taylor, perhaps unwittingly conflating postmodernism with chaos theory, proposes the simultaneous elimination of tenure and departmentalization, imagining a university in constant and irremediable bureaucratic flux, with a transient faculty continually reassigned to new working groups. Meanwhile, the antitenure mice have been nibbling away at it for thirty years, simply by hiring faculty off the tenure track, either full-time or part-time.

From one perspective—that of nationwide trends and averages—the battle for tenure is already lost. Raw data collected by the U.S. Department of Education and then compiled by the AAUP shows that from 1975 to 2007 the percentage of American faculty either tenured or tenure eligible was gradually cut nearly in half, from 56.8 percent to 31.2 percent, while the percentage of contingent faculty rose from 43.2 percent to 68.8 percent (AAUP, "Trends") and is now 70 percent or more. The actual number of tenured positions has not significantly declined. Instead, the bulk of hiring has been off the tenure track. Yet on numerous elite or liberal arts campuses, the picture continues to look entirely different. At many of our most well known institutions, tenure is alive and more than well: it remains the primary model for faculty hiring. And, here and there across the country, institutions have rethought their addiction to foraging for fast-food faculty and have instead been replacing expendable part-timers with permanent employees.

In the remainder of this chapter, I first dramatize the differences between the worlds with and without tenure and then explain why tenure is beneficial to all faculty, both those who do and those who do not have it. Finally I suggest some of what we must do if the problem of contingency is not to continue weakening higher education. One of the unexpected consequences of the immense increase in the number of contingent faculty is that in many places they constitute a new subculture. That means the ignorance of tenured faculty members—once limited to not knowing either who their contingent colleagues were or under what conditions they worked—now has an unsettling added dimension. Most tenured faculty members do not understand the culture of contingent faculty—the interests, priorities, beliefs, values, work patterns, or social and professional relations that shape their daily lives. "You are not us," the implicit rebuke of the tenured faculty to their contingent colleagues, has evolved into "we are not you," the rallying cry of part-timers themselves.

It is hardly surprising that part-timers have a distinctive culture, given that their life experiences are quite different from those of tenure-track faculty. Gather a group of young part-timers together, and you will not witness the ongoing conversation about tenure expectations typical of traditional assistant professors. In states where it is permissible, you are more likely to hear people trading information about how to get unemployment benefits in the summer. For those teaching at several institutions, an obsessive focus on one department's politics is not a given. They will not be so likely to talk about local opportunities for research funding, since there is a good chance they are not eligible for it. They will probably not be sharing news about the new computers issued to department members. Given that they may have no office space and no place to gather, they may never meet their peers. If they do, they are more likely to discuss next semester's employment prospects. When part-timers from different schools get together, they inevitably compare institutional differences, employment practices, contracts, and benefits. They focus on the coping strategies unique to their tenuous identities.

Increasingly, one common element of contingent culture is disdain for tenure. Yet the benefits that a stable, dedicated, tenured workforce offers to departments composed of tenured and tenure-track faculty cannot easily be overstated. I know my colleagues' published work. I know the subjects of their current research. I am familiar with their course syllabi. I have built (or avoided) personal relationships with them over time. When I advise students about forming faculty committees, enrolling in courses, or planning a curriculum, I know how to balance faculty strengths and weaknesses. When we hire new faculty, we vet them exhaustively and come to know their intellectual commitments months before they arrive. Even in moments of intense departmental conflict, in-depth knowledge of the players puts both advocacy and aggression in context. We are a community—with all its stresses and rewards—not a traveler's hub. And our students are part of that community; in time they master its resources and risks. They too need not travel blind.

The other world of tenure, the contingent world dominated by tenure's absence, is nothing like this. Substantially a world of part-time employment, there your transient "colleagues" pass unnoticed, like ships blind to each other's passage beneath the noonday sun. Yet even that blunt metaphor is inadequate, since it entails potential daytime visibility. Some departments concentrate part-timers in evening courses. Since those contingent faculty members only feed on the curriculum at night, they are sometimes nervously referred to as "vampires." Perhaps that is a useful provocation. If it triggers a moment of recognition, tenured faculty may realize that their contingent colleagues are *our* vampires. We called them up and assigned them to our darkness. They are us, the faculty.

At institutions relying on contingent teachers, the appearance of new faculty or disappearance of continuing faculty is often unmarked. There is no sense of community. The college is literally not a meeting place, a space of interaction, for its faculty, many of whom may retreat to the parking lot immediately after class to travel to another teaching job. A department in an institution staffed with contingent faculty is often essentially a structure filled with nameless bodies. The campus is recognizable only through its buildings and its students. In institutions without tenure, academic freedom and shared governance are often nonexistent.

A department of tenured faculty may succumb to posturing and bombast, but even that is preferable to the world without tenure and academic freedom, where the climate is too often ruled by fear—fear of losing your job, fear of consequences for speaking frankly. If you believe part-time faculty have academic freedom, you should talk to them and learn how they design their courses so as to avoid controversy and the potential loss of their jobs. Most tenured faculty members have probably spent their entire careers without feeling the need to exercise that sort of caution. They may often enough want to encourage controversy. Yet institutions relying heavily on vulnerable contingent faculty still hypocritically claim they are teaching their students through the example of intellectual courage. Not that tenured faculty members are necessarily eloquent or outspoken. As Matthew Finkin and Emanuel Donchin have succinctly pointed out, tenure is not a guarantee that everyone will be courageous, but it is a method for protecting the few who are.

Yet the protection that the combined force of tenure and shared governance gives significantly diminishes the necessity for constant, disabling wariness and for intellectual choices shaped by estimates of personal and political vulnerability. Remarkably, many contingent faculty members nonetheless remain fiercely dedicated and give excellent service, though the contradictory pressures to be forthright and cautious make the world without tenure fundamentally schizophrenic.

The world without tenure is also fractured on other grounds. The part-time faculty member with a full-time job in another industry, moonlighting to teach a course at an area college, is less likely to need a sense of community at the supplementary educational workplace. The retired full-time faculty member, returning to part-time teaching, may miss some lost elements of collegiality, if they existed in the past, but is not guaranteed to be so disenchanted with his or her lot.

There are also significant disciplinary and methodological differences in the level and character of the alienation faculty without tenure may feel. Humanities, science, or social science faculty who service students more elaborately—either by teaching small classes or grading individual papers—but whose fragmented jobs may curtail interaction with students may well feel more alienated than faculty delivering lectures to large audiences or teaching strictly technical courses in the increasingly instrumentalized higher education environment. Delivering large lectures or evaluating multiple-choice tests does not instill an equivalent level of identification with individual students, and it can take less time, though preparing lectures for the first time or writing exam questions can be labor intensive. Those contingent faculty members who put more time into each course may also find their institutional anonymity and invisibility—and diminished contact with students—more painful.

In its most comprehensive, institution-wide forms, the alienated world without tenure is consolidated across an economic and cultural divide. The two worlds of tenure—one with tenure, one without—are increasingly serving different populations. Tenure is becoming concentrated in elite institutions, where it serves elite students and offers faculty elite identities. The world without tenure is more and more the home of the poor, most notably in community colleges. Offered to poor students, to working-class students, to disenfranchised minorities—often enough by alienated faculty—untenured teaching too easily becomes a second-class education. The very disadvantaged students who most need extra attention from faculty are thus being denied it. As George Kuh writes, "getting prompt feedback, discussing grades and assignments, and discussing ideas out of class—we know that the more frequent the contact the better" (29). As Vinnie Tirelli and Marc Bousquet both persuasively argue, our two-tier higher education system is fundamentally a class system—both for faculty and for students. Sympathy for contingent faculty has led many of us to suppress such concerns, but new statistical evidence suggests that contingent faculty have only half the time to give to class preparation. And we have learned that students who take their introductory courses from contingent faculty have lower retention rates. Timothy Schibik and Charles Harrington, for example, in a study of one university found "a statistically significant negative relationship between a freshman's first-semester level of exposure to part-time faculty and second-semester retention" (18).

The problem is immensely exacerbated by the two other major institutional consequences of tenure's structural absence: diminished or nonexistent academic freedom and diminished or nonexistent shared governance. But of course, these two matters are codependent. Curtailment of one enhances curtailment of the other. The AAUP has long known that job security underwrites academic freedom both individually and institutionally. Without a clear majority of faculty possessing job security, a climate of fear may prevail. In 2004, the AAUP censured the administration of Philander Smith College for dismissing a professor who violated an injunction against contact with the media; censure was removed in 2008 after a new president rescinded the policy. Without strong shared governance provisions the faculty loses control over the primary areas of its responsibility.

More deeply, faculty members lose all control over their own fate, and they typically lose the right to peer review and proper grievance procedures. The world without tenure is a world of administrative fiat—first over all elements of shared governance, then over academic freedom as it applies to faculty speech in public and in the classroom. Although the world of faculty contingency has seen numerous serious curtailments of faculty speech in recent years, the bedrock denial of faculty agency is in shared governance. Stripping an institution of all procedural safeguards then enables assaults on individual freedoms as occasions arise. To survive at all, faculty then must suppress their fear enough to function, but it is with them all the while nonetheless.

At present, the two worlds—with and without tenure—seem sharply divided. Yet in some critical respects they are becoming steadily more similar. The most critical cultural overlap is in administrative impatience with the element of faculty authority in shared governance. In too many elite institutions faculty have carelessly let thorough faculty oversight over programmatic development, budget allocation, and educational mission wither. Administrators have filled the vacuum and are increasingly frank in their contempt for the delays inherent in democratic process. We have learned too often that when the bedrock of shared governance crumbles, erosion of academic freedom soon follows.

One sees evidence of this connection at many institutions with tenure. Pressure to revise faculty dismissal proceedings may rise. At many institutions a general commitment to across-the-board improvement of department quality is replaced by a pecking order based on each department's capacity to raise external money, again without the faculty senate's consent. Sometimes, as at Rensselaer Polytechnic in New York, administrators find excuses actually to restrict a senate's right to determine its membership and thus who will participate in shared governance. And increasingly, some institutions, among them my own, are becoming reluctant to fund unprofitable humanities and social science research, something the last two generations of tenured faculty never imagined would happen.

I am not predicting that tenure will disappear from the world that presently has it. I am, however, arguing that the erosion of shared governance is a strong national trend that cuts across both worlds. Thus, I am predicting that as shared governance declines and managerial administration rises, tenure and academic freedom will mean less than they have for nearly half a century. The two worlds of tenure are more interdependent than they may appear. It is, for example, obviously easier to try out decision making by administrative fiat at institutions with a decisively disempowered faculty. Although such efforts are not coordinated, knowledge about them spreads through administrator networks to other campuses. The contingent world without tenure is a living laboratory for higher education as a whole. The results of experiments conducted there will not bring good news to any of us.

Will institutions without tenure and academic freedom effectively destroy tenure and academic freedom at those institutions that have them? Not likely. Will the world with tenure and academic freedom be gradually corroded and transformed by the world without them? Almost certainly. The slow but nearly inexorable spread of contingency from the first to the second group of schools—a spread fundamentally facilitated by passive faculty at some of our best institutions—gives fairly reliable evidence of how trends at one kind of institution can influence others.

My dichotomous model now needs further qualification. As we all know, at many institutions the two worlds of tenure coexist, with vulnerable and protected faculty often enough sharing the same building but remaining invisible to one another. Surely academic freedom carries less weight where the percentage of faculty with tenure or on the tenure track is a minority of those teaching. A majority of the faculty at such institutions typically has little role in shared governance and no job security. Is the meaning of tenure itself at such institutions undergoing change? Ask yourself how many schools now credit vacated faculty lines to administrators for reassignment to whatever department they choose, when it was only a generation ago that tenured faculty in a given department automatically had power to decide the fate of vacated lines.

It would certainly help in evaluating this problem if we had comprehensive institution-by-institution data on trends in faculty hiring, not simply national averages. It would also help if we knew what percentage of courses are actually taught by tenured faculty at each institution, but accurate information on the role graduate-student employees play in instruction is particularly elusive. The figures I presented earlier on the declining number of tenure-track faculty do not include teaching done by graduate-student employees; thus, the percentage of courses taught by contingent labor is actually higher. Yet even in the absence of these data, we can begin to ask certain critical political and philosophical questions. One conclusion we can draw is that the meaning of tenure is not only individual but also institutional. Far too many faculty members think the only thing that matters is whether they themselves possess job security. But they have less of it than they think if it does not include structural support for due process, peer review, and shared governance. Tenure is something faculties possess both individually and collectively, and its collective character varies.

Tenure is also something we possess nationally. It is sustained by the remarkable consistency of the six-year probationary period won by the AAUP's 1940 statement and its more than two hundred organizational signatories. Despite substantial national variation, a rough normative consensus about tenure procedures prevails. That consensus, however undermined now, reinforces related expectations about academic freedom. Without those expectations, arbitrary dismissal would be far more common and restrictions on faculty speech perhaps universal.

To some degree, the survival of tenure and its reinforcement of academic freedom in many elite private universities, flagship public institutions, and liberal arts colleges constrain practices at schools heavily reliant on contingent labor. Tenure at the institutions that have it helps anchor faculty freedoms at other schools. This is something many faculty members do not understand. Without the anchor institutions enjoying tenure, the educational system as a whole would falter. The professoriate as a whole cannot survive in its present form without a significant number of anchor institutions with tenure. Though the cultural and professional power that the standard of tenure wields is surely not only diminished but also still further threatened, it remains a critical component of faculty status and AAUP effectiveness nationwide, even at some schools without a single tenured professor.

Yet by creating a huge class of contingent faculty without job security, we have guaranteed widespread resentment against tenure in the national faculty workforce. The alternatives to tenure, however, are all deeply flawed. They have value *in relationship* to tenure—as partial security for those who lack tenure—but not as independent, stand-alone replacements for the tenure system as a whole. Renewable term contracts, for example, may not be a serious problem for those quietly doing their teaching and research in fields an institution values, but they clearly put faculty critics of institutional mission and administrative decision making at risk, as I have certainly discovered myself.

As I mentioned earlier, in November 2006 the AAUP's Committee A on Academic Freedom approved a historic extension of job security and due process rights to part-time faculty. The document was the product of extensive ethical, political, and professional negotiations. The standards it puts forward, growing out of decades of contingent faculty activism in the California Faculty Association, the Coalition of Contingent Academic Labor (COCAL), and elsewhere, were negotiated *in relation* to the AAUP's 1940 standards for tenure. Put crudely, part-time faculty members were granted far more job security than most of them possessed beforehand, but notably less than comes with traditional tenure. If tenure did not exist—and was not still widely enforced for nearly a third of faculty nationally—the AAUP would have had little hope of winning assent to granting a series of real but lesser rights to part-time faculty. On the other hand, the country could certainly reach a tipping point where too few tenured faculty remain nationally to anchor any sort of job security and academic freedom for anyone else. That is now real reason for concern. We could see the percentage of tenured faculty decline to 10 percent within a generation.

The process the AAUP went through is not unlike what union negotiators go through in seeking a degree of job security for contingent faculty. Their rights are negotiated *in relation* to the better working conditions tenured faculty enjoy, either at the same institution or elsewhere. Strong union support can make a tremendous difference for contingent faculty. The contracts negotiated in Vancouver, Canada, and by the California Faculty Association (www.calfac.org/) make that apparent. Both two-year and four-year colleges in British Columbia support pro-rata pay for part-timers, though the very best provisions have been negotiated by the Vancouver Community College Faculty Association (www.vccfa.ca/). Instructors who teach half time receive 50 percent of the salary a full-time instructor would receive at the same rank. Not only do part-timers receive medical benefits; they also receive funds for professional development and accrue vacation leave. In time, after proving themselves, they automatically become regular faculty (Longmate and Cosco). That is the model U.S. community colleges should adopt.

None of this would be possible without the existence of still better benefits for tenured faculty. The result of doing away with tenure is thus likely to be a pervasive backsliding to at-will employment. Even multiyear contracts would be more difficult to put in place under those conditions. Another way to say this is that we have a system in place that has become far too exploitive of far too many people, but it will not be improved or reformed if we abandon its best guarantees. Although many part-timers will not believe me, let me put this clearly: you would be worse off if tenure did not exist.

What would happen if faculty unions were negotiating employment security in the absence of tenure? Obviously right-to-work states would be largely cut loose from any consistent policies. And the unions would be subject to the give and take, the gains and losses, of job-security negotiations in other industries. You could then look to the auto industry for a model of the academy's future. Negotiated buyouts for faculty eligible for retirement would be supplemented by god only knows what sort of managerial inventions for jettisoning faculty. There would be no set of guiding principles for faculty employment with any realistic influence on higher education practice. Tenure can be guaranteed by a legally enforceable union contract, but it cannot be literally invented by one.

The other lesson faculty members must relearn—a term I use because many once knew this—is that we are not powerless, despite how powerful the national trends undermining tenure may be. The collective meaning of tenure can only be reshaped and altered collectively—either by faculty passivity or action. Perhaps more than anything else, faculty members need to rethink their identities so that they include a component of collective agency. No matter how strong any given faculty senate may be, every campus also needs an effective AAUP chapter. There needs to be an organized faculty voice prepared to speak truth to power. The faculty needs a principled, collective voice of a sort many senates cannot provide. Faculty cooperation with administrators needs to be balanced by frank public discourse and, when necessary, by organized resistance. Only that way can tenure's central role in defending academic freedom be preserved.

As the battle over tenure, academic freedom, and the future of higher education in the United States unfolds, one player above all remains central to any hope the faculty may rationally entertain: the AAUP. The organization is sometimes too slow to adapt and often too slow to react, hampered as it is by the very deliberative and consultative processes that are critical to the high quality of its policy statements and investigative reports. And the AAUP is sometimes too cautious in asserting its values, restrained as it sometimes is by the quasi-judicial character of its methods. The AAUP needs to rebalance its internal equations, learning from the strategic interventions of its local chapters, its state conferences, and its brother and sister unions. In recent years, the AAUP has gradually and powerfully adapted and certainly has repeatedly spoken with great eloquence. Nationally, too many faculty members are distracted and ill informed. Without the AAUP, the game is lost, which is why all faculty members should join the organization and link their activism with that of a national organization.

Yet activism on the basis of current personal identifications alone will not suffice. We must find ways of reaching across the great divide between tenured and contingent faculty that do more even than extend workplace justice to our exploited colleagues. Workplace justice is, to be sure, the first essential step. Without that, nothing follows. And there are conceptual hurdles to be overcome if the most challenging bar to equity is to be dealt with successfully.

That bar is, of course, the access to full-time tenurable jobs. We must begin by realizing we have *not* in fact overproduced PhDs over the past forty years. We have underproduced appropriate, nonexploitive jobs. The students are there to teach, in more than enough numbers to warrant full-time tenurable positions for faculty. Given that, part of the challenge is to find ways of moving contingent faculty to tenure-track slots.

Two conditions must be met for that to work. First, we all need to admit that institutional needs and faculty roles differ. A community college is not likely to have the same faculty job requirements as a research university department that conducts a national search as an effort to hire someone with sound prospects for having a major influence on the discipline. A community college that hires contingent faculty carefully will often be hiring people fully qualified for tenurable positions. Those institutions should be pressed to adopt the Vancouver model for automatic upgrading to tenure-track positions. Creating a tiered faculty when there is no educational justification for doing so is particularly inexcusable. Second, working conditions must be established that enable contingent faculty to function without disabling stress levels. A part-time faculty member who teaches for twenty years without health care, job security, academic freedom, and vestment in a retirement system, or without earning a living wage, may no longer be an appealing candidate for a full-time job. As I said at the outset, this system breaks people. On the other hand, a unionized part-time faculty member who receives all these benefits is likely to be psychologically healthy and quite ready to transition to full-time employment.

One of the dangerous developments in part-time faculty culture, however, is the conviction that the sheer number of part-time positions should be protected, despite the damage it is doing to academic freedom, the status of the faculty, and the quality of higher education. One can understand the source of the conviction: solidarity with part-time colleagues, a sense that there is potential part-timer political and institutional power in numbers, and rational anxiety that a part-time job is the only teaching job many people can get. Nonetheless, efforts must be made to discourage this conviction from taking root. The relevant principle is clear: no part-time faculty member should lose his or her job as a result of converting a position from part-time to full-time. Conversion to tenure should be offered to all qualified continuing part-time faculty and should otherwise take place no more rapidly than the voluntary departure from contingent positions. But conversation itself must be a universal faculty commitment.

The deeper problem arises with those elite institutions well on the way to creating two classes of faculty members clearly based on different responsibilities and workloads. The tenured faculty teach graduate and upper-level undergraduate courses, direct dissertations, and conduct research. The part-time faculty teach more courses, mostly at an introductory level, have no contact with graduate education, do less research overall, and earn less money. Many schools have sought to avoid the appearance of a faculty class system and the pressure for universal tenure by limiting the number of courses a part-timer can teach. That model has unfortunately evolved into a ruthless, irrational system in which "freeway fliers" cobble together a de facto full-time job by teaching at several schools. As a result, the institutional restrictions on teaching loads have become merely abusive. In 2008, California passed legislation increasing the part-timer eligibility to a 67 percent teaching load at any given school. It is likely that such restrictions will continue to erode.

The gains that some contingent faculty have won through collective bargaining—multiyear contracts, peer review, grievance procedures, dismissal only for cause after a probationary period—have done a great deal to secure them a degree of academic freedom and job security. Strong, enforceable grievance procedures are particularly important to part-timers if academic freedom is to prevail. Modest funds for professional development are appearing in some contingent faculty contracts as well, since it is in everyone's best interests to help all long-term faculty stay current in their fields.

Gains in part-time faculty remuneration would benefit from better comprehensive data collection and distribution. That may require help from disciplinary societies, since many institutions maintain detailed part-timer data only at the departmental level, and disciplinary organizations thus may provide the best contact point for data collection. After a difficult struggle within the MLA, the organization agreed to publish its one-time 1999 data on part-time faculty salaries department by department, as its Delegate Assembly had mandated, rather than by geographical averages, as staff preferred. Within a few months, faculty members at over twenty institutions had written in to say they had been able to use the specific institutional salary rates to win salary increases. Such data collection should be regular. I also believe disciplinary societies should risk publicizing best and worst practices in contingent hiring, perhaps in a list of ten best and ten worst schools. The risk of doing that is alienating those schools and having to rely thereafter on alternative means of data collection; the benefit is the pressure to change.

Administrators who recognize the appeal of a stable, reliable, poorly paid workforce may also see broader union-negotiated agreements as a managerial gain. And, indeed, some provisions (save low salary) also represent major benefits for the faculty involved. The breakthrough contractual gains gradually assembled by the three-thousand-member AFT lecturers' union of the University of California, which now seem miraculous to most part-timers, may come to be commonplace: expectation of continued employment after six years, protection from dismissal based solely on student evaluations, evaluation by your lecturer cohort, strong grievance procedures.

At a number of distinguished campuses, including Rutgers, related proposals for career "teaching track" faculty, as distinguished from research faculty, have surfaced. Even from a coldly managerial perspective, this emerging model for career lecturers or teaching-only faculty offers advantages. No rational administrator needs the "flexibility" to dispose of his or her introductory composition, foreign language, or math teachers en masse. American high schools will not soon be making such college-level courses unnecessary. Meanwhile, as administrators will be pleased to see, provisions such as peer review, if well administered, mean that proletariat faculty will become self-policing. There is little reason other than bloodlust (the desire to break the souls of contingent faculty), the lust for power (the reluctance to cede any authority over faculty worker bees), or simple fear of change for administrators to resist this new dispensation. It may eventually be coming to a campus near you.

The downside of this model, at least at research-oriented institutions, is clear: the final, decisive installation of a permanent two-tier faculty, with a permanent underclass of faculty who may never really earn a middle-class income and who are ideologically severed from their formally tenured colleagues, not only by compensation but also by fundamentally different notions of what a faculty member does and what a university's mission is. The counterargument is compelling: that system is already in place, and we are morally and professionally responsible for our long-term contingent faculty. More than half our college teachers nationwide are already underpaid and intellectually marginalized, coopted for a service job called college teaching. The same argument applies to efforts to lift teaching caps for "part-time" faculty. The claim that we are not using "part-time" faculty for the same teaching responsibilities as tenurable faculty is a fiction sustained by artificial limits on the number of classes they can teach at a given school. In the present climate of "freeway fliers," our only humane option is to better the lives and secure the academic rights of the academic underclass. There is no other way to secure academic freedom and no other practical way to assure that contingent faculty can fully serve their students.

If, however, the tradeoff—institutionalizing academic McJobs—seems thoroughly depressing, that is because it is. More and more, two different kinds of lifetime jobs and two diverging professional cultures will coexist in countries that structure the higher education workforce this way. The Rutgers proposal to create Tenure Track Teaching Appointments, or TTTs—coauthored by long-term activists and advocates for part-timers Zoran Gijac, Karen Thompson, and Richard Moser and rejected by the Rutgers University Senate in 2009—in my view concedes too much in its effort to win approval. It appropriately seeks "a more stable and professional teaching corps" but then recommends that TTTs produce "scholarship on teaching methodology, curriculum development, pedagogical practices and theory" (Rutgers 8). Academic freedom means that faculty choose their own intellectual commitments and are free to change them over time. TTTs are effectively being urged to abandon the disciplinary work and aspirations embodied in their doctoral dissertations, unless those dissertations had a pedagogical focus. It is especially unfortunate to pressure faculty to concentrate their intellectual lives on introductory service courses. John Barth notoriously taught introductory composition courses at SUNY Buffalo for years, but no one urged him to stop writing novels. It is also fundamentally unjust to bar PhDs capable of teaching more specialized courses in the areas in which they have been trained from ever doing so. Finally, my friends at Rutgers unwittingly reverse the vampire metaphor cited earlier: "TTT faculty can consistently release active faculty from teaching one course per year and make their research more productive" (ibid. 10). I suppose tenured faculty should then thank their little TTT brothers and sisters for freeing them up to pursue the higher life. All we can really do to undermine this widening internal split is to work away at the edges of this powerful economic engine of change. We can begin to bridge the cultural differences between the two groups.

The difficulties of seeking wholesale conversion of part-timers to traditional tenured lines are further illustrated by the efforts of yet another union, the Professional Staff Congress (PSC), representing City University of New York (CUNY) faculty. With roughly eight thousand part-timers employed in the system, negotiators sought the brass ring—conversion to full-time tenurable slots—in their 2005–7 contract negotiation. They won a hundred such conversions, with part-timers justly pointing out that it would take eighty years at that rate to convert all of them. As talks for the next contract were winding down in 2008, the administration offered only fifty more such positions. PSC negotiators had to battle fiercely to obtain a hundred conversions over two years. As a result of the pattern set in the previous negotiations, they were really only fighting for an exceptionalist benefit, rather than a structural one. The PSC leaders and negotiators, all highly dedicated, are pledged to seek more fundamental changes in the status of part-time faculty in their 2010 negotiations. Stay tuned.

In the long run, only structural benefits will suffice. Some structural benefits pave the way for full conversion. Approving contingent faculty for committee work or advising and paying them for it brings them into the department and makes them recognized colleagues. Paid office hours increase student contact and institutional identification. The more contingent faculty assume the full range of faculty responsibilities, the more natural it seems to convert them to tenure-track positions—if a conversion mechanism is in place. Meanwhile, there is a rational alternative to instituting a permanent two-tier faculty at serious research institutions. Grant long-term teaching faculty tenure but build a sunset provision into the arrangement. In other words, agree to hire no new faculty in those positions, so that the two-tier system eventually disappears. Obviously that solution would require the political will, faculty solidarity, and administrative determination to commit sufficient resources to make it a reality.

Yet entirely reversing the thirty-five-year nationwide trend toward perma-temping the faculty is not only a huge goal but also almost certainly an impossible one. In the meantime, however, even as we secure better working conditions for contingent faculty, we must also do more still to bridge the alienating gap between tenured and contingent faculty and between institutional types. Work of this sort needs to be done within all academic disciplines, but it is more critical for some than others. Those disciplines that can generate outside resources are much more secure in the corporate environment of the contemporary university. The humanities and interpretive social sciences, however, are increasingly vulnerable, and overreliance on contingent faculty seriously enhances that discipline-specific vulnerability.

In order to sustain the humanities and interpretive social sciences and enable them to enrich American culture—a culture otherwise destined to be set in fascist stone, sustained by uncontested platitudes—we need to redefine the communities dedicated to these kinds of research. They need to embrace all those who produce, interpret, and disseminate ongoing interpretive research. The work these scholars do extends well beyond major publication to include teaching graduate and undergraduate students, reviewing and evaluating the scholarship of others, and interrogating the state of the university, a field of scholarship, and the discipline as a whole.

Put simply, humanities and social science research would be worth little if it were not disseminated to new generations of students. It would have much less chance for impact if it were not evaluated in book reviews or in longer essays. The meaning and impact scholarship can have, the cultural work a book can hope to do, can be transformed by the kind of in-depth reflection other scholars can offer.

I am suggesting that we need a level, nonhierarchical model of subdisciplinary and interdisciplinary research communities that encompasses the whole range of teaching and research activities, the whole range of teaching positions, and the whole range of academic institutions. We need to find ways of honoring and recognizing all the kinds of contributions people make to their particular research communities. Peer review and recognition of teaching, for example, could include evaluation of how faculty incorporate and interpret recent research in their teaching. In order to protect themselves from administrative aggression and public indifference, the humanities and interpretive social sciences need the solidarity and sense of shared mission that broad-based research communities could promote. These research communities would also necessarily embrace the whole range of academic teaching and research positions: part-time faculty, full-time faculty ineligible for tenure, academic professionals, and the tenured and tenure-track faculty who were once the bedrock of the teaching staff. It is not just a question of recognizing different kinds of work when salary or tenure decisions are made, a suggestion made repeatedly in the past. It is a question of how to use intellectual commitments to create meaningful faculty cohorts and build genuine cohesion.

Promoting research communities is one critical way to unify our diverse group of academics, something that must happen if diverging interests are not to divide these constituencies still further and turn them against one another. Those who wish to suppress humanities and social science research so as to diminish its influence on current and future generations—and to curtail enhancing critical citizenship as a central goal of higher education—will welcome the primary identification of research with elite institutions. The notion of research communities can demonstrate instead that the combined production and dissemination of research unifies all of higher education, from Harvard University to Dade County Community College, from faculty with named chairs to faculty with part-time appointments.

Disciplinary associations usually have defined divisions or interest groups that accurately name potential research communities, but their meaningful activities are often limited to planning convention sessions or editing a journal. They may do little else to unify their membership. And they do not typically make outreach efforts to contingent faculty or to the two-year sector. Much more would need to be done, not only to broaden membership but also to recognize, promote, coordinate, and publicize all the teaching and writing that research communities do. Such communities would also need to confront the special pressures that contingent faculty face.

Publication itself often blurs the line between teaching and research, since not only publishing new historical information or unknown primary texts but also disseminating interpretations of texts and social forces often has direct classroom impact. Research communities would also need to give more full recognition (and more serious evaluation) to the impact that major textbooks have on the culture. The need for a sense of community in higher education is in fact still more pressing than even the multiple assaults on humanities research might suggest. Two generations of tenure-track faculty—obsessed with their careers and identified almost exclusively with their academic disciplines—have been distracted and inattentive as the character of campus decision making has been gradually transformed. This trend has been accelerated by the growing number of contingent faculty lacking the job security that undergirds academic freedom and shared governance.

When I began interviewing and writing about contingent labor in the academy over twenty years ago—first focusing on graduate-student employees in a series of essays leading up to *Manifesto of a Tenured Radical*

and then on contingent faculty in *Academic Keywords* and *Office Hours*—
it was the violence done to them as human beings and the sense of professional injustice that drove my work. When I began thinking about contingency, it did not seem a fundamental structural problem, let alone a potentially fatal one. Yet like other members of my generation, my career as a tenure-track faculty member, which began in 1970 and ended in 2000, when I gave up tenure and began teaching part-time, coincides precisely with the growth in contingency. Most of us on the tenure track over the past four decades have moved in lock step with a frequently invisible and steadily increasing cohort of minimum-wage colleagues. If the fundamental cultures of contingency and tenure continue to diverge and evolve, it will become increasingly difficult for the two groups of faculty to find common cause. The odds against restoring the dignity of the professoriate and securing academic freedom are not good. Tenured faculty are now a dwindling minority. They can regroup and reach out to their more vulnerable colleagues, or they can watch higher education diminish as an institution, abandoning its critical function and its political value in a democracy. Is there really a choice between acquiescence and activism?

[4]

Barefoot in New Zealand

Political Correctness on Campus

> Most scholars of the Middle East, especially graduate students and
> untenured professors, understand very well that there is a heavy
> price to pay for publicly supporting Palestinian national aspirations
> and very little support for research projects that do not fit into the
> policy-driven priorities of most funding agencies.
>
> —Beshara Doumani, "Between Coercion and
> Privatization" (38)

> A shift toward more visible pro-Palestinian or anti-Israel senti-
> ment has been profound on some campuses, prompted, in part,
> by the winter war in Gaza. Where some describe a correspond-
> ing disintegration of civil discourse or a scapegoating of Israel for
> a complex set of problems, others celebrate a newfound space in
> which to be critical of Israel—to mount a challenge to what they
> see as a dominant discourse. . . . "We've seen a more shrill tone to
> much of the criticism of Israel," . . . said David A. Harris, executive
> director of the Israel on Campus Coalition. . . . "We see dozens
> and dozens of examples of 'die-ins' and [displays of] tombstones
> and public displays that are intimidating to some."
>
> —Elizabeth Redden, "On Israel, Shifted Ground"

Although few students or faculty on American campuses who are on
either the Right or the Left of the political spectrum are inclined to
acknowledge each other's perspective, members of both groups feel
beleaguered, isolated, outcast, and underrepresented in their higher education environments. What is more, divisions within these groups mean
that some are castigated by others who share many of the same political
beliefs. Where the Left is concerned, as cultural and political history tells

us, today's conflicts are only the latest episodes in a long-running, multigenerational, now multimillennial story that entails fractious disputes about one's right to claim a place on the certified Left. That such a history exists does not, however, make today's fractious disputes less painful either to participants or to observers.

One visible recent split on the Left concerns the war in Afghanistan. The split crosses all campus disciplines, involving not only the social sciences and humanities but also the sciences and the professional schools. As Michael Bérubé reported on his weblog, when some faculty long identified with the Left argued that a military response to Al Qaeda in Afghanistan was necessary and action to remove the Taliban defensible—even though they typically did not endorse the Bush administration's wantonly brutal, failed tactics there—they found themselves essentially pariahs among many on the campus Left. Once the 2003 war in Iraq was launched, there was no social space in which to give qualified support to one military action and thoroughly condemn the other and not be treated with contempt. That was my own stance, and I simply gave up attending campus meetings on the Iraq war, because my only choices were to remain silent (not my style) or be personally denounced. I was better off avoiding the campus and instead criticizing the Bush administration in print, where I could articulate distinctions between the two sites of aggression. I am not, to be sure, suggesting that American campuses as a whole opposed the war in Afghanistan but, rather, that in specific progressive settings on campus there was often no socially and politically viable way to take different positions on the two wars.

As identitarian politics fragment and crisscross the categories of Left and Right still further, we now have even more versions of inner exile on campus than we have ever seen before. "Can't we all get along?" In a campus political context, we would have to answer, "Apparently not." What, then, are the prospects for committed but civilized campus debate, discussion, and advocacy? Can we do better? *Should* we try to get along? What pitfalls should be carefully avoided?

Determination to exaggerate or misrepresent their own and other people's psychological alienation is certainly a contributing feature of the current scene. For David Horowitz and Anne Neal, self-appointed higher education authorities, there is no doubt that the Right on campus is silenced, discriminated against, and thoroughly alienated—*and* that the Left reigns supreme and freely terrorizes everyone. But people on the Left are just as likely to feel besieged. Some of the progressive faculty attacked in Horowitz's notorious book *The Professors: The 101 Most Dangerous Academics in America* now feel endangered by increased scrutiny. Untenured and part-time faculty members feel vulnerable when they engage in progressive advocacy. Anecdotal accounts suggest that self-censorship, prevalent during the McCarthy period, has returned to shape faculty behavior.

Genuine identity-based discrimination does exist on college and university campuses. But so do equal treatment, special privileges, and hystericized political correctness. The highly variable climate from campus to campus, even department to department, makes it difficult to generalize. In some departments and on some campuses, lesbian faculty members with progressive commitments remain victims, whereas in others they are valued colleagues, often identified with leading areas of research. African American faculty members in some settings get recruitment bonuses and in others have their progressive research commitments questioned. The sense of repression that Doumani describes in the epigraph to this chapter would in some departments be unrecognizable, in others dominant.

The list could continue, and only careful quantitative and qualitative investigation will provide a clear nationwide profile, but several high-profile cases suggest there is one area where tension and misrepresentation reign supreme: campus incarnations of the Arab-Israeli conflict. Although there are players and forces with campus impact from both sides, an exceptionalist victimology has evolved in which each beleaguered campus cohort considers its suffering unique. It does not help matters that the off-campus political struggle involves trying to win moral legitimacy for one side and withdraw it from the other, a pattern that does not enhance rational debate on campus. To some degree, that pattern mirrors politics in the Middle East itself, though the campus is not a scene of life-and-death struggle and thus potentially could be a site for sober self-assessment; but that has been the exception, not the rule.

For Barnard professor Nadia Abu El-Haj, Columbia professor Joseph Massad, former DePaul professor Norman Finkelstein, and some of their advocates, the pro-Israeli lobby is all powerful; there is no other force of consequence. Those who have watched the movement to boycott Israeli universities gain some purchase in the faculty union in Britain in 2002 and then spread to Canada and the United States during Israel's 2008–9 military action in Gaza may feel differently. The Canadian Association of University Teachers rejected the boycott but did pass a resolution condemning Israel's actions in 2009, and resolutions condemning Zionism and Israeli policy were put forward by the Modern Language Association's Radical Caucus at the association's Delegate Assembly meeting in both 2007 and 2008 (Jaschik, "Moderate MLA"). The winter of 2009 saw Israeli Apartheid Week and divestment movements unfold on scores of campuses (Redden, "On Israel"). Indeed faculty and students with sympathies for Israel encounter implacably pro-Palestinian attacks in multiple settings; these include departments where no candidate who has written in support of Israel in general or a two-state solution in particular would even be considered for a job. The prohibition would apply most strongly when Middle East studies is part of the job description, but it can extend to positions for which it is not directly relevant to the advertised area of teaching and research.

In 2009, I received a number of faculty emails of the "AAUP can run, but it can't hide" variety, demanding that the organization endorse a boycott of Israeli universities. In 2005, the AAUP issued a statement condemning all academic boycotts, which essentially formalized what had long been the organization's practice. The AAUP had endorsed a general economic boycott of South Africa years earlier, a boycott that had collateral effects on higher education, but consistently rejected boycotts singling out universities. There were both practical and theoretical reasons. In Israel, as in many other countries, universities remain centers of dissent; thus, the AAUP does not want to cut off the dialogue with faculty and students. The organization is fundamentally in the business of promoting, not curtailing, academic freedom. It is also virtually impossible to set universally applicable criteria to use in adjudicating whether moral issues in a given instance should trump academic freedom. In cases where the nation-state is massively in violation of international standards for human rights—as in Nazi Germany—one might argue that a boycott focused on universities alone is either pathetically inadequate or misguided if universities have been absorbed as pure instruments of party and state.

Finally, in singling out universities, comparisons between institutions in different countries become critical. Israeli universities have unquestionable problems, but none rises to the level of what takes place at both Arab and non-Arab institutions in other countries in the Middle East. Syria is a police state; the complete absence of academic freedom there compares with conditions in North Korea, Myanmar, and Zimbabwe. As Human Rights Watch detailed in its 2005 report "Reading between the 'Red Lines,'" in Egypt the security presence at universities is pervasive, reaching down to the classroom level; its institutions are not sites of free inquiry. Iran presents a mixed and unstable picture, but its president called for a purge of liberal and secular professors from universities in 2006 (Tait), and its recent history includes incidents of extreme violence and repression, culminating in mass arrests and dismissals of faculty members and alleged shootings on campus in June 2009 in the aftermath of a national election widely criticized as fraudulent. In Morocco, a relatively liberal state, no one can dispute Islamic doctrine or criticize the king. Throughout the area, there are both religious and political obstacles to academic freedom. Indeed many of these institutions developed in states preoccupied with a national security state mindset, and the institutions still reflect that history (Stork). Some people on American campuses may thus feel that the exclusive focus on Israeli universities is fundamentally unfair. Indeed, one may reasonably deduce that boycotts focused on Israeli universities have been advocated precisely because American universities harbor significant anti-Israeli constituencies.

The AAUP meanwhile generally cannot take up individual cases abroad in the absence of involvement with American students or faculty or potential impact on U.S. practices or policies. There is a need for international monitoring of academic freedom and investigations of violations, but that will first require comprehensive international data and then an appropriate international organizational structure. The New York–based organization Scholars at Risk has begun the important task of gathering information about academic freedom worldwide. Meanwhile, campus debates about international academic freedom are often conducted in almost complete ignorance of global conditions.

Whether the relevant competing forces are equally empowered on campus is difficult to estimate and often irrelevant, since the only two things that often matter are how power is exercised in a given venue—whether the venue is a rally, a political meeting, a study group, a lecture series, or a department—and how people perceive their situation. In truth, the two constituencies are never equally balanced in any given setting. Yet the only chance for rational dialogue and a process that honors academic freedom is to credit people's perception of being under assault and thus to entertain a fiction of equal stress and anxiety. That pro-Palestinian and pro-Israeli constituencies have not been equally empowered throughout civil society also colors campus perceptions and sometimes influences campus decisions. Certainly the fact that the U.S. government continues to support Israel gives opportunities to mount claims of unequal power, even among those who have little respect for American foreign policy, just as it adds to anti-Israeli moral authority. And again, the warring forces are not equally empowered on every campus. Faculty at Columbia University, for example, where pro-Palestinian colleagues have faced extraordinary and sometimes unprincipled assault, are more likely to feel beleaguered by "the persistence of the Zionist lobby in smearing" (Robbins 341) their colleagues than are faculty at many midwestern universities. Indeed, Columbia has become the de facto epicenter for the forces that Robbins decries.

Faculty members at Columbia were confronted by virulent public protest when Rashid Khalidi was named to an endowed chair, a protest that developed into a wholesale attack on the Department of Middle East and Asian Languages and Cultures. An aggressive website maintained by Daniel Pipes's organization Campus Watch added to public opposition. "Columbia Unbecoming," a documentary produced by the David Project's Center for Jewish Leadership, attacked Columbia professor Joseph Massad's teaching. Like Horowitz, the David Project disingenuously asserted that it was defending, rather than undermining, academic freedom. Efforts were mounted in Congress to oversee Middle East centers at U.S. universities, which would clearly have violated academic freedom. Meanwhile, alliances between neocon members of the Bush administration, conservative think tanks, and pro-Israeli Christian fundamentalist groups added to the sense of a converging conspiracy (Beinin). Although it is not rational to take all this as an orchestrated campaign by the American-Israel Public Affairs Committee (AIPAC), the sense that major efforts to intervene in academic freedom were under way is fully justified. As Beshara Doumani writes, "in the post-9/11 political climate, there is no field more radioactive than Middle East studies" (31). Unfortunately, this situation has sometimes led to a reactive rejection of moderate, independent views on the Middle East within the field itself.

As major fractions of the Left have grown increasingly hostile and unforgiving toward Israel, the once progressive view that Israel should trade land for peace, recognize a Palestinian state with East Jerusalem as its capital, and provide reparations for land appropriated in 1948 is now likely to get denounced as Zionist. The only socially and politically acceptable stance for some people in academia is that Israel has no right to exist, has no moral or political legitimacy, and must be dissolved into a larger regional nation-state. The grave risk to Israeli Jews in a one-state solution should not be an unacceptable topic of discussion. Nor should all protests against violence perpetrated by Israel be automatically considered anti-Semitic. Certainly the demand that Israel guarantee equal citizenship for all within its borders—Palestinians and Israelis alike—has nothing to do with anti-Semitism; it embodies genuine democracy and human rights. Similar demands might be made of other nations in the area. Nor does rejecting any consideration of the mystical conviction that Israel has a divine right to control all of "Judea and Samaria" represent bias; it is a claim that one may evaluate politically or anthropologically, but it is not a proposition worthy of serious consideration in the academy. It is nonetheless clear that some attacks on Israel—including those relentlessly put forward on the MLA's Radical Caucus listserv by Grover Furr—are colored by anti-Semitism. Finally, history does not often warrant unqualified moral legitimacy for any major nation-state. Both the founding of the United States and the country's subsequent expansion were, after all, grounded in the genocide of Native Americans, and imperialist episodes have repeatedly marked American history. Power and international agreements have more relevance to the matter than a blameless or morally unblemished national history, the latter being difficult to find or certify.

Bringing all these issues to bear on campus curricula, program planning, hiring, and tenure decisions can make them impossible to negotiate. Campus discussions about these matters are properly separate issues, not an appropriate symbolic terrain on which to fight a cultural simulacrum of the Arab-Israeli war, but we seem increasingly to be doing exactly that. The prolonged and well-organized attacks on El-Haj, Massad, and Finkelstein were real and amounted to fighting a war by other means. False, inexcusable characterizations of their work were widely distributed and endorsed. External efforts were made to influence internal university decisions. Some faculty regrettably joined those efforts; they have every right to criticize a colleague's scholarly publications or political writings, either in print or in conversation, but should refrain from publicly attacking a colleague's right to tenure. There were real threats both to academic freedom and to shared governance in these cases. People writing from outside the university were exercising their free speech rights, but the job of universities is to protect the process from unofficial external influence. Since Finkelstein settled with DePaul and signed a nondisclosure agreement, thereby eliminating the possibility of his cooperating with a full-scale AAUP investigation, we are less likely to know how public controversy affected his case.

Massad and Finkelstein were very much controversial public intellectuals before their tenure reviews took place, El-Haj rather less so (Kramer). Massad and Finkelstein had been widely praised and attacked in print and online, both by scholars and by members of the public. Nonetheless, faculty familiar with academic freedom would have reason to expect their right to a job would not be threatened by extramural controversy. Although the high-profile organized attacks on these professors' tenure decisions are a new and immensely troubling phenomenon, they may have been inevitable. All it took was one figure like Alan Dershowitz to come up with the idea of fighting Finkelstein's tenure to trigger a series of such incidents. Tensions in Middle East studies as a result run high on all sides. And the attacks on prominent scholars have inevitably had a chilling effect on many others, both within the field and outside it.

Campus relations over the Middle East first of all need greater self-awareness and collective honesty about the impact of identity on political debate. It is clear that you do not have to be an Arab or a Jew to experience a high degree of sympathetic identification, even to feel yourself virtually part of a wounded population. The spread of identity politics has certainly made empathic, fantasy identification easier. One curative move would be to accept Michael Rothberg's wise analysis throughout his book *Multidirectional Memory* that neither experience nor representation of collective suffering is a zero-sum game in which acknowledging one group's suffering has to trump another's, absorbing all space and oxygen so that only one historic injustice can gain a public hearing. Rothberg argues persuasively that coming to understand one historical injustice can in fact make us more receptive to understanding others. On campus that would mean agreeing to stop seeking to be agents of the victims of first rank and instead negotiating as strategic, though not historical, equals. I am not foolish enough to imagine that people would not rank Jewish and Arab victims in their heads; rather, I am hoping for modest interpersonal restraint. As claims, accusations, and counterclaims escalate, the need for this kind of campus diplomacy only increases. Nothing in this prescription assumes that the parties are equal or that their arguments should be carefully "balanced" against one another. It does not presume that they need actually to respect one another's positions. Rather, it argues for a purely performative civility.

The price we pay otherwise is that identity politics and its effects rule over professional decisions. And the examples I have cited so far are not the only highly publicized instances in which politics have compromised university decision making. The decisions by "patriotic" Colorado politicians to make public statements attacking Ward Churchill's tenure, statements immediately condemned by the AAUP, are the most well known examples. The 2008 decision by the University of Michigan Press to stop distributing Pluto Press books—disingenuously characterized as a matter of principle based on Pluto's manuscript review procedures, but clearly grounded in resistance to Pluto's pro-Palestinian list—is a case in point (Jaschik, "Michigan"). There is some evidence as well that departments are gaining the right to trump one another's hiring decisions in the area of Middle East studies, another dangerous precedent.

If self-righteousness and a sense of unique victimhood as a result come entirely to dominate the perceptions of campus players, then the dangers to academic freedom will only get worse. Already, reasoned comments on senior job candidates in Middle East studies, history, political science, sociology, and literature are occasionally characterized as "uncollegial" when the substance of differences among faculty members in the hiring department is actually political, and the comments themselves are well within professional norms. Of course, critiques of potential hires *can* cross the line and become abusive, even actionable. Nonetheless, wide rhetorical latitude needs to be preserved for full consideration of candidates' strengths and weaknesses to be possible.

Faculty hiring is clearly an area where political correctness can control the process on controversial appointments in some departments. Beginning appointments are rarely at issue, because applicants are not questioned about their political beliefs, and few dissertations telegraph a writer's politics. Since the overwhelming majority of appointments are at the less expensive junior level, the problems I am describing substantially affect only a small percentage of faculty appointments. Senior scholars, however, may well have done a wider variety of work, and some of it may engage political questions directly. If some convictions are judged unacceptable, it can result in good candidates being ruled out, less qualified candidates being interviewed and hired, and conscientious faculty being thoroughly alienated because their views about a candidate cannot gain a hearing. Indeed, they may be castigated for exercising and communicating their professional judgment. Middle East studies is a prime site for this sort of conflict in a number of disciplines, not just in Middle Eastern studies programs themselves. The AAUP may well have to address the problem in a future report.

Because the climate and practice can vary widely from department to department—even in the same institution—it is thus primarily a department-level problem, at least in the sense that it may not require institution-wide remedies, though it certainly needs institution-wide discussion. But if a department head signs on to the suppression of departmental opinion and asks the dean to punish a faculty member whose professional take on particular appointees is unpopular, then it becomes a broader problem. I have seen both progressive and conservative faculty treated this way by deans, even at major universities. At the University of Illinois, an irresponsible dean supported a homophobic department head's harassment of a progressive black lesbian scholar, first refusing to speak with her, then threatening her if she proceeded with a formal complaint. The scholar left the university as a consequence.

Two concepts are increasingly coming into play to restrain outspoken or ideological outliers on the Left or the Right. Once again, it is critical to realize that both ends of the political spectrum can be targets. Strategic and improper use is increasingly being made of accusations of "creating a hostile work environment" or of "lack of collegiality." The first of these categories is legally based and requires elements of gender or race for the claim to apply, but a university administration can trigger an internal investigation on the flimsiest of bases. Moreover, some institutions are beginning to invoke the hostile-work-environment charge as a way to stifle dissent, as when they claim that perfectly civil disputes about educational policy create a hostile environment for one side or the other. These principles, thought to be progressive victories when they were put into place, are now coming back to bite us. Although the impulse to take any victory offered is difficult to counter in the United States, it is always best to ask how people at the other end of the political spectrum will use a procedure once it becomes available.

The AAUP explicitly condemns the use of collegiality as an independent criterion in tenure decisions. But collegiality is now undergoing mission drift, and the AAUP may need to expand its analysis. In the Finkelstein case, a standard for collegiality was inexcusably applied to his publications, making the forceful critique of other scholars' published positions a new ground for termination. The prevailing rhetorical standards vary not only by discipline but also by field and subfield, but scholars need to have the right to challenge rhetorical conventions by employing the rhetorical strategies of any discipline or subdiscipline in their work. Academic freedom, in other words, should protect the right to transpose rhetorical conventions from one field to another without being penalized, except by the peer-review process when submitting manuscripts for publication. Claims about collegiality are being used to stifle campus debate, to punish faculty, and to silence the free exchange of opinion by the imposition of corporate-style conformity.

Another version of the collegiality argument is implicit in the falsely confident distinction between advocacy and scholarship. Since the 1915 Declaration, the AAUP has been historically overinvested in quiet rationality and sweet reasonableness as the only ethical models for professional interaction. Following this lead, some people have been inclined to place faculty members on the Left—such as Finkelstein, Churchill, or Joel Kovel—in a separate category of polemical writers and thus disallow their scholarly publishing credentials. But many peer-reviewed journals accept highly polemical work, and some subdisciplines are routinely polemical. And books often have both highly polemical and neutrally evidentiary passages. The standards for scholarship can also be subtly influenced by campus expectations for face-to-face interaction. It is as if Churchill and Finkelstein were faulted for creating a "hostile environment" in their prose.

Sensitivity to and enforcement against hostile environments on campus, meanwhile, can be Orwellian. At the University of Illinois, a white anthropology graduate-student employee was investigated for months after he approached an African American graduate employee for advice. A student in one of the white student's classes used the word "nigger"; the grad student was upset and wanted advice about how to handle the problem. The African American grad student filed a complaint that the white grad student had created a hostile environment by telling him the story. The complaint should have been dismissed immediately instead of being allowed to fester so long. On yet another major research university campus, a faculty member was severely chastised and financially penalized for arguing on behalf of Israeli scholar (and admittedly polemical public intellectual) Benny Morris for a position in a Middle East studies department and against the less widely published pro-Palestinian scholar whom the search committee had recommended. The grounds in this case included lack of collegiality and contributing to a hostile environment. While Morris's increasing conservatism is not in doubt (Morris), neither is his status as a major historian in question (Gorenberg). His appointment would be a coup for any university.

One contributing factor in these incidents is that abuses of power identified and debated in the 1970s and 1980s—including gender and racial discrimination, sexual harassment, and behaviors creating a hostile working environment—are by now explicitly prohibited by a formidable array of official campus codes, guidelines, and regulations. This is not bad in itself, representing long, hard work by many passionate and well-intentioned people. But now it is also a tool that serves the powerful as much as the powerless. Administrators, as always, find new uses for such tools, including uses beyond their intended function. And many formal regulations, such as speech codes, are flatly unconstitutional.

But administrators are not the only culprits. These incidents are part of a larger pattern in which the Right and the Left—both on and off campus—use established regulations or attempt to create new ones in order to advance a political cause. Horowitz is eager to see universities investigate what he regards as inappropriate political speech in the classroom, meaning any historical reference not falling precisely within the typically brief course description. Though Horowitz's examples are becoming increasingly ludicrous—as when he helped a Pennsylvania State University student file a formal complaint that a course in effective social science writing covered public attitudes toward global warming, arguing, as Robin Wilson reports ("Using New Policy"), that global warming "is a matter of environmental, not social, science" (apparently sociologists cannot write about attitude formation!)—such investigations themselves have a chilling effect. Unfortunately, some faculty members are willing to endorse opportunistic political strategies in their own interrelations.

The intrusion of politics into senior faculty hiring, however, rarely rises to the level of formal proceedings. More often it plays itself out in a series of intellectually substandard, coercive, and embarrassing departmental debates. This brings me to the central story of this chapter—and to an explanation of my presumably incomprehensible title.

Not long ago my department was considering appointing a faculty member teaching in New Zealand to a senior position. Just before an offer would have gone out for a campus visit, someone Googled the candidate's name and turned up a letter to a New Zealand newspaper in which the candidate had contributed to local debates about whether it was appropriate to go barefoot in public places. The letter suggested that it was uncivilized not to wear shoes and that it promoted the transmission of disease. One of my colleagues decided the letter was an attack on the Maori people and thus racist and circulated a petition to that effect, demanding that the candidacy not go forward. After negotiations among potential signers of the petition, the claim was modified to say that the language in the letter was "articulated to racism and colonialism," which fell short of a personal accusation of racism but amounted at least to a claim of intellectual limitation and fundamental insensitivity.

On that basis, nineteen of my colleagues were willing to sign. The department atmosphere immediately became highly charged and unstable. Some faculty members were not approached with the petition, and some of them were deeply upset as a result: were they not asked to sign, they pleaded, because people thought they were racist? What was missing from these anxious testimonials was an account of physical nausea, a common consequence of the conjunction of guilt and cowardice. At the same time, given the intellectual independence of the department's African American faculty, it is not surprising that several of them did not sign. That ought to have signaled that the petition was not an unambiguous test of racial sensitivity. As news of the petition and its growing number of signatures spread through the department, it became increasingly difficult for people to speak against it. Watching academics mass like lemmings atop the fatal cliffs of ideology is never pretty. Although some proponents disingenuously characterized the petition as a call for further discussion in the face of an appointment that appeared to be a "done deal," in point of fact the petition was an intervention destined to close off discussion, to make it impossible to proceed with the appointment.

Once the politically correct interpretation of the candidate's letter had taken hold, it was essentially impossible to stop the impending train wreck. One colleague who did have the courage to speak against the interpretation of the fatal letter to the editor later characterized his own delivery as "too ironic, passing, and nervous," suggesting the considerable emotional difficulty of speaking out forcefully. My own comments had no effect on those who signed the petition. Meanwhile, a colleague with some knowledge of New Zealand argued that the debate there had nothing to do with race, that the only people who went barefoot there were white hippies, and that the candidate's letter to the editor had to be seen in that context. No one listened to him either. Six months later, in Australia, I met two faculty members who had grown up in New Zealand and were now teaching there. I asked them about the whole incident. They had no doubts. The Maori people, they informed me, would never go barefoot in public. Indeed, they were relatively formal and had detailed codes about acceptable social conduct. They would never, for example, casually sit on the edge of someone's desk. Furthermore, only one section of New Zealand had a climate suitable for going barefoot, and there, indeed, some white hippies did so. Thus, the petition amounted to a call for an expression of racial solidarity with what, under the circumstances, we might describe as an indigenous population of white hippies. Australian aborigines, on the other hand, did go barefoot, so a similar debate in Australia would have a very different character.

But my colleagues, including people I very much admire, had no interest in accurate information about the historical and cultural context. They were also unwilling to consider whether their assumptions about Maori culture were fundamentally racist. After all, it was the language in the letter that was pertinent. What did it matter if it was not "articulated to racism and colonialism" in a New Zealand barefoot context? It was surely so articulated in the sands of the Kalahari or in the Mississippi delta. But, in any case, high dudgeon about a single letter to the editor, however eloquently flaunted, was not the central matter. For white faculty, this was, in part at least, about proving themselves to colleagues of color. And for a very few faculty, it was about racializing department decisions that had, thankfully, never been racialized before. It was about changing the configurations of self-consciousness and the lines of power in the department. The prospective appointment was a target of opportunity for a broader professional and political agenda. One of the casualties of success was academic freedom as we had exercised it for decades. All this culminated in a department meeting, which I will not describe because it was confidential, though I will say that more than one colleague later described it as "the meeting from hell." Indeed one faculty member cites the meeting as one reason he left to accept a job elsewhere. Suffice it to say that the position was not offered to the candidate from New Zealand. Notably, I have not provided the person's name, gender, rank, institution or area of specialization. That is not only so as to protect that individual's privacy; it is because the whole controversy was about local, national, and international politics, not about the candidate in question.

For at least a few of us, this controversy was a transformative moment—the point when the department ceased to be the department we had known for decades, when efforts at group coercion replaced discussion. Thereafter, all senior appointments would be promoted or disparaged with hyperbolic praise or hyperbolic denunciation. A department that had made wonderful partner hires in the past suddenly began making some indiscriminately while terrorizing others, always accompanied by inflated claims about the candidate's strengths, meanwhile putting an excellent prospective partner candidate through the torments of the damned. Each candidate was either a descending angel who would save us from ourselves or a venomous and ignorant assassin who would spread dissension everywhere. Unfortunately, the universally overheated character of every evaluation made it impossible to recognize that an actual sociopathic personality might be under consideration for a faculty appointment.

And, as always happens, giving in to one version of identity politics led to the encouragement of others. A department that had disenfranchised women—or readily denied them faculty appointments entirely—until the 1980s had steadily healed itself since then. Although by the start of the new millennium only 40 percent of the department's sixty-five faculty members were women, salary discrepancies had been repaired and department politics and decision making were basically gender neutral. But when a new rhetoric program proposed by a female faculty member was under discussion in 2009, suddenly critics of the plan who argued their case calmly and rationally were accused of sexist bullying. It would be unfair to say the New Zealand contretemps was the cause of all this. It did not help, for example, that literary studies nationally no longer had a conceptual center that would hold. What is less debatable is that the New Zealand incident was the first of a series of highly abusive department events that undermined civility in fundamental ways. By 2007, faculty members began to leave in larger numbers than we had ever seen before. By 2009, we were hemorrhaging colleagues.

It was not only the national climate that encouraged this departmental shift away from academic freedom and civilized debate. It was also because we had hired a large number of faculty members in a few years, and they had not been integrated into departmental culture. For better or worse, however, that process of integration had historically never been either overt or planned; it was inertial and carried out by example. With a sudden influx of new colleagues, very different models of faculty identity could be put in place, especially since successful candidates had to win their jobs over the bodies of the rest of their graduate-class cohort. In the light of the emerging character of higher education, it may have been inevitable that we would eventually endure our own local episode of frenzied political correctness. Given the demographics of the profession, other departments on other campuses are experiencing similar pressures over hiring and thus face similar possibilities.

I have talked about this case at length not simply because I know it well but also because it enables me to testify to the reverberating impact of a highly politicized hiring debate. Exquisitely intelligent, ethically meticulous, and discriminating faculty were turned into the obverse of themselves: bullies, liars, and opportunists. The process was more like a reenactment of *Lord of the Flies* than departmental democracy at work.

When things reach that point, gentle appeals to decency and reason—the only recourse that seemed available to our department head—may have no effect. The only solution may be to try to take senior appointments out of the political arena, though the necessity for a tenure vote makes that difficult. Colleagues would have to be willing to honor the decision of a small, fair-minded hiring committee. Indeed, the same damaging impulses can spread to other areas, most notably internal tenure decisions, as we saw in the El-Haj, Massad, and Finkelstein cases. Then, as we saw dramatically in the 2008–9 academic year, people both on and off campus may be tempted to prevent people they disagree with from speaking on campus.

Among the conclusions one can consider is that Horowitz and other right-wing culture warriors have mistakenly focused on political mistreatment of students, a phenomenon that is far less prevalent than he suggests. But then he has never taught in a university and has no real knowledge of faculty decision making. The critical issue is the politicization of faculty self-government at the departmental level—and the willingness of some deans to support the department head's will at any human cost. Horowitz is too ill informed to understand that a senior job candidate in the humanities or social sciences is just as likely to be rejected for being too Left as for being not Left enough. Faculty commitments on the Right can be equally finely calibrated when disciplines like business and economics do their hiring. Indeed faculty culture remains socially conservative. Except for the far Right, no one much minds faculty politics in scholarly publications, which may well be ignored in the public sphere, unless the reader's own commitments are challenged, but public activism on the Right or the Left makes many faculty uneasy. What some faculty are more than willing to do is to mistreat one another and to politicize their own decision making.

Given the rather vicious way local and national politicians can conduct their business—the crude characterizations of opponents, the false rumors, the eagerness to destroy careers—is there any reason to expect universities to do better? Perhaps not, but countries need spaces where passionate but reasoned debate can be conducted, where advocacy can partner with relative civility. The alternative in too many public conflicts is to reach for real or symbolic weapons and kill one another. Institutions of higher education are one of the few places that can offer an alternative model, though that need not mean forbearing to denounce positions one believes to be genuinely damaging.

Nor does the alternative model mean that passion needs to be suppressed, though it does need to be moderated. The idea that all university dialogue needs to be conducted in a calm, dispassionate, unvaryingly respectful way in fact makes the university less useful as a social model, because then the university seems unrealistic and irrelevant. The University of Michigan has an interesting and atypical policy that permits brief interruptions of speeches for protests, with the proviso that the presentation then be allowed to continue. I saw that happen at the University of California at Berkeley in April 2008, when a speech by law professor and torture-memo author John Yoo was interrupted and then allowed to continue. Conservative law students in the audience whom I interviewed afterward denounced the interruption as an example of "heckler's veto," but that exaggerates the impact. Too many campuses enforce a stifling and inflexible imposition of reasonableness on public events, while tolerating faculty discussions that are genuinely uncivil. When those discussions embody political conflicts, the results can be particularly ruthless, since everyone thinks that much more than local interests are at stake. They imagine themselves to be actors on the world stage.

Part of what is critical is for campuses to set aside political considerations in tenure decisions. Whether you agree or disagree with Finkelstein, El-Haj, and Massad, they all meet long-established academic criteria for tenure. Finkelstein, of course, lost his job; El-Haj kept hers. Massad's case was successfully reconsidered after initially being recommended for a terminal contract, rather than tenure. If he had lost his bid for tenure, academic freedom would have suffered a telling defeat, and the role of politics in university decision making would have required urgent rethinking. At the same time, the sometimes hyperbolic character of hiring discussions needs to be reined in and based more consistently on careful analysis.

The university needs to be a place where faculty and students can voice political opinions forthrightly and passionately and where they will not be punished for doing so. The only realistic answer to "can't we get along on campus?" is "not always." But we need to establish spaces and define circumstances in which civility and mutual respect can prevail, among them being departmental decision making. To do so across all campus contexts would impose an Orwellian corporate conformity of its own sort. And transgressions against standards for good decision making and productive communication can also be instructive. Over the years, we learn as much from bad decisions as from good ones. As a teaching environment, the campus instructs by error as usefully as it does by success. Bad decisions indeed tend to haunt us, remaining teachable moments that last for decades.

What I have sought to emphasize here, however, is that the dangers to critical thinking on campus come not just from the organized Right outside the university but also from internal intolerance and self-delusion. To the extent that the Right has succeeded in putting progressive students and faculty on the defensive, it has made it harder to acknowledge problems and find the will to address them. Thus, though political correctness is not the all-defining campus cultural force the Right makes it out to be, it does operate, in some contexts absurdly. We can do better.

We are now confronted with the need to make some rather nuanced decisions and set some rather difficult standards for ourselves. The need grows partly out of unintended consequences. Having argued repeatedly that "the personal is political" in the 1970s and 1980s, we find ourselves now in a world where "the professional is political." I played a role in the development of that notion myself, having repeatedly chastised tenured faculty with progressive publication histories for failing to support job actions by graduate-student employees. What I would *not* do is allow such judgments to influence either a tenure or a hiring decision. Similarly, I might disagree at many points with El-Haj, Finkelstein, or Massad, but as I said earlier, I would support their tenure. Would they do the same for me? I have no idea. Whether my inclinations amount to a personal code of professional ethics or standards that should be universal remains to be seen. But it is time for all of us to be discussing such distinctions.

The Ford Foundation has established one of its "difficult dialogues" programs on the issue of the Arab-Israeli conflict on the campus of the University of California at Irvine, and we may all be able to learn from that effort to promote rational debate (Gomez). A conviction that one is absolutely in the right is certainly not a hopeful way to begin that political discussion. Recognizing and at least provisionally validating one another's experience is a first step. Collectively identifying and acknowledging productive and unproductive behavior is another. Simply determining to set aside our political differences in tenure decisions is a parallel critical step. The campus does not need to be a consistently ideal human community, but it needs to ask what the components of such a negotiated community might be.

[5]

The Future of Faculty Unionization

Unionization is important to all employees as a means to redis-
tribute both wealth and power through their participation in
workplace decisions that affect their employment. For professional employees, the legally enforceable right to collectively bargain over such decisions is also a means to protect the standards
of their profession.

—Risa Lieberwitz, "Faculty in the
Corporate University" (300)

I keep waiting for the other shoe to drop. At campuses across the country, jackbooted university managers have trod all over faculty rights for a
decade. Shared governance is too often at best the object of administrative contempt. Faculty control over the curriculum is whittled away by
reliance on part-timers with no input and by online degrees designed by
bureaucrats. Academic freedom is simultaneously compromised by policies for email use and campus servers and threatened by continuous right-
wing assaults from outside the university. Independent faculty research in
science, engineering, and agriculture is increasingly undermined by reliance on product-oriented commercial support. Tolerance for "unprofitable" humanities and social science research is on the wane. And the burgeoning class of contingent faculty without health care, retirement plans,
due process, job security, or true academic freedom make college teaching a new form of wage slavery.

Unfortunately, the faculty as a whole has one foot in the cradle and
one in the grave. It is generationally divided between those too young to
know any better and those waiting to retire. They all need to buy good
union-made shoes and organize. Among the only cohorts that justify
hope are those union activists with a broader social vision, including

veterans of the graduate-employee organizing movement, the core of dedicated but aging AAUP members, and those faculty scattered across the country who combine realism with activism. Without fundamental changes in faculty attitudes and ambitions, the kind of higher education we know will not long survive, except to some degree at the wealthiest institutions.

Despite all the trends that give clear warnings, many faculty members are simply hoping for the best. Faculty members regularly point to their handbooks as guarantees of tenure, due process, and shared governance. As anyone seriously involved in collective bargaining knows well, handbook provisions in many states are not worth much unless they are mirrored in a legally enforceable contract. Though the legal status of handbook provisions not supported by union contracts varies from state to state, there is often very little reassuring case law bearing on the issue. Overall, there is little warrant for relying on handbook guarantees. As events in Louisiana after Hurricane Katrina should have taught all of us, events discussed in chapter 7, faculty handbooks can be tossed aside under the right conditions. Nor does it take a natural disaster for some administrations to revise them unilaterally.

When I wake up each morning and put on my own shoes, I keep wondering if it is the day I will be walking arm in arm in solidarity with my colleagues. I believe that public higher education is ripe for a new wave of collective bargaining campaigns. I believe faculty at private institutions will someday seize the power inherent in numbers. Exactly when the tipping point will come I cannot say, but history suggests that worsening conditions eventually produce resistance. The other shoe will drop. Exploitation will engender organization.

Opportunities for collective bargaining received a major, Depression-era boost from the 1935 Wagner Act, which fueled the rapid expansion of industrial unions. The act did not, however, apply to public-sector institutions, and it was not until 1970 that the National Labor Relations Board (NLRB) ruled that private colleges and universities came under its jurisdiction and thus could bargain under the provisions of the legislation. It was in fact changes in state law offering government workers bargaining rights that most fueled the growth of academic unions (Garbarino 3). The Taylor Law did so in New York in 1967, and faculty at the City University of New York (CUNY) and in the State University of New York (SUNY) system soon took advantage of the opportunity. A series of states in the Northeast and Midwest followed. Beginning in the late 1960s and extending through the 1970s, public-sector academic organizing flourished.

At first, the AAUP rejected collective bargaining, but some of its own chapters sought recognition as bargaining units anyway. That helped lead the AAUP's National Council to endorse collective bargaining as an option for its chapters in 1971. The association's annual meeting ratified that policy change in 1972, and the following year the AAUP issued its "Statement on Collective Bargaining," which supported the contention that unionization could reinforce the full range of faculty professional values. A decade of union activism followed. It was fueled by a number of additional economic and cultural forces. Average faculty salary increases generally exceeded the rate of inflation in the 1960s, but failed to do so thereafter. Increases in institutional size and in the number of departments encouraged adoption of more formal shared governance procedures that could best be established through structured negotiation. The difference the AAUP has made to faculty bargaining has been in two areas: establishing the right of each institution's faculty to set its own priorities and emphasizing shared governance and academic freedom principles in contract language. Thus, for example, Gary Rhoades reviewed a large number of collective bargaining contracts and found a much higher incidence of careful financial exigency procedures and safeguards in AAUP contracts (91). The AAUP also has a strong appeal to research-oriented faculty, though the organization's ability to take advantage of that appeal has been undercut by the Supreme Court's decision to make organizing at private universities exceedingly difficult.

In the 1980s, the drive toward faculty unionization slowed. It is not difficult to list the forces that have largely stalled the drive to organize more campuses. Organizing at private universities came to a virtual halt, and the union movement ran out of states with positive legislative environments for public-sector organizing:

1. The 1980 Supreme Court decision in *NLRB v. Yeshiva University* blocked the faculty there from organizing for collective bargaining by declaring them "managerial employees," based primarily, as Risa Lieberwitz summarizes it, "on the evidence of faculty autonomy over academic matters, including curriculum, teaching methods, grading policies, and student admissions, which the Supreme Court found to be managerial duties carried out by the faculty in the interest of the university" (283). Six years earlier, in *NLRB v. Bell Aerospace*, the Court had identified as management those who "formulate and effectuate management policies by expressing and making operative the decisions of their employer." That hardly captures the self-perception of faculty, and the NLRB characterized Yeshiva faculty instead as professional employees, a category eligible for collective bargaining. The Court ruled otherwise, finding that "faculty must be aligned with management," another surprise to many of us. The NLRB only has jurisdiction over private universities, but the *Yeshiva* decision means the NLRB cannot certify union drives and supervise elections for faculty at private universities. Faculty at private universities could still win recognition by consent, but that is considerably more difficult in the current antiunion cultural climate. There is also the possibility that Congress could legislate to overrule *Yeshiva,* but that would certainly require a coalition of national unions making it a priority. The era of growth in private-university academic organizing, which began in 1970, thus came to an end a decade later.

2. Public universities are governed by state law, but twenty-two right-to-work states, especially in the South and the West, have laws that prohibit agreements between unions and employers that allow for the collection of mandatory union dues. With the exception of Florida, such regulations have effectively eliminated faculty organizing at public institutions in those states. The difficulties are both obvious and not so obvious. Not having mandatory dues certainly keeps a union in organizing mode and in touch with its membership, which is a good thing, but mandatory partial dues for nonmembers, as in a union shop, provides greater resources. An exclusively voluntary membership can also skew membership to more activist faculty whose values are not representative of the faculty as a whole (Eisenberg). That can alienate especially those senior faculty who rely on their status to negotiate individual deals and can leave a union mostly in the control of junior faculty.

3. Despite unreliable shared government practices, faculty at elite research universities have largely felt secure enough not to seek collective representation. Although tenure and academic freedom were, ironically, themselves secured by collective action, they have helped sustain an ideology of individual autonomy. Just as faculty can hardly be described as "managers" across the whole range of university responsibilities, so too are faculty not autonomous in many areas of their professional lives. Nonetheless, the fiction holds. Given that faculty are as vulnerable to misinformation as any other human beings, it is perhaps not surprising that antiunion campaigns have succeeded in persuading some faculty members falsely that collective bargaining will usurp shared governance or that it will make all campus interactions adversarial. In fact, as Barbara Lee showed, as early as the 1970s it became clear that collective bargaining regularly strengthened faculty senates (28). Collective bargaining can restore shared governance to a campus where it has declined or can establish it for the first time. A union can play a major role in strengthening faculty morale. When all parties bargain in good faith, moreover, collective bargaining is a method for conflict negotiation and resolution, not a route to maximum antagonism. It provides procedures and a time line for grievance resolution. It can establish raises and benefits based on good-faith negotiation. Faculty at elite schools, however, worry that unions would encourage mediocrity, rather than a meritocracy, and thus would undercut familiar practices such as merit pay, though there is no reason why any level of commitment to merit pay cannot be won in negotiations if a majority of the faculty members on a given campus want it. What is especially significant is that many faculty unions have "sought with substantial success to limit administrative discretion in setting salaries . . . by some combination of negotiated criteria and peer review in the distribution of merit-, market-, and equity-based selective increments" (Benjamin, "Faculty Bargaining" 43). Certainly AAUP-style collective bargaining gives a local the right to define its own values and priorities. Whether public institutions will have the resources to grant faculty significant differential financial rewards over the next decade is doubtful. What is more, merit pay only works if there is enough salary money available and if a sufficient group of faculty members are *not* meritorious. Certainly faculty members in 2009 with multiyear contracts

were glad to have their contractually negotiated raises guaranteed in the midst of a recession.

4. Increased numbers of contingent faculty means that more faculty are inherently more difficult to organize, not only because they are more dispersed and transient but also because they are substantially constrained by fear, though no one would claim that contingent faculty are covered by *Yeshiva*. Keith Hoeller has argued that adjunct faculty need their own independent national union, because the major existing faculty unions give priority to the interests of full-time, permanent faculty and rarely win decent salary raises or job security for part-timers. Certainly any form of organizing that puts more pressure on existing faculty unions to better represent adjuncts is to the good. Yet an independent national union for contingent faculty would take years to create and could not be effective without a sizable strike fund. It would also solidify the cultural division between tenured and contingent faculty and thus leave the professoriate decisively split in half.

Under these conditions, relatively few major prospects for faculty organizing remain. Most, though not all, of the campuses most likely to organize already are organized. To fight that trend, in 2009 the AAUP launched an experiment in joint organizing with the American Federation of Teachers (AFT), aiming to combine the AAUP's academic credibility and expertise with the AFT's greater financial resources and legislative clout in some states. There is some hope, because the material and psychological working conditions of faculty are changing, and job satisfaction is declining for both full-time and part-time faculty. Certainly the growing influence of managerial administrative ideology undercuts the fiction that collegiality, mutual respect, and shared authority govern campus decision making. Although, as Michael Mauer points out, "the weak position of organized labor off campuses—arising out of outright hostility in its various forms in addition to the widespread perception that unions are simply powerless" (388–89)—reinforces faculty reluctance to think seriously about collective bargaining as an option, the fact is that roughly 40 percent of full-time faculty at four-year colleges and universities are organized for collective bargaining, and very few campuses contemplate abandoning it. As I suggested earlier, the possibility exists that we will see a resurgence of interest in collective bargaining on campus.

Nonetheless, a series of questions remain: When will the balance of self-interest tip toward collective action? Are we ready for that day? Do we have unions that can hail faculty frustrated by a commercialized university mission they no longer recognize? Do we have unions that can simultaneously invoke practicality and idealism, wages and academic freedom, self-interest and community responsibility? Do we have unions that can overcome the antagonism toward collective bargaining that is widespread in American culture and perilously linked to faculty's belief in their independence and individuality? Is there any chance the public would admire us in the wake of a new wave of faculty unionization? What sort of unionization would enhance our status in the public eye? Those are the questions I begin to answer in the rest of this chapter.

Devotion to academic freedom and shared governance, founding staples of AAUP collective bargaining, are certainly essential components of faculty unions worthy of both our own devotion and public support. Indeed, unionization will be increasingly necessary nationally to shore up these values. But much education will be required before the public either understands or endorses these values. Just turning faculty into articulate defenders of academic freedom and committed participants in shared governance would be a considerable task. If a faculty union were to approach the average new assistant professor with a call to join up and help strengthen shared governance, the most likely response would be "what is shared governance?"

Getting the public to understand academic freedom is a still more daunting goal. It would require sufficient resources to produce and place magazine ads and radio and television spots explaining key elements of the concept. It would be a multimillion-dollar campaign. Meanwhile, unions need to recover their historical devotion to the public good if they are to refurbish their image. What better place to do that than a college or university campus? What better place than that to harness students' idealism to the faculty's capacity for articulate advocacy?

We might begin by turning the campus itself into a workplace laboratory for social justice, helping to organize our weakest brothers and sisters on campus, from contingent faculty and graduate employees to secretaries and cafeteria workers. A faculty union should make universal workplace justice its first priority. The AFT faculty union at Eastern Illinois University includes in the bargaining unit contingent faculty teaching 50 percent time or more. The full-time faculty made their contingent colleagues their first priority in their 2006 contract negotiations, winning them higher salary increases and the possibility of multiyear contracts. It was not easy. Some tenured faculty and some administrators objected. But everyone I have talked with since—both faculty and administrators—are now proud of the results.

Tenured faculty should insist that all workers have health care, a living wage, and due process rights. Insist that all students from poor and lower-middle-class families receive a free college education. Insist that the huge gap between the highest paid administrators and the teachers on the line be closed. Then turn outward and demand the same commitments from local industry and local government. A faculty union should be a force that galvanizes community commitment to a better life for all. It should be a source of public inspiration and solidarity.

We all know that many Americans now regard unions as little more than group efforts to harness greed and avoid work. Worse still, many union members themselves lack an understanding of unions' larger cultural role. Thus, many of them vote against their economic and political self-interest in national elections. In the 2004 presidential elections, some National Guard members who voted for George W. Bush have surely since paid with their lives in Iraq. Across the United States, no doubt some union members who decided that the risks from gay marriage were greater than the risks from lax enforcement of workplace safety rules voted for George W. Bush and also paid with their lives. Others simply lost their pensions or their health care, as Bush-appointed judges decided that hard-won provisions applied to the life of the contract, not the life of the employee.

Faculty's fear of collective action—revulsion at the thought of having their imperial, transcendent individual agency smothered in mob rule—is their version of horror at gay marriage, a form of false consciousness learned at the cradle of the academy. It is part of the ideology that grew out of the identification of communism with fascism that was installed in faculty culture in the 1950s, when it seemed to some that all mass consciousness was demonic. My hope is that losing power over the curriculum, watching institutional mission morph from education into job training, watching administrative salaries soar, witnessing the sheer number of administrative positions multiply like the triffids of the 1962 science-fiction film, and seeing the teaching profession reduced to the academic equivalent of fast-food employment will lead faculty to realize that their self-interest does not reside in group impotence.

Far more than bread and butter is disappearing from the university table. So self-interest at some point mandates that faculty opt for the only kind of agency—collective agency—that can enforce principles of academic freedom and shared governance, that can contractually restrict the use of contingent labor in the classroom, that can enforce due process, and finally, that can reverse the flow of power from the faculty to the administration that has eroded the faculty's role for a generation.

For more than a decade, in a series of books and essays, including *The Knowledge Factory* and "Should Academic Unions Get Involved in Governance?" Stanley Aronowitz has been arguing that faculty unions need to get more involved in governance issues. He has also urged unions to take on a broader social mission. As he wrote at the end of his 1997 essay "Academic Unionism and the Future of Higher Education," "unions are now faced with the awesome task of becoming institutions of alternative as well as resistance. In short, they are challenged to accept responsibility for the academic system rather than remaining representatives of specific interests of faculty and staff within its technocratically defined boundaries. The challenge is to become agents of a new educational imagination" (213). There really is no choice. The workplace issues for faculty now involve rapacious redefinition of the fundamental character of higher education and the role of the faculty. The nature of the job is changing—and not for the good. When only one faculty member holds the last good job in the United States, the job will not matter. The last tenured faculty member in the United States will not possess academic freedom.

But even an AAUP-style union that embraces shared governance in all its aspects cannot win public admiration, let alone hail young faculty, students, and staff. If faculty self-interest writ large and small are equally imperiled, they cannot be repaired by anything less than a redefinition of faculty identity. We need to encourage models of faculty identity that combine careerism with social responsibility. We need to encourage faculty to realize that their lives are not complete, their identities not whole, unless their personal ambition is matched by community commitment. We need a notion of community that is actually empowered by faculty advocacy. At the end of chapter 3, I recommend a new component of community identity, one not dependent on collective bargaining. Here I explore what unions can contribute.

Faculty collective bargaining must be at the center of the project to redefine faculty identity. Faculty collective bargaining needs to lead the effort to reverse the trends and restore unionization's progressive ambitions and its utopian heart. To say that this call will fall on deaf ears is more than an understatement. It is not clear that faculty have the social ears to hear this challenge. Certainly there are relatively few faculty leaders in AAUP collective bargaining units (CBs) working toward this goal, except perhaps those who have been part of citywide living-wage campaigns. So it is not as if I can claim I am speaking to an incipient yearning in the hearts of faculty unionists.

Indeed, the course of faculty unionism on many campuses has been in the opposite direction. Far too many locals have never replaced the dynamic leaders who founded CB chapters in the 1970s. A disturbing number of locals have lost the organizing impulse and let their memberships drift near or into minority representation. Only reluctance of their enemies to take on the battle protects them from decertification challenges. And here and there local ideology has grown corrupt or jaded. Moldy bread and spoiled butter dominate the issues of the day, as when members of a tenured-faculty union become convinced that every dollar granted part-time teachers is a dollar lost to them, as when members of a tenured-faculty union do not care whether their contingent colleagues have health care or a living wage.

But I am not sure a vulnerable union near minority membership is the least inspiring state for a campus. At least that kind of local broadcasts a message of weakness that calls for change. After three decades of union activism and visits with still more local CB leaders over the past several years, I have a different model for my image of a worst case local: one that is fat and happy with a faculty that is deaf, dumb, and blind.

Although I realize what I say will mortally offend many people in the movement, I believe one of the most disabling kinds of unionism is exemplified by a well-functioning, staff-run local that includes virtually no engaged, well-informed faculty members. There are locals out there where the faculty are effectively ventriloquists' dummies, parroting staff views without dissent or variation. If such a local has agency fee (which mandates that all faculty, whether they join the union or not, must pay a portion of union dues) and a sufficient revenue flow, the staff can often argue for (and sometimes deliver) salary increases, protect benefits, and conduct aggressive grievance hearings.

In such a local—if the office is well managed and efficient and does not squander resources—the faculty need not think about the union. It never moves out of the deep background of their lives. There will of course be a faculty executive committee and local officers. Yet they may stand for election and be replaced every year, so that the officers never really learn what is happening before they are out the door. But they tend in any case to be well indoctrinated; their opinions on all issues are thoroughly scripted by staff. If anything arrives in their mailboxes that might cause them to think differently, they can be relied on either to ignore its content or simply to discard it unread. Often a staff member is the only person who has regular contact with other locals or with the union's national office. All knowledge of the outside world of collective bargaining is colored by the staff member's interests and shaped by the staff member's perspective. Despite the published claims about the independence of the faculty in AAUP unionism, the AAUP is no more guaranteed immunity from this sort of passive faculty unionization than is the AFT or the National Education Association (NEA). Whatever the benefits of nonparticipatory unionization have been in the past—the main one being its facility at freeing up the faculty to pursue their other interests—the main problem is that nonparticipatory unionization will not be able to adapt to the social activism I believe unions must embrace in the future.

Though instances are rare, staff-dominated unions can also drift into malfeasance. The possibility that absolute power will corrupt absolutely is always there. Some time ago I had experience of one local where the staff was apparently hiring friends or relatives to do make-work and perhaps spending union funds irresponsibly in other ways. The faculty finally rose up and fired the staff, taking over the union and relying on a substantially reduced number of employees to do the routine necessary clerical and administrative work thereafter. The faculty took control of the union again. With reduced overhead, the local now has the resources to begin building a significant strike fund. You might think it should have been obvious all along that a strike fund was more valuable than two new assistants to the executive director, but apparently not.

I am certainly not against having a staff. I am simply against their operating in a vacuum of faculty engagement and in the absence of real oversight and authority. Some graduate-employee unions notably limit staff tenure as a way of avoiding power being disproportionately vested in long-term employees. If grad-employee unions—which rely on staff not only for administrative services but also for sustaining collective memory through changing membership—can survive regular staff turnover, so can faculty unions. Although local staffing needs and priorities will differ, the issue of staff longevity needs to be on the table for discussion. So does the issue of staff size. There are good reasons to keep union staffs relatively lean, among them being to make faculty volunteerism necessary.

The issues are obviously different for a statewide or international union, for which a substantial staff is necessary. A local may be able to function with a bare-bones staff in a way that a state organization or an international cannot. In the case of the larger unions, a partnership between leadership and staff, well exemplified by the California Faculty Association but only intermittently in evidence at the AAUP, is essential.

A local dominated by a single faculty leader is not, however, necessarily better than one dominated by a single staff member. Some of the same problems exist, with most faculty easily becoming disengaged, detached, and ill informed and with one person filtering all information provided to members. It is entirely possible that a local can be led to act against its own best interests under those conditions. And, of course, like dictatorships, one-person union leaderships often have no capable successor in the wings. Disintegration may be the outcome of the leader's death or departure. In such cases, the only recourse may be for the national office to step in and guarantee the local's continuing operation. Indeed, an inability to create new generations of local leaders is one reason why locals sometimes become steadily more dependent on a powerful national staff.

The ideal union is thus one in which a significant, if evolving, core of faculty activists remains thoroughly engaged and responsible for setting policy. Policy should grow out of a democratic dialogue among numerous well-informed people. Such a collaborative union is far more likely to be effective in monitoring shared governance, academic freedom in both research and teaching, and the whole range of campus issues for which the staff really does not have day-to-day input, let alone a role in negotiating with the administration. No single faculty member has enough disciplinary or policy expertise to do everything. A core of faculty activists also has a better chance of winning their colleagues' attention when more-active solidarity is necessary. And it is likely that only an engaged faculty can broaden a union's horizons to encompass workplace justice for the community as a whole. Inspiring students to join that cause is also a faculty, not a staff, responsibility. Utopian unionization must be an engaged, collective enterprise, not simply an efficiently administered bureaucracy.

I have no illusion that I can easily gain a hearing with the faculty who I believe most need to hear this message. My most likely audience is those who feel their vested interests lie in rejecting everything I am saying. But we have to start somewhere if unions are to lead the way in resisting the relentless corporatization of university culture. There are those of us who believe American education needs not only to retain but actually to enhance its capacity to empower students to become critical participants in a democracy. A largely vulnerable and contingent faculty is far less able to voice unpopular views, to resist the reduction of education to job training, and to assert control over the curriculum and faculty hiring. To be effective in the far more challenging managerial regime we face, the faculty needs an organized voice that can negotiate legally enforceable agreements. That voice is called a union.

If such a faculty union has majority membership and a healthy core of activists, it will be able to negotiate with the administration as equals over the key educational issues about which the faculty has both interests and expertise. Not all those issues entail opposing every senior administrator. Here and there the corporate university still harbors deans, provosts, chancellors, or presidents who understand and cherish academic freedom. There are even some administrators who honor shared governance. A faculty that exercises its will effectively can empower a sympathetic administrator to act.

Yet sympathetic administrators are exceptionally vulnerable today. Governing boards seek aggressive managers intolerant of shared governance's complications. Administrators who truly endorse academic freedom may feel seriously isolated among their peers. The social pressures among senior administrators to conform to a managerial model are substantial. Faculty affection and support for sympathetic administrators may limit overt attacks on them from unsympathetic peers but may not stop covert campaigns to undermine a "disloyal" dean, provost, or president. Just consider how exposed and isolated an administrator who endorses collective bargaining would be today on a typical non-CB campus. I have no solution to offer, just a warning: a lone progressive administrator may not be able to survive in the contemporary corporate university.

Despite the crude character of a good administrator/bad administrator distinction, it remains useful and necessary in many contexts. You often have to know who your friends are. What this dichotomy misses, however, is the structural character of higher education governance. We all decry the proliferation of a managerial class of career administrators peopled by folks who have either never spent time in a classroom or have long forgotten the experience. What we may miss is the coercive character of social relations in this expanded group and the impact managerial socialization has on faculty organizing. These people are trained to resist unionization and then, if they fail, to help ensure you become a business union, rather than a broadly progressive social force. The excessive number of administrators facilitates their collective conformity to these goals. They work together. They breed together. They cultivate their faculty allies, reward them, and incorporate them into collateral socialization processes.

During the first two decades of my career, I regularly worked closely with senior administrators, many of whom were dedicated to improving the whole range of disciplines on campus. Then, in the 1990s, the upper administration joined with the Association of Governing Boards in believing that advocates of collective bargaining should be barred from shared governance roles. A corporate logic began to take over the central administration, and "unprofitable" humanities disciplines lost the core of their support. My preference is still to collaborate with the administration, but not when none of its senior members is committed to academic freedom.

In that environment, an enlightened administrator is to be treasured, however vulnerable. On my own campus, a sympathetic chancellor (Nancy Cantor) was able a few years ago to grant graduate employees bargaining rights—against the wishes of most other campus administrators—in response to a building occupation that followed a vote for recognition (Nelson and Watt, *Office Hours* 139–43). That application of force gave the chancellor warrant to act decisively. Reasoned argument had failed to win the day for twelve years, though it had certainly educated people and prepared the ground. But collective agency and activism was required to close the deal. Yet in the end, the chancellor was essentially run out of town by conservative administrators and alumni.

The faculty similarly need activism from time to time to build alliances across the moats that divide disciplines. A faculty union that goes more than a generation without a strike can lose sight of its potential for solidarity. A strike in support not only of faculty interests but also of principled employment for the whole campus community could create goodwill for a decade or more.

How might an enlightened faculty union transform higher education into an industry devoted to social justice? A socially responsible humanities and social science curriculum, partly developed with union funds, might, for example, engage an instrumentalized university mission critically. It could examine all the economic practices that structure a student's education. One issue that such a curriculum might raise—as a prelude to faculty unions embracing it nationwide—is the desirability of free public higher education throughout the country. As Mark Dudzic and Adolph Reed point out, "What issue could possibly be closer to the consensus view of the American dream?" The total bill for tuition at public institutions of higher education—community colleges to universities—is about fifty billion dollars. That would be a truly progressive stimulus package.

Too many campuses, following the Stanley Fish employment model described in chapter 7, at present amount to instructional manuals for workplace exploitation. Teaching by example, they teach students how to break employee morale, destroy families, withhold basic rights, and deny self-representation. As Richard Shaull put it in 1994, "There is no such thing as a *neutral* educational process. Education either functions as an instrument that is used to facilitate the integration of the younger generation into the logic of the present system and bring about conformity to it, *or* it becomes . . . the means by which men and women deal critically and creatively with reality and discover how to participate in the transformation of their world" (34).

When Yale University historically fired many of its workers during the summer, rather than assigning them to other tasks—a practice that turned long-term employees into seasonal workers who could be rehired year after year while being denied benefits (Wilhelm)—it constructed its students as participants in class oppression. Now all who benefit from the exploitation of contingent teachers are complicit in a system founded on injustice. And as Marc Bousquet has shown us in his account of the University of Louisville's ruthless partnership with UPS, some universities have found new ways of turning undergraduates into disposable workers. To grasp how intricately the contemporary university can brutalize both students and teachers, one has to read the "Students Are Already Workers" chapter in Bousquet's *How the University Works*. The Louisville students do back-breaking work at the UPS sorting hub from midnight to three or four in the morning, all for wages of roughly $120 a week. Then faculty, who also teach classes during the day, show up to advise them as they come off the line in the middle of the night. As the corporate university has evolved over the past twenty years, it now exploits *both* teachers and students in the workplace. Perhaps the clearest indication of that development, as Jeffrey Williams has warned, is the pervasive increase in student debt. That is a new configuration for higher education, and unions need to instruct all of us in its modes of operation and to take the lead in resisting its human costs.

I am not suggesting that a union negotiate with the university about the overall curriculum. I am suggesting that a union educate the faculty comprehensively about the campus's employment environment, that the union support the faculty's right to teach about such matters, that the union develop educational materials for students and faculty, and that the union fund course development in this area for interested faculty. The institution's employment practices are relevant to every student in every class, no matter what the subject matter. Academic freedom means that faculty members can take some modest amount of time to raise such issues in any class they teach. That much can be reinforced in a faculty handbook or union contract.

While such issues are being taken up in classrooms, the union should stand behind all campus workers. Whenever possible, it should not only endorse but also help organize all employee groups. It should be an advocate for all groups, whether or not it represents them in collective bargaining. On those campuses where the administration has partnered in exploiting undergraduate workers, unions have a special responsibility to publicize the fact and seek reform. Even a nonunionized private-university faculty could take on these tasks. Certainly any AAUP chapter could do so. It would not hurt, for example, for parents to see faculty unions as the defenders of their children. A union's support for and monitoring of academic freedom should be part of a comprehensive progressive agenda.

Organizing drives would also benefit from recasting and expanding the social profile of unionization, not only because it would have wider appeal but also because it would be harder to resist. A card drive advocating comprehensive workplace justice would be significantly more difficult to misrepresent. At the very least, the arguments *against* "a living wage and health care coverage for all campus workers" and "fair representation for the faculty in shaping the curriculum" would be more vulnerable.

Those faculty leaders who forged unions decades ago understood themselves to be joining a cause. If successors have often not stepped forward to fill their shoes, it is not surprising. Maintaining an ongoing organization is hardly equivalent to jousting with dragons to establish one. Meanwhile, many unions since have sold themselves on the basis of disengagement: "Give us your dues, and we'll take care of business. You'll be free to concentrate on teaching and research." Yet we do not need to galvanize all our members to reinvigorate unions with a sense of mission. We need to inspire a core of activists in every local, to put forth a new, more generous, cause around which faculty unions can mobilize and recruit new members. Such efforts may also require a triggering event, a rallying point, such as a university's decision to freeze unrepresented workers' salaries. Unions are not prevented from advocating on behalf of workers they do not formally represent. Meanwhile, the conceptual ground can be established in advance.

The 2008–10 recession provided a test of the capacity of campus unions to see themselves this way. Some unions met the test, while others did not. Confronted with proposals for universal furloughs and salary freezes, some activists argued that lower-paid workers should not suffer. Some proposed cutting administrative positions, rather than faculty lines. Many argued for community-wide debate, rather than the imposition of solutions by administrators.

The general changes I am advocating are partly a recovery project. They challenge unions to recover their historical devotion to the public good, while shaping it to new times and conditions. Faculty unionization as a vehicle for narrow self-interest has no future. We need to envision a day when people outside the academy look to a unionized faculty with admiration, when they see a union as the single most enlightened and democratic force on campus. We are a long way from the dawn of that day, but its fundamental elements are not unimaginable. Principle itself is not outside the boundaries of faculty identity. It just needs to be deepened, expanded, rethought, and applied anew. Faculty unionization now has a long enough history for us to realize that campus unions, like all other cultural and political institutions, need not only to be continually strengthened but also to be regularly rebuilt and reconceived. We have now reached that time. If the faculty can lead the way to recovering public faith in unions, they will indeed have done due diligence for the country as a whole. Nothing less will assure their necessary role in preserving academic freedom.

[6]

Graduate-Employee Unionization
and the Future of Academic Labor

Our data analysis pointedly suggests that unionization, in itself, has not undermined the mentoring relationship. There are, however, other factors that do undermine it. A primary one occurs when faculty members or university administrators make explicit a conceptualization of graduate students as resources for the university to use as it sees fit. This conceptualization is more evident on campuses where shared governance has deteriorated.

—Patricia J. Gumport and Daniel J. Julius,
"Graduate Assistants' Bargaining" (58)

In my early 20s I had a job playing Papa Smurf at a mall. All I could see out of the tiny screen hidden below the nose of my gigantic and sweaty cartoon character costume were droves of hyper children. Some hugged me, some tugged on me, and some just ran away from me in fear. The worst of them would step right up to me, stare directly into my face, and declare sneeringly "You're not real!" Little did I know that being badly paid, abused, disrespected, and rendered invisible wasn't unique to being a Smurf. Life as a part-time instructor in the university system turned out to be scarily similar. From the very first semester much of my experience as a working graduate student challenged me—the exploitation of students as TAs and RAs; the strange, unspoken economy of faculty attention and support; the administrative pitting of students against each other for small amounts of funding.

—Alison Hearn, "Exploits in the Undercommons"

The movement for graduate-employee unionization is the single most promising development in higher education over the past two generations. It began with the formation of the first such union at the University of Wisconsin at Madison in 1969, followed by the University of Michigan a year later. Graduate employees at the University of Oregon won their recognition election in 1977. Several campuses in Florida followed, but the effort took form as a genuine movement in the 1990s, with the universities of Kansas, Iowa, and Massachusetts and the State University of New York and University of California campuses winning recognition and negotiating contracts.

The movement arrives at a time when much of the news about the industry is not good—from casualization to corporatization to the predominance of careerism and lack of community responsibility among many of the full-time tenurable faculty. As good a statistical indication of several of these destructive trends as any is the more than 50 percent decline in AAUP membership from the 1970s to the 1990s, a decline I evaluate more fully in chapter 8. Once again, faculty who see themselves as exclusively devoted to their careers and their disciplines—who are unconcerned with the principles and goals that unite the professoriate—are less likely to join in the defense of academic freedom.

One key element of graduate-employee unionization is how it responds to and helps us reverse several of these developments. Of first importance, of course, is the potential for unionization to raise the wages, benefits, and working conditions of all contingent workers in the academy and its proven capacity to spread workplace justice to other industries in a given area. But equally critical is its other clear legacy: its capacity to create new, socially and professionally responsible subject positions or identities for both graduate students and faculty. The movement for graduate-employee unionization is the best source of future faculty members devoted to both their personal academic work and their community responsibilities. Graduate employees are also often more alert to problematic working conditions and threats to academic freedom than tenure-track faculty, who typically have far more elaborate protections against abuse. Graduate employees thus work in an environment rife with opportunities for raising consciousness about academic freedom and for socialization that embodies a more comprehensive notion of professionalism. To a large degree, that socialization can be provided by their peers. Graduate-employee activists learn to work collectively for the common good, meanwhile learning advocacy and organizing skills. They are at the core of a generation that has the potential to reverse the dominance of identities based, ironically, on disempowered self-interest among the faculty.

Faculty unions also need the new blood and the focus on professional principles that graduate activists bring when they graduate to faculty status. A disturbingly large number of faculty unions formed in the 1970s or later have not grown a sufficient cadre of new, younger leaders. As I pointed out in the preceding chapter, some have also let the practice of recruiting new members slide and have thus seen their percentage of membership drop to the point where decertification at the hands of administrators or faculty opponents is a real risk. There is nothing quite like a leader who has been through a founding organizing drive. By far the largest pool of such people now is graduate-student union activists. Those activists should be cultivated as the faculty leaders of the future.

Graduate-employee activists also gain personally by acquiring skills in self-presentation that play extremely well in job interviews and in department life, because they have learned to present arguments convincingly to strangers, learned to listen carefully, and learned the psychological complexities of negotiating advocacy as part of interpersonal relations. At the same time, they learn to juggle competing demands on their time, moving back and forth between organizing their colleagues and taking courses or writing their dissertations. They live with demands on their time that can be all consuming, while also realizing that such responsibilities reach a point when they must be passed on to others. When union activity is combined with AAUP membership, graduate employees can add to this mix a deep knowledge of the principles that sustain and link academic freedom and job security.

The AAUP's ability to help organize graduate students for collective bargaining has unfortunately been hampered by its dues structure. Graduate students pay about forty dollars in annual dues, with a five-dollar supplement if they are organized as an AAUP collective bargaining unit. A freestanding AFT graduate-employee bargaining unit may pay union dues of 1.8 to 2 percent of salary. That provides enough money to staff a

local grad-union business office, pay part-time salaries for grievance officers and organizers, while still funding support from state and national
offices. The AAUP's dues structure does not. Yet it is the AAUP that can
offer graduate employees identification with academic freedom and other
faculty-oriented values. I have urged the AAUP to devise a dues structure
that facilitates realistic organizing possibilities. For there is another reason why the AAUP needs to be more involved in grad-employee organizing: most existing graduate-employee contracts have no guarantees of
academic freedom or protections for shared governance speech.

Based on the long-term experience of faculty unions in both Canada
and the United States—and on decades of graduate-employee unionization at the University of Wisconsin and the University of Michigan—a
clear pattern emerges about the practical benefits that union members
can expect. Improvements in health benefits are often the most immediate gain, supplemented by gradual progress on compensation. But
the more fundamental difference unions make, I believe, is in grieving
unfair or unsafe working conditions and in securing workplace rights.
Unions have the authority to establish workplace justice. Whole classes
of employees for the first time have the advantage of dispassionate, well-
informed third-party negotiation of exploitive practices, negotiations,
moreover, that guard against retaliation against the victims.

Faculty in well-run programs (in which I include my own department)
or in fields such as law that do not generally hire graduate students to teach
often have no idea how many graduate employees nationwide lack basic
workplace justice. The AAUP has now issued a revised set of national
rules for graduate employees that can help rectify some of the more widespread problems ("Graduate Student Employees"). In doing so, the organization has learned from benefits built into graduate-employee union
contracts and sought to make them universal. First on the list is strengthened academic freedom guarantees for those with teaching responsibilities. Then it is necessary to mandate clear letters of employment, laying
out both responsibilities and expectations for renewal. Several new
graduate students at Yale recently got very brief letters employing them
as assistants in courses, without any further specifications of their duties.
They showed up in class, waiting for the actual instructor to arrive, and
after fifteen minutes retreated to the department to ask what was up. They

were then clearly informed for the first time that *they* were the instructors. Having learned from the NYU experience, discussed later in this chapter, the AAUP will also prohibit firing graduate employees on strike. And it will establish strong due process requirements for employees confronted with termination midcontract.

Faculty unions should help enforce these standards, since even the strongest faculty union cannot establish workplace justice by looking solely after its own academic freedom and economic interests when graduate employees and contingent faculty are being denied those rights or being exploited on the same campus. It should also be a fundamental ethical and professional principle for existing faculty unions to help organize graduate employees, part-time faculty, and full-time faculty off the tenure track. The AAUP has been encouraging its full-time-faculty unions to do just that, and some have answered the call and succeeded. Not long ago, the AAUP's full-time-faculty collective bargaining unit at the University of Rhode Island took full responsibility for the successful drive to organize graduate employees and then integrated servicing of the new bargaining unit into existing chapter activities. The unit is now seeking to do the same for part-timers, a significantly more difficult task. The AAUP's Rutgers chapter, now jointly organized with AFT, has long had units for full-time faculty, graduate employees, and part-timers, and it now has a Service Bureau that handles needs on an integrated basis.

But not all AAUP chapters or locals have been sympathetic to graduate-employee unionization. During the 1995–96 graduate-employee strike, the Yale AAUP chapter was largely hostile toward the Graduate Employees and Students Organization (GESO). My own AAUP chapter declined to endorse the national AAUP policy in support of graduate-employee collective bargaining rights, despite the fact that I had written the policy and had given sworn testimony on behalf of our graduate employees before the Illinois Labor Relations Board. The NYU AAUP chapter opted to devote its energies and resources into a more spontaneous, and effective, formation called Faculty Democracy. Now that graduate students have full membership and voting rights in the AAUP, the opportunity exists to revitalize rather dormant AAUP chapters such as Yale's with local membership drives concentrating in part on graduate-student membership.

On the other hand, some non-AAUP faculty unions behave as if every dollar won by contingent teachers is a dollar taken from their own pockets. Yet denying contingent faculty a living wage and salary parity actually helps keep tenure-track faculty salaries low in a number of disciplines. A faculty union that either passively or actively collaborates in the exploitation of its brothers and sisters has simply lost its soul. At some level, it has become an arm of administrators devoted to extracting labor at its lowest possible cost. Worse still are those faculty unions that grieve their own workplace inequities while tolerating the mistreatment of contingent faculty or graduate employees down the hall.

Interestingly, one of the major groups of graduate employees who benefit from negotiation or formal arbitration of their grievances are those who work in engineering or science laboratories. Work weeks of a hundred or more hours can be reduced to a humane level when a union intervenes. Bizarre or repressive regulations in the contracts for lab assistants—breakage fees for dropping a glass beaker, requirements to work double-time to compensate for taking Christmas off—can be eliminated through union negotiation. Paradoxically, these are among the most difficult graduate employees to organize, not only because they are often relatively well compensated financially but also because they feel exceptionally vulnerable. Labs are often constructed around a core of foreign students who are anxious about visa renewal. If their families remained in their home countries, they may be less stressed by long working hours. For all these reasons, they are more readily influenced by false propaganda from administration spokespeople, propaganda that is often enough grounded in a mix of antagonism and ignorance (Benjamin, "Faculty Bargaining" 52–63). I believe unions should work together on a national educational campaign aimed at these employees and their supervisors. Meanwhile, emerging unions often agree to leave them out of the bargaining unit, a strategy administrators are sometimes willing to accept.

Faculty attitudes toward collective bargaining have always varied, especially at institutions where there are wide differentials in compensation by discipline. Tenurable faculty also show disciplinary differences in their approach to campaigns for graduate-employee unionization. Few humanities faculty members see themselves as employers. Even if a graduate employee is assisting in a large lecture course, humanities faculty are generally happy to see them better compensated. Running a lab staffed with graduate employees is another matter. There faculty can be corrupted by the temptation to extract the maximum labor at the lowest possible cost, because they supervise their workers directly and benefit professionally and financially by the work they do. Most laboratory faculty obtain funds for graduate employees' salaries through the grant application process, and they worry that a union contract will increase compensation before a new grant cycle will enable them to obtain additional funds. A responsible administration would begin setting aside enough indirect cost revenue to deal with this possibility as soon as a unionization drive gained strength. Instead, most administrations prefer to exploit faculty anxiety.

One of the most unethical faculty practices in both science and engineering labs is that of deliberately delaying PhD completion in order to retain experienced graduate employees as long as possible. It is a widely recognized national phenomenon, but in my experience neither department heads nor graduate-school deans do a very good job of policing the problem. It is another area where a union can step in and make a difference and another reason why training in academic freedom and workplace ethics needs to be built into faculty culture.

The past thirty-five years have seen successful drives for graduate-employee unionization at public universities in the East, the Midwest, and the West. Both experience and careful studies have shown that campus relations are improved, not damaged, by unionization—even in more volatile lab environments—though administrators often claim otherwise. The movement picked up speed in the 1990s and was supported by sometimes eloquent and witty state court opinions in such venues as Kansas and California. When the NLRB first ruled in favor of New York University graduate employees, it thus had not formal federal precedent but substantial state argument defending the notion that graduate students could be both students and employees, according to the roles they played at different times during the day.

The NLRB, of course, has jurisdiction over private universities, and there the story of graduate-employee unionization has been more troubled. Generation after generation of grad-employee activism has been sustained at Yale University, but the Yale Corporation in its hostility to all forms of unionization, now moving toward a century-long history (Nelson, introduction to *Will Teach for Food* 3–43), has successfully wielded administrative and legal power to prevent these employees from realizing this right recognized by the United Nations. The activists I worked with at Yale in the days during and after the historic grade strike, when grad employees withheld end-of-the-semester grades, are now long gone; many are tenured faculty elsewhere or union organizers in other industries. The struggle for unionization at New York University has its own long, unique story. Recognized by the NYU administration after a positive NLRB ruling, the union negotiated a strong contract and then was effectively decertified when the NYU president took advantage of an NLRB reversal to stop bargaining a new contract. He was not required to do so; he chose to disenfranchise his employees. Detailed analyses of the NYU events can be found in *The University against Itself*, edited by Monika Krause and others. But here I deal with the political and strategic issues at stake in the NYU story, so as to encourage realism in those who take up this cause. Because despite the benefits of graduate-employee unionization—and despite the hard evidence that it does not undermine faculty-student relations—administrators routinely fight the prospect to the grave and beyond. Those who participate in grad organizing campaigns will obtain the great gift of experiencing the solidarity of group struggle, a benefit alone worth the effort, but they should also be prepared for the challenges they will face.

Neither at Yale nor at NYU were strikes successful at winning or restoring union recognition. There are lessons to be learned from these and other struggles, however, that can help prepare the ground for future organizing campaigns and job actions. The most obvious lesson appears to be the most difficult for those of us within the campus bubble to internalize: the withdrawal of teaching labor never wields sufficient force to bring an administration to the bargaining table. It is easy to succumb to the expectation that a classroom strike will matter. The classroom is at the center of our lives and many of our social relations, but a forced vacation does not communicate imminent peril to students, who assume they will end up graduating anyway. Parental protests do not wield decisive power either. It is a storm most administrators assume they can weather. The major economic pressures fall on the strikers themselves—unless they plan carefully to assure the reverse.

A strike is a major emotional event; for some academics it will be the first powerful collective action they have ever taken, and the experience may prove life transforming. The eloquence, passion, and dedication of long-term graduate-employee activists is never less than inspiring. At NYU, a major local and national mobilization took place, drawing in teaching assistants, undergraduates, faculty, and external allies. Like the multigenerational struggle at Yale, it included events embodying unforgettable solidarity. It is thus surely forgivable to romanticize the experience. But it is best to avoid romanticizing the projected outcome. A cold calculation of likely results and strategies is in order.

I recently told a large faculty union planning to reduce its dues that they ought instead to use the excess money to build a substantial strike fund; even if they never had to use it, its existence would limit the administration's confidence in its ability to break a strike. That particular union had the power to build a one-million-dollar strike fund in three years, hardly enough to cover salaries for a long strike but enough to cover health insurance costs, and that alone would make a considerable difference. Graduate-employee unions cannot build comparable financial reserves, but they can accumulate more modest strike funds. And the focus on economic issues helps everyone realize their centrality. Political power can also be effective—if it is real, not merely symbolic—but it is economic power that can be decisive. The NYU strikers eventually received their most dramatic political support in the form of a letter jointly signed by New York's two U.S. senators, but there was little evidence of any politicians applying behind-the-scenes pressure: quietly delaying building permits and contracts, complicating inspections, refusing multiple forms of cooperation, orchestrating public embarrassments for administrators, and the like.

The first and most necessary form of economic pressure is cooperation from other unions in blocking all deliveries to campus. It is certainly easiest to prevent deliveries to a self-contained campus with its own clearly defined boundaries and with a limited number of entrances. An urban campus such as NYU, with buildings owned by multiple businesses in the same area, presents much greater difficulties, but it is still possible to map major delivery sites, loading docks, and other points where pickets can inhibit deliveries. Few drivers will pass a Teamster picket. Construction sites can also be shut down with union cooperation. A campus administration may be able to hire nonunion day laborers to keep some projects going, but somewhere in the supply chain a union is likely to be in place. During a 2006 strike by an AAUP-affiliated faculty union at Eastern Michigan University, the people who drove concrete trucks were nonunion and willing to pass picket lines, but the workers who loaded the concrete were unionized and honored the strike. Decades ago, a strike at the University of Wisconsin was won in part because conservative faculty pressured the administration to settle when food deliveries to animal labs were prevented and long-term experiments were on the verge of collapsing. The NYU strikers were unable to organize effective cessation of campus deliveries; that was an early sign that their strike was in trouble.

The United Auto Workers (UAW) might have done more to help the NYU students at that point, but my own view is that it is unwise to rely on even a strong national union to win full local cooperation from other unions in blocking deliveries. A history of campus support for other unions can be a critical component. Join the picket lines of other striking unions. Attend their rallies with signs identifying your own local. Honor and publicize their boycotts. Meet with their leaders to offer assistance and build relationships. Build local solidarity, both because you believe in it and because you know you will need it yourselves in time. Then add the component of advocacy from a national.

Any disruptive job action should also be timed to begin immediately after paychecks are distributed, so that participants have some waiting power. Strikers and their allies should also consider boycotting all local businesses, or at least those that refuse to support the strike, so that business owners have reason to pressure an administration to settle. That will also increase the amount of publicity a strike can generate. In a large city, it will be necessary to define a zone of impact, since one cannot expect to bring New York City or Washington, DC, to a halt. But denial of patronage can still be part of a successful strategy, especially if it is honored by all campus workers and their friends.

Solidarity is obviously a critical component of effective economic actions of this sort. Students, faculty, and staff who join such efforts in large numbers can bring considerable power to bear on an administration. In a small town where the college or university is the major employer, a coordinated economic boycott can be decisive. Withhold rent, mortgage, and utility payments. Organize caravans to shop in another city or, better still, in another state, if you are near a border. Many businesses do not have sizable ready cash reserves. They cannot long endure a sharply curtailed cash flow. Even large utility companies are vulnerable to cash-flow interruptions.

The absence of sufficient solidarity can be disastrous. That was one of the key lessons of the Yale grade strike, where sufficient effort did not go into educating undergraduates about any of the issues at stake. They did not understand that their instruction was being delivered by exploited workers. They did not understand that crossing a picket line is a significant ethical and political decision. I still wince at the memory of the anti-GESO editorials and cartoons in the Yale student newspaper. At one level, the Yale organizers had great publicity; their posters were clever and striking. But they had not done enough of the hard work of undergraduate instruction to build real commitment in the student body. At NYU, graduate-employee support for the UAW-affiliated union was strong across the whole range of disciplines, and there was a core of dedicated faculty support. But far too many other faculty members were indifferent or antagonistic. More time to educate faculty would have helped, though timing was partly out of the union's control, since the strike was prompted by the president's action.

Strike timing is nonetheless both complex and critical. Some of the people involved in planning the NYU strike, including the national UAW leadership, held that delaying a strike would undermine its credibility and chances for success. Others—among them NYU graduate activists and Yale graduate employees playing key leadership roles in the NYU events—counseled caution. A standard union warning is that it is easier to go out on strike than to come back to work victorious. There really was no effective winning strategy in place at NYU. Since, for example, a strike usually brings at least a temporary halt to negotiations, plans must be in place to make it too costly for management simply to wait out the strikers. Those who preferred waiting longer before striking at NYU—waiting until support was assured—were almost certainly correct.

One obvious reason why relying on the local influence of the national UAW would have been unwise is that the UAW simply does not have the political power in New York that it has in Michigan. It cannot even rely on the same level of cooperation from other UAW locals in New York. Dealing with a private university, rather than the public institutions it dealt with in organizing University of California graduate employees, put the UAW at a still further remove from political influence. Corporate anxiety about the UAW's potential political power was an effective component of a strike threat, but the added demands accruing to an actual strike presented a greater challenge. It is also necessary to be realistic about prospects for cooperation in a fragmented and sometimes competitive labor movement. The obvious place to turn for help would be to other unions representing college faculty, but if those unions not only see themselves as competing to represent the same groups but also are inclined to make tactical decisions based exclusively on a narrow view of their self-interest, then they are unlikely supporters.

The legal landscape, to be sure, may well have changed by the time this book is published. The United States now has a Democratic president who acted quickly to appoint sympathetic NLRB members, and this new NLRB is likely to reverse the ruling that denied working graduate students their employee status (Jaschik, "Return"). But the NLRB has lost much of its credibility. It is now so fundamentally and irredeemably a political agency that any sense that it can apply labor law fairly may be lost. Indeed, over time we could still face a whiplash sequence of Republican- and Democratic-appointed NLRBs reversing each other's rulings. At the very least, therefore, we also need federal legislation guaranteeing all graduate employees the right to bargain collectively.

Meanwhile, the Mafiosi in charge of the elite private universities strung along the eastern seaboard are also following these events. They too are anticipating another NLRB reversal. By the spring of 2009, alternative union-busting plans were being worked out at NYU and elsewhere. Once again, the fraternity of Ivy League presidents was in collusion to deny graduate employees their rights. NYU may shift some portion of funding for humanities and social science graduate students from assistantships to fellowships, taking on a major new expense designed simultaneously to improve support for some students and to retain power and control by breaking the graduate-employee union (Jaschik, "New Ideas"). That will either leave adjuncts to do the teaching now done by graduate employees, or in reality department heads and directors of graduate study may have to take on a new and unwelcome managerial role, urging graduate students to supplement their fellowships by teaching if depart- ments are to meet their instructional needs. Then the newly minted graduate-employee adjuncts could join the adjunct union—*if* they meet the minimum teaching requirements specified in the adjunct contract. If not, those requirements will have to be lowered in the next contract negotiations, with job actions looming if the university resists. Of course, adjuncts and graduate employees ordinarily have somewhat different priorities and grievance issues. Whether those can be worked out to cre- ate a viable union remains to be seen. Certainly it is divisive to put in the same union graduate students with a high priority to be awarded teaching and adjuncts with a much lower priority. There are also many graduate employees at other area schools now teaching in less-than-ideal condi- tions, among them CUNY grad employees faced with teaching de facto remedial classes much too large to mentor appropriately. They would be very happy to teach at NYU instead. What NYU president John Sexton and his loyal dean of graduate studies, Catharine Stimpson, have done is to maximize conflict among New York's contingent teachers in a new strategy for union busting.

One lesson for both graduate students and faculty at private universi- ties seems increasingly clear: take advantage of the NLRB when possible, but otherwise ignore it. An employee group with campuswide solidarity can get whatever recognition and negotiating power it needs. Stand firm with secretaries and maintenance workers in their organizing drives and job actions. Then ask for their support when your turn comes. No admin- istration can stand against a campus when a strong majority of all its labor groups supports a job action. Many existing faculty unions were recog- nized by consent in the 1970s, not by the use of state or national labor law. In today's antiunion atmosphere, consent will now be forthcoming only with the application of force, but the principle is the same. Even in states that bar collective bargaining for public employees, faculty and students can force informal but effective negotiating. An AAUP chapter can discuss salary and working conditions with Mississippi or Alabama administrators if it chooses to do so, and it can place many sorts of poten- tial job actions and noncooperation on the table as points of negotiation.

The challenge is to take possession of the power inherent in numbers and agency. The prevailing identities of recent generations have worked against that recognition, but growing activism among graduate employees and part-time faculty is beginning to change the pattern.

This kind of organizing also requires a mix of wit and courage. Nonviolent civil disobedience may be a critical component, but only if economic pressures are in place. And sufficient solidarity must be present so that arrests are engineered day after day. For me, this is one of the unforgettable lessons of Vietnam protests: you have to make daily life unmanageable. The California Faculty Association has learned to give key administrators no peace. Place chanting pickets outside their homes. Disrupt every meeting they attend with sardonic or inspiring public theater. Arrange building occupations and street demonstrations every week. The goal is protest without end. Plan actions for members with different levels of commitment. You will certainly have some people willing to do almost anything nonviolent. Use them. Divert others to less confrontational support.

At NYU, strategies such as this ran into some difficulty because of cultural differences between the more activist students, some of them graduates of global justice movements, and the more staid leadership of the national UAW. There was a more anarchistic, opportunistic element among the students that made the UAW leadership uneasy. When a planned occupation of administration offices in Bobst Library ran into difficulties, the students argued for more aggressive tactics. The UAW insisted instead that the occupation effort be abandoned. In truth, it can be very helpful to have a seemingly uncontrollable element within a movement.

No employee group, it must be clear, acts simply out of self-interest in such struggles. Every union defeat empowers administrators elsewhere. Every union victory sets a precedent other campuses and other industries will find it increasingly difficult to resist. The issue is the worldwide exploitation of workers in all industries. The call is to rise up and take possession of economic justice. A university president who earns a million dollars while denying classroom teachers a living wage is a criminal. He or she stands in opposition to all the values to which higher education has traditionally been dedicated. As I argued earlier, a campus that exploits its labor force educates all its students in the logic of exploitation and sends them forth to practice it with untroubled consciences.

At a November 2006 invitational conference called "Terrorism and the University," held at John Jay College of Criminal Justice in Manhattan, the president of NYU gave a keynote speech touting his unflinching dedication to high principle. Despite political and cultural pressures to compromise, he assured the audience, the satellite campuses that NYU was establishing in the Persian Gulf region would not eliminate course components offensive to local tastes. Art classes would show slides of classic female nudes despite objections. As he rose to speak, Eric Lott of the University of Virginia and I stood and prominently turned our backs on him, silently protesting what I regard as his administrative terrorism in denying his graduate employees the right to negotiate their working conditions. The next day, I told conference attendees that I did not expect John Sexton to honor such rights in the Persian Gulf either. I anticipate that his satellite campuses—like so many others—will staff their courses with underpaid and unrepresented part-time faculty. The combination of high culture and wage slavery is the hallmark of the contemporary university. The city on the hill is built atop a mountain of hypocrisy.

Two weeks after I talked in New York, the news came through that the University of Toronto was planning to deny its part-time, or sessional, faculty access to research grants, a deplorable but typical act of deprofessionalization and dehumanization. This proposal was defeated by union solidarity and a worldwide petition and letter-writing campaign. In the state of Washington, faculty unions too often exclude their part-timers from negotiated wage increases. Part-timer activists such as Keith Hoeller are writing editorials to draw attention to this tradition. Once again, we face not only local but also international pressures to adopt exploitive employment practices, because the globalized economy has made all such practices interdependent, co-present. The familiar adage "act locally, think globally" has been supplanted by forces that relentlessly internationalize local forms of exploitation. How higher education does or does not perform its commitment to human decency, how it does or does not enact community responsibility, now has the power to shape worldwide standards in all industries. Collective action is the one and only way we can guarantee that the academy's impact will be salutary, rather than malicious. Graduate-employee activism can be an inspiration for other campus groups to join in group advocacy and organizing.

As the logic of corporatization is globalized and new opportunities for exploitation arise, the need for activism increases. American universities have been led to establish satellite campuses in other countries in part by the burdens placed on international students by the Patriot Act and the Department of Homeland Security. If Arab students cannot come to us, we will go to them. Homeland exploitation thus encourages us to secure profits by exploiting our academic labor force elsewhere. If local faculty resistance is a problem, circumvent it.

Will faculty at schools throughout the country let administrators get away with such initiatives? The experiences at the University of Illinois, detailed in chapter 2, merit a general warning. The potential for mischief in UI's Global Campus alone is limitless, because it sets a precedent both for other ways of severing faculty from their traditional areas of responsibility and for increasing reliance on exploited labor. We must resist. And while we can write and speak as individuals, most effective action must be collective. Perhaps twenty years of graduate-employee activism will wake up my faculty colleagues to a broader oversight role. Responsible, community-focused, internationally engaged unionization and AAUP membership are among its components.

The university is now being subjected to sustained political, cultural, and economic assault. Yet to theorize the contemporary corporate university is to recognize that there was nothing inevitable about its formation. It did not have to be, and it can still be dismantled. Set a two-hundred-thousand-dollar limit to faculty salaries and a three-hundred-thousand-dollar limit to upper administrative salaries. Limit coaches to three hundred thousand dollars as well. At my institution, the executives working for the president earn more than three hundred thousand dollars; I would cut their salaries by 50 percent. Redirect the money saved to hiring assistant professors, raising part-timer salaries to parity and graduate-student-employee wages to the cost of living, and eliminating all tuition payments for poor and lower-middle-class students. Deny administrators the right to fund gratuitous pet projects at the expense of a principled campus salary schedule. If administrators refuse to comply, sit in their offices, sit in front of their cars, block campus streets, block access to buildings, picket their houses. Use nonviolent civil disobedience to force change. Or if that seems too confrontational, form a union and negotiate these matters at the bargaining table. Increasingly, graduate employees and contingent faculty are doing just that. The key decisions about the job system and the academic workplace are made on your own campus when budget priorities are set and governance practices established. Take the money and a role in decision making in your own hands. You have nothing to lose but your colleagues' chains. As the AAUP has argued for nearly a hundred years, academic freedom cannot survive without job security and shared governance.

7

On Weakened Ground

The AAUP, Pedagogy, and the
Struggle over Academic Freedom

Might not a teacher of nineteenth-century American literature,
taking up *Moby Dick*, ask the class to consider whether any parallel between President George W. Bush and Captain Ahab could
be pursued for insight into Melville's novel?
> —AAUP, "Freedom in the Classroom," revised version

Without the substantial erosion of tenure, a by-product of the
corporate model of downsizing and outsourcing, groups such as
ACTA and Horowitz's Center would not pose a serious threat. In
this case, neoliberal capitalism is the primary ingredient for right-
wing reaction.
> —Eric Cheyfitz, "Framing Ward Churchill" (232)

Academic freedom is being eviscerated.
> —Ellen Messer-Davidow, "Caught in the Crunch" (400)

For decades, academic freedom has seemed a relatively stable feature of
the psychology and practice of academic life. As of 2006, over two hundred organizations had signed the AAUP's 1940 "Statement of Principles
on Academic Freedom and Tenure." From the start, to be sure, there were
inherent disparities between secular and religious institutions. Among
schools chartered by different denominations, expectations about faculty speech and student intellectual freedom vary considerably, and those
expectations have themselves sometimes shifted substantially when
church leaders, politics, and doctrine changed. Wanting to maximize
the academic freedom of faculty at religious institutions, the AAUP has

worked hard to keep them on board, emphasizing that doctrinal constraints need to be made explicit and public, so that students and employees know what to expect before they enroll or accept employment. Not infrequently, however, religious institutions step over the line, and the AAUP must launch a formal investigation. In religious institutions in many countries, of course, that delicate dance has no counterpart. There may simply be no credible equivalent of academic freedom for faculty and intellectual freedom for students. This history is worth recalling because religious intolerance and doctrinal inflexibility now threaten academic freedom worldwide. In the United States, it is one general source of discontent with classroom freedoms and thus helps establish a climate of resistance to progressive pedagogy.

In this respect, as in many others, academic freedom has always been an arena for cultural struggle, rather than an eternal verity perfectly embodied in every institution and sustained unchanged over time. Both for religious and secular institutions, the AAUP's very visible investigative reports on academic freedom and tenure—and its continuing need to censure a limited number of institutions—provides an evolving handbook of guidelines and markers for administrative behavior that crosses a line. Yet the means available to cross that line—and the cultural contexts in which the struggle for academic freedom is waged—evolve over time. And thus, both the meaning and the material embodiments of academic freedom change no matter how stable its official definition may seem. The most dramatic recent revelation about how much the status of academic freedom and shared governance can change overnight came with the educational aftermath of Hurricane Katrina. More about that at the end of this chapter.

In two specific ways, academic freedom has been steadily put at risk over two generations. The first of these is embodied in a generational shift now in place for nearly four decades, during which what the organization sometimes calls ACLU-style AAUP membership—represented by faculty members who make an individual decision to join purely on a principled basis, as many people do for the American Civil Liberties Union—has drastically and disastrously declined. Faculty members who take a job at an AAUP collective bargaining chapter of course often join almost automatically, but nothing compels them to learn much if anything about the national AAUP's activities or commitments there-after. Thus, I often visit CB units where few members read *Academe*. If you read the magazine regularly, you will be pretty well informed about the issues confronting higher education and you will have ready access to the AAUP's policy statements and investigative reports. But that does not prevent some members from tossing their copies in the trash before they leave the mailroom. Purely voluntary ACLU-style AAUP member-ship has gradually declined, both in real numbers and as a percentage of AAUP membership overall, though it is reasonable to assume that, when AAUP membership grew rapidly in the 1960s, joining then was also a relatively unreflective decision for many faculty; it was simply what new faculty did. In any case, the consequence for academic freedom has been severe, if largely unnoticed—namely, that many faculty who joined the profession over the past forty years have no knowledge of the history of academic freedom, little capacity to define or defend it, limited awareness of the mounting threats to its continued existence, and no active local AAUP chapter to defend faculty rights and values.

Through one of my presidential initiatives, the context of which I describe in chapter 8, the AAUP started a program to correct this prob-lem in the fall of 2007, sending twice-monthly educational emails about its history and current activities to nearly four hundred thousand faculty. Of course, every new generation needs to be educated about its culture's ethical norms, just as each new member of a profession needs to be social-ized to the profession's standards and values. Academia has now failed to perform that task adequately for two generations.

Ignorance about the principles of academic freedom and its relation to good shared governance practices has deepened alongside the other long-term trend eroding academic freedom. The subject of this book's third chapter, this trend has been largely invisible except to its victims: contingent faculty, part-time teachers and those hired full-time off the tenure track. The AAUP throughout its history has consistently asserted and reinforced the necessary bond between academic freedom and job security. Indeed, Robert Post has emphasized that "the ideal of academic freedom was formulated precisely to transform basic American under-standings of the employment relationship between faculty and their uni-versity or college" (62). If they can fire you for what you say, you really do not have academic freedom, either in the classroom or in print. After fighting reliance on part-time faculty for decades, the AAUP decided it was necessary to confront reality and win them a degree of job security and due process.

The reality that the organization faced is this: the professoriate is now composed largely of part-time faculty who can often be terminated without stated cause or due process. From a profession characterized by a high degree of job security, we have become one characterized by complete insecurity of employment. Drastically underpaid, most part-time faculty who rely on their teaching for their whole financial support have no reserves and no capacity to sustain even brief job loss. Many of them practice elaborate self-censorship to avoid offending students, parents, or administrators. Most tenured faculty, on the other hand, have remained willfully oblivious to this fundamental crisis. In an ideal world, the tenured faculty would guard the rights of part-timers and vigorously defend their academic freedom. That does occasionally happen, but it is not the characteristic dynamic of academia's class system. Faculty with secure jobs have nonetheless themselves also paid a price for the fundamental disempowerment of large segments of their colleagues. A fragmented tenured faculty has no deep experience of solidarity to draw on and little collective experience of asserting its rights. The parameters of academic freedom are thus often set by senior administrators, rather than by faculty discussion and consensus. Administrative tolerance for progressive pedagogy, should external critiques of such pedagogy gain political power, will be nonexistent on many campuses. We no longer have the infrastructure necessary to defend academic freedom on campus.

Many of the patterns I have described in this book are fairly visible long-term trends susceptible to predictive analysis. If faculty want to marshal the resources to counter them, they can do so, assuming they recognize their historical situation and can learn to act collectively. But other forces—predominantly political—are also having a significant impact on academic freedom, and they are all fundamentally variable and unpredictable. As a result, the future of academic freedom is both uncertain and unstable. The faculty now stands on weakened cultural and political ground, but its ultimate fate is neither set nor secure.

Perhaps the most widely publicized political affront to academic freedom is the multipronged assault on faculty speech in the classroom and in course syllabi. Heavily funded by individual conservative donors and by right-wing foundations alike, this ideologically coordinated effort embraces several organizations and a number of spokespersons who have gained national visibility through the campaign. There is, of course, no argument to be made against their right to promote their views, but that does not prevent people sympathetic to academic freedom from detailing how damaging this campaign may prove to be.

The American Council of Trustees and Alumni (ACTA), founded by Lynne Cheney and currently led by its president, Anne Neal, has historically helped "train" college and university boards of trustees to distrust their progressive faculty and now engages in a broad campaign to smear both current faculty and a range of humanities disciplines. ACTA's published report "How Many Ward Churchills?" (May 2006) is its most indicative publication. The report argues that hundreds of courses across the country are designed to deliver the message "that the status quo, which is patriarchal, racist, hegemonic, and capitalist, must be 'interrogated' and 'critiqued' as a means of theorizing and facilitating a social transformation whose necessity and value are taken as a given" (3). In short, "indoctrination is replacing education" (3).

Though ACTA does not trouble itself to draw the distinction, there is a difference between the assumptions listed in the first half of their prototype message and the activist appeal in the second. Many faculty convinced of the first set of claims are reluctant to embrace the agenda announced thereafter when they are teaching. ACTA is also satisfied with what is, in effect, a Google search for key terms. The appearance of words such as *race, class, gender,* and *sexuality* in a syllabus is all the evidence they think they need to prove that a course is driven by a political agenda. But they do not lay the blame exclusively on individual leftist faculty. They find that a series of entire academic disciplines and specializations have been thoroughly corrupted by "the message." So their demand that these views be "balanced" by others is really a demand that disciplinary consensus be compensated for with extradisciplinary political perspectives. That counters the whole notion of professional training and expertise that underlies not only the AAUP's concept of academic freedom but also the departmental structure of the contemporary university; it opens academic debate to any alternative point of view with political influence.

The litany of complaints about leftist biases—which are echoed by David Horowitz—includes a number of theses or conclusions that many of us consider to be important advances in our understanding of human culture. In a debate with me—broadcast on C-Span2 on March 17 and 18, 2007—Horowitz complained about a University of Arizona syllabus that "assumes as an uncontroversial fact that 'gender is socially constructed.'" Horowitz insists students be informed that there is disagreement about this matter. My guess is that most instructors do in fact mention the opposing argument, the traditional claim that maleness and femaleness are fundamental, immutable categories. But I doubt that many contemporary humanities or social science faculty give equal time to the earlier view; they would not consider it professionally responsible to do so.

There is widespread consensus in many fields that—whatever the spectrum of physical differences between men and women—the *meaning* of gender is socially constructed. Horowitz, on the other hand, as he argued in a debate with me in Eugene, Oregon, on May 19, 2008, believes anatomical differences between the male and female brain mandate greater facility for men in such fields as music and math, a view, as he seems unable to understand, that is itself socially constructed. He goes on to claim that faculty members who promote the theory of social construction typically say society is controlled by "a patriarchal ruling class that imposes passivity on women so that men can oppress them." But the theory of social construction is politically neutral; it would apply as well to a society dominated by women or to one where gender was politically irrelevant. Underlying the Neal/Horowitz position here is presumably the continuing conservative complaint about relativism, which the Right considers a left-wing plot, though that is hardly the case. The Right thinks relativism denies the existence of values. Instead, relativism concludes that they are a source of struggle, that they must be fought for because they are not guaranteed.

Horowitz also complains constantly that faculty teach in areas in which they do not have professional credentials and that this is part of the politicization of the academy. Professional credentials, for him, are the product of a doctoral education. But people acquire new areas of expertise throughout their careers. They do so by reading, talking, attending lectures, and thinking. My PhD is in English and American literature, but my publications include several books each about areas not part of my formal training: higher education and the Spanish Civil War. As a result, I have been asked to lecture about each topic both here and abroad. My refereed publications prove my expertise in these areas, but I might well have taught courses on these subjects—without publishing—after wide reading.

In our 2007 debate, Horowitz asked me to endorse some further mechanism to formalize faculty acquisition of new areas of expertise. I cannot imagine what he would have in mind. A written test? A review board? Neither he nor Neal has much understanding either of the life of the mind or of the life of academic disciplines. The discipline I studied in the late 1960s in graduate school has precious little to do with the discipline I represent now. No faculty member in my graduate program would even have recognized the names of most of the American poets I have written about over the past twenty years. And while in graduate school, I could not have named them myself. In addition to taking on new areas, faculty members assume responsibility for disciplines that themselves become radically new enterprises. But Horowitz's proposal also trespasses on the academic freedom acquired with a terminal degree. The doctoral training I had cannot be said to encompass much of whatever expertise I might now claim to possess. My PhD in effect credentialed me to grow and change, to supervise my own intellectual development. There are, in any case, informal mechanisms in place to vet requests to teach in new areas. My department assigns me courses to teach based on the requests and proposals I submit, and my colleagues are aware of my new interests through conversation and publication, the latter of course being externally reviewed. If I asked to teach Shakespeare, I would certainly have to justify the request.

Some years ago, when I applied to my university's Scholars' Travel Fund, administered by our Research Board, to attend the annual meeting of the Modern Language Association (MLA) to give an invited paper on the state of higher education, the fund's administrator refused the request and told me they would never again fund me to speak on higher education because I had no formal training in the subject. At the time, I had already published a number of books and essays on higher education. Faculty in my campus's College of Education had assigned some of my books as texts. What is more, the invitation meant that my disciplinary organization judged me qualified. In the amusing note I received from the Research Board, the administrator informed me that I was an expert on the Spanish Civil War and on modern poetry, but not on higher education. How she confidently distinguished between two areas of knowledge acquired after the PhD—the Spanish Civil War and the politics of higher education—I cannot guess. In any case, the refusal was a genuinely unwarranted imposition of political opinion. She did not like what I was saying about higher education and thought to silence me. It was also, more fundamentally, a violation of academic freedom. Although I was not an AAUP officer at the time, I called the national office and asked if they would take the case. They expressed some pleasure with the opportunity. My department head let the administrator know this, and she backed down. I am not sure that I want her—or anyone else—running Horowitz's kangaroo court to judge more recently acquired scholarly expertise.

Horowitz repeatedly agues for some sort of rough balance in the scholarly texts assigned to cover controversial issues. This would require not only an equal-time provision but also elaborate mechanisms for oversight of course content. That would seriously constrain the ability of faculty to teach what they believe to be true and necessary. Students and faculty alike would lose the pedagogical benefit of an individual faculty member's passionate take on the discipline, his or her idiosyncratic set of interests and areas of expertise. We would lose much more in limiting academic freedom in this way than we could possibly gain.

The AAUP's statement on controversial speakers on campus has some relevance here. It rejects demands that any particular event embody a "balance" between opposing positions. It rejects the idea that a given group must invite speakers representing different points of view. And the AAUP certainly rejects any notion that faculty should be required to represent points of view discredited by their disciplines. The AAUP believes balance is achieved over the long term by the full range of views students are exposed to in classes, in public lectures, in conversations, and through the media. All this is part of their education. Horowitz regularly cites global warming as a case where students may now only be exposed to one point of view. Apparently he never watches television. The AAUP trusts students to evaluate and accept or reject the opinions they encounter in the classroom and in the culture at large.

When I debated Horowitz in Washington, DC, a large banner was stretched across the stage: "TAKE POLITICS OUT OF THE CLASSROOM." This is an increasing focus of conservative critique and presents an extraordinary threat to academic freedom. When the AAUP clarified its 1940 statement on academic freedom and tenure in 1970, it advised professors to avoid the "persistent" intrusion of extraneous material into a class. I take "persistent" to refer to bringing outside material into the classroom so frequently that the ability to teach the course's advertised content is impaired. Even then, I regard the warning as ethical and professional advice, not the logic for a regime of surveillance.

A complete prohibition on political speech not relevant to the subject would disable American pedagogy. Some faculty members teaching on April 5, 1968, the day after Martin Luther King was killed, among them a chemistry teacher at Wesleyan, realized they wanted to devote the class to the previous day's assassination. Many of the teachers who found themselves teaching an 8 a.m. class on September 12, 2001, in the hours before campuses canceled classes, among them a law professor at the University of Virginia, found it necessary to discuss the attacks on New York's World Trade Center the day before. If teachers thought they could ignore the previous day's events, their students may have thought otherwise, though one NAS member has informed me that she is still proud that her philosophy class on Monday, December 8, 1941, made no mention of the Japanese attack on Pearl Harbor the day before. For those classes that did take a break from the syllabus to confront Pearl Harbor—whether the class was on chemistry, home economics, or international politics—students might well have been "persistent" in bringing the subject up again later in the semester. There is room in many classes to devote a modest amount of time to topics not in the curriculum. Sometimes life gives us little choice. Academic freedom embraces the right to address such imperatives.

When Finkin and Post take up this issue, they use what is a classic AAUP investigation of a 1960s case, that of first-year history professor David E. Green at Ohio State University. Overwhelmed by King's assassination, Green walked into his class the next morning and told students he was "suspending the curriculum" to "offer some personal remarks." Students were permitted to leave if they wished. They later testified that they understood it was not a normal class meeting. Green delivered an impassioned presentation about race in America, capping it off by burning his draft card in protest against all violence, a common enough symbolic gesture at the time but nonetheless a federal crime. Had Green not burned his draft card, the matter would not have attracted the attention of the press or mustered the anger of the board of trustees. Despite the incredible political tensions of the time, a faculty hearing committee was both sympathetic to Green and gentle in its recommendations, concluding that he had acted unwisely but avoiding major sanctions. Then the Ohio State president stepped in and successfully urged the board to fire Green immediately, without allowing him to see the committee report before the board met and without giving him an opportunity to defend himself at its meeting. The AAUP's investigation that resulted in censure found numerous procedural errors in the president's handling of the case but managed along the way to find Green an inexperienced but sympathetic figure as well. Not so Finkin and Post, who forty years later give Green no quarter, insisting that he "had no right to commandeer the class for a 'teach in' on his personal political views" (100). Whether the former University of Virginia president who set aside his class on constitutional law to discuss the attacks on the World Trade Center the day afterward would meet with the same fate were his case discussed in *For the Common Good* I cannot say, but not all Committee A veterans would side with Finkin and Post on this issue. Some of us believe national tragedies can trump the syllabus for a day, whether for an open discussion or an impassioned lecture.

Those are some of the most dramatic occasions that would justify shifting from the syllabus to another topic, but there are many examples of lesser political issues that can, in my view, be treated the same way. Those include issues specific to campus life. Thus, one might well decide to spend part of a class every semester discussing the employment conditions on campus—and the politics of campus power relations—that make student education possible and establish its financial conditions. These are matters relevant to every class. Ruling discussion of them illegitimate or unprotected by academic freedom is itself a political act. When my campus administration announced severe limits on political expression during the 2008 presidential campaign, I spent twenty minutes discussing the matter in the seminar I was teaching.

One of my good friends was devastated when a graduate student in the Army Reserves whom she was advising was called up for active duty and then killed in Iraq. If my friend had chosen to talk about this to her students, I would consider it her right to do so. In the end, it is the instructor's responsibility to decide what is or is not relevant to the moment in which he or she is teaching. Does that mean there are no abuses of academic freedom? Certainly there are. But academic departments are equipped to handle them, and departments tend to know the participants best.

There is a prevailing view in the academy that dispassionate, decathected argument serves us best. As Matthew Finkin has put it succinctly, pedagogical "freedom is accorded equally to dispassionate dissection and to committed partisanship" (88). Indeed, as Ernst Benjamin has argued, "open advocacy may better safeguard a student's right to form an independent judgment than the implicit bias inherent in the presumption that the faculty member's presentation is simply factual. . . . Advocacy not only need not lead to indoctrination but also is often the antidote" ("Some Implications" 307, 311). When this bias spills over into an ideology devoted to neutrality and balance, we risk projecting the illusion that the public sphere is a reasonable and reliable space. The relentlessly reasonable classroom may reinforce confidence in the reasonableness of the nation-state in which it resides. Nonetheless, over forty years in higher education I have found that the overwhelming majority of faculty members are reluctant to reveal their political views to their students. Yet I believe that students benefit from hearing committed advocacy from their professors. It helps them learn how to advocate for a position themselves. When the AAUP first addressed these issues in 1915, it had in mind a still significantly rural country and a much more impressionable student body. Neal and Horowitz would like to maintain that image of the infantilized student—vulnerable to faculty advocacy—because it is politically useful to them. But as successive waves of new media overtook the country—from radio to film to television to the Internet—the naive and unformed undergraduate largely disappeared. Today's students visit the city on television and in cyberspace before they leave the farm. They arrive well stocked with their own political opinions and ready to defend them. Good luck to any faculty members who think it will be easy to change their minds. Of course, there remain differences in sophistication among students; undergraduate juniors and seniors are less impressionable than freshmen. One might, therefore, have different personal teaching standards for political speech in beginning and advanced courses.

Although the 1915 Declaration is one of the best things the AAUP has ever written, it has never been the last word on our principles. Our most thorough statement on student rights, still the best such statement in existence, dates from 1967. Like all efforts to speak for all times, the 1915 Declaration is necessarily marked by its historical moment. Its approach to students embodies at moments a protective, in loco parentis model of student innocence that is far less applicable now. Yet the 1915 Declaration is also somewhat conflicted in its views. Though it warns us that a student should not be exposed to faculty opinions "before he has sufficient knowledge and ripeness of judgment to be entitled to form any definitive opinion of his own" (299), it also suggests that "the average student is a discerning observer, who soon takes the measure of his instructor" (296). My students do not delay the process of opinion formation.

Fundamental to both Neal's and Horowitz's organized campaigns is an effort to confuse the public by eliminating any distinction between advocacy and indoctrination, despite a substantial scholarly history of efforts to differentiate between the two practices. Any faculty effort to *advocate* for a given position, they would have us believe, is an effort to *indoctrinate* students. Advocacy, of course, encompasses a vast range of rhetorical strategies, including strategies that summarize, compare, and contrast alternative positions. It is fundamental to the search for truth.

A number of the contributors to *Advocacy in the Classroom* (Spacks, 1996) and *The Future of Academic Freedom* (Menand, 1996) make serious efforts to distinguish advocacy from indoctrination. Nadine Strossen, then president of the ACLU, argues that "advocacy is diametrically different from expression that is 'inculcating' or 'indoctrinating.' . . . Advocacy is intended to open minds; inculcation is intended to close them"

(73). As Louis Menand writes, "indoctrination isn't just bad pedagogy; it's bad advocacy" (16). Myles Brand, former president of Indiana University, acknowledges that there is "a gray area between strong advocacy and proselytizing" but emphasizes that "faculty members are expected to have a point of view; they are expected to advocate for a position" (10–11).

Yet defenses of advocacy—along with efforts to carve out some space for political remarks not connected with the course subject matter—are fundamentally inadequate unless they embrace the reasoning central to the AAUP's 2007 statement on the subject, because many political comments that Horowitz and other conservative critics would consider wholly unacceptable are fundamentally *not* irrelevant to the subject. A basic feature of human culture is that anything can be potentially connected with anything else; the capacity to make those connections is fundamental to human consciousness. Political commentary often derives from an instructor's efforts to draw analogies and comparisons between different bodies of knowledge and different historical periods. Thus, the AAUP insists that both instructors and students can reference contemporary political life to illuminate a course's subject matter—whatever academic discipline the course represents and whatever the catalog description and syllabus say. The answer to the question posed by the AAUP's "Freedom in the Classroom," quoted in the epigraph to this chapter, is thus emphatically yes. A teacher of *Moby-Dick* can, if he or she chooses, compare Ahab and George W. Bush as obsessional leaders or invite students to do so. As I suggested in the introduction, what is perhaps most bizarre or unrealistic about the objections to a Bush-Ahab comparison is that the analogy is already out there, in circulation, not only in the popular press but also in Melville scholarship, including a 2002 *London Review of Books* essay by Jeremy Harding and a 2005 book by Andrew Delbanco.

Analogies between a ship captain and a head of state are hardly incomprehensible. Is Iraq for Bush a contemporary incarnation of the white whale? Debates about presidential power are a staple of American history. It is perfectly valid for an instructor to deal not only with what a novel might have meant in its own time but also what it may mean in ours. A literature class taking up such comparisons could help students understand the continuing vitality and relevance of the humanities.

Committee A included the Bush-Ahab sentence in its report because it recognized that people can easily sign on to a principle (the right to reference contemporary politics) without really confronting what it entails. Nonetheless, it knew the passage would draw fire. Indeed, I led with it in the press release that accompanied the report. The committee paired the Bush sentence with one about Bill Clinton, not because it had any illusions that "balance" was possible but, rather, to make it clear that political analogies are an equal-opportunity realm. Views of Clinton's personal ethics, however, were not a hot topic of debate in 2007; the Bush sentence got all the attention. By far the most interesting discussion came in response to a Stanley Fish column in the *New York Times*, predictably a critique of our report. The online comments— over a hundred of them—demonstrated definitively what a rich conversation comparing and contrasting Bush and Ahab could do. People agreed, disagreed, and offered scores of alternative analogies. It was like an impromptu national classroom: witty, passionate, sardonic, inventive, instructive, outraged. Most important, it demonstrated the power of references to contemporary life as a way to engage people at their most articulate. I could offer no more persuasive evidence in support of "Freedom in the Classroom" than the 112 numbered comments on Fish's essay.

Given that the half-life of this online exchange has no doubt already expired, it is worth preserving it by summarizing it in some detail. Fish argues that literary, rather than political, parallels to Ahab would be more appropriate: "Milton's Satan, Marlowe's Faust, Byron's Cain, Bram Stoker's Dracula, Shakespeare's Iago, Jack London's Wolf Larsen." H. S. Rockwell III points out that these references "would almost certainly fall on mostly deaf ears. The sole character on the list that most students might know is Dracula! But that knowledge would most certainly have been gleaned from comic books and vampire movies, not from Stoker's book. Furthermore, given the strict conventions of vampirism, Dracula does not fit very well on the list: what he does is in his nature and completely out of his control. Ahab makes choices; Dracula doesn't" (comment no. 26). Another reader endorses the practicality of the analogy: "I've yet to come across students for whom these exemplars would be at all meaningful. So comparing Ahab to Bush seems much more of a pragmatic decision, and not a political one" (no. 49). But Matthew Carnicelli asks, "Why compare Bush to Ahab when Santino Corleone is more applicable?" (no. 17). Cae Fu proposes that "it would be Mr. Cheney who would make a better Ahab analogy, since he seems more intensely motivated by fury than does his employer" (no. 30). J. Forman suggests Cheney could be more aptly compared to Shakespeare's Iago (no. 36). Another reader claims, "Jack in *Lord of the Flies* is a more apt comparison. Bloodthirsty, one-sided, appealing to the worst in people, not terribly bright" (no. 90). Michael Murray offers Elmer Gantry or Inspector Javert (no. 92). H. R. Coursen sardonically remarks that "the comparison with Ahab is, of course, illegitimate. Ahab acquires a grandeur, even in his mad and 'fiery hunt' after the White Whale, that Bush will never come close to achieving" (no. 54). Bob McGivern adds that the analogy "does a disservice to the foresight and planning exhibited by Ahab in achieving his goal" (no. 68). But Don Tapken counters that "the oath sworn by the *Pequod's* crew might certainly cast light on the Senate vote to authorize force" (no. 55), and James Valle endorses the comparison with Bush: "Ahab was a leader who perverted his mission. Utilizing a potent mixture of charisma and authority, he set his men a goal other than the one he and they were supposed to accomplish. He obviously had it in mind to do this from the very start of the *Pequod's* voyage" (no. 80). In any case, as D. S. Rudman points out, "the comparison does not have to be a good fit to be effective for learning" (no. 56).

William P. Ferris takes *Moby-Dick* out of the literature classroom:

> I may be the only one on this email list who has actually taught *Moby Dick* in a college course, asked students to think of leaders to compare to Ahab, and watched them come up with George Bush, among many others. . . . The course is one on leadership and management in an undergrad business major and in an MBA program. We use fiction, drama, autobiography and management theory books to examine leadership and management topics in a popular elective course. . . . Ahab gets compared to all the Presidents, to certain CEOs in business, and even to people the students know, like their coaches and the bosses on their summer jobs. A big issue is how Ahab hires the crew on with the expectation that he will lead them on a lucrative trip accumulating whale oil and then they will return to their families. . . . Then

he changes their mission. . . . And how about the crew becoming persuaded that they would be making the seas safer for their comrades back in Nantucket by the end? Sound familiar? (no. 61)

As one of the respondents adopting a pseudonym argues, "If you were trying to get your students to relate the fictional character of Ahab to a current well-known figure, one they *already* know as a path to understanding that character, who would you choose? He has to be a leader, there has to be an obsession, and there has to be a dangerous task that puts all at risk for questionable benefit. It is unfortunate that our President might be well qualified for that role" (no. 27).

Joe Safdie cites a paragraph from Thomas More's *Utopia* (1516) that he recently taught in a British literature class and asks whether Fish would forbid him "from drawing the obvious political parallel":

Once upon a time they had gone to war to win for their king another kingdom to which he claimed to be the rightful heir by virtue of an old tie by marriage. After they had secured it, they saw they would have no less trouble in keeping it than they had suffered in obtaining it. The seeds of rebellion from within or of invasion from without were always springing up in the people thus acquired. They realized they would have to fight constantly for them or against them and to keep an army in continual readiness. In the meantime they were being plundered, their money was being taken out of the country, they were shedding their blood for the little glory of someone else, peace was no more secure than before, their morals at home were being corrupted by war. (no. 100)

Another respondent quotes a 1963 remark by poet Robert Lowell, from his collected *Interviews and Memoirs* (77), with certain relevance: "If I have an image for us [America], it would be one taken from Melville's *Moby Dick*: the fanatical idealist who brings the world down in ruin through some sort of simplicity of mind" (no. 72). Fish would prohibit teachers from making contemporary analogies with either the More or the Lowell texts. That kind of dialogue is fine in the *New York Times*, he would argue, but not in the classroom. Again, academic freedom allows faculty to make their own decisions about that issue.

When I debated Fish about politics in the classroom at the University of Illinois in October 2003, I described how I drew analogies in class between Vietnam War–era poetry and current events. The students had been assigned to read several antiwar poems before class. Then I read them aloud, substituting George Bush's name for Lyndon Johnson's and Iraqi place names for Vietnamese. Passages about the earlier president's Texas machismo, conveniently, did not require revision. Here is a brief example from Robert Duncan's poem "Up Rising." My substitutions are in brackets:

> Now Johnson [Bush] would go up to join the great simulacra
> > of men,
> Hitler and Stalin, to work his fame
> with planes roaring out from Guam [Saudi Arabia] over
> > Asia [Iraq] . . .
> And men wake to see that they are used like things
> spent in a great potlatch, this Texas barbecue
> > of Asia [Afghanistan], Africa [Europe], and
> > > and all the Americas [the Middle East] . . .
> and the very glint of Satan's eyes from the pit of the hell
> of America's unacknowledged, unrepented crimes that I
> > saw in Goldwater's [Cheney's] eyes
> now shines from the eyes of the President
> in the swollen head of the nation (81–83)

My first point was to demonstrate that, contrary to widespread disciplinary belief, topical poetry does not always age rapidly; it often remains applicable to subsequent events. The second point was to raise the question of whether Duncan's apocalyptic, mythic rendering of Vietnam had any relevance to our understanding of Iraq. I mentioned that I was opposed to the war, but I hardly needed to say more: Robert Duncan, Allen Ginsberg, Denise Levertov, Robert Bly, and Adrienne Rich did the work for me. Fish quickly responded, "If I were Cary's dean, I would fire him immediately!" I have the impression that the AAUP would come to my defense.

Fish's column about the Bush-Ahab analogy was one of several that led to his 2008 book *Save the World on Your Own Time*. To Fredric Jameson's famous motto "always historicize," which involved, among other things, a call to contextualize the understanding of texts, Stanley Fish has responded with a manifesto rejecting all forms of contemporary political contextualization. The book mounts a giddy, principled, single-minded endorsement of educational irrelevance. Its motto, "always academicize," is promoted for every course within every discipline. "To academicize a topic," he tells us, "is to detach it from the context of its real world urgency" (27) and focus on its antecedents, its rhetorical history, and its argumentative claims. Those claims should be "offered as objects of analysis rather than as candidates for allegiance" (87), "dissected and assessed as arguments and not as preliminaries to action on the part of those doing the assessing" (26). Faculty who do anything else are not doing their jobs. Fish thus endorses a rejoinder to his *New York Times* op-ed that complains, "under Fish's rule, a faculty member in the South in the 1950s could not embrace and urge the idea that segregation is wrong" (29, quoting Ben Wallace on huffingtonpost.com). Not only can Fish faculty not advocate for fundamental social justice, but students are to be silenced as well. "Preferring (or dispreferring) values on the part of anyone, teacher or student, is just not a proper academic activity" (69). As Fish baldly asserts, students have no right to freedom of expression that encompasses advocating for their views: "students do not have any rights except the right to competent instruction" (123). The AAUP disagrees.

Fish is proud of the results his method will produce: "there will be less and less pressure in the class to come down on one side or the other and more and more pressure to describe accurately and fully the historical and philosophical antecedents of both sides. A political imperative will have been replaced by an academic one. There is no topic, however politically charged, that will resist academicization. Not only is it possible to depoliticize issues that have obvious political content: it is easy" (28). No one is likely to disagree with Fish that it is beneficial for students to acquire skill at dispassionately dissecting arguments. Nor are many people likely to argue that a class rigorously restricted to that and only that would build valuable intellectual discipline. But if the whole enterprise of higher education were to be so constrained, it would deprive students of the benefits of committed debate, of advocating for one point of view. It would eliminate the opportunity for students to test and learn advocacy skills in preparation for using them in the world outside the university. It would substantially deprive higher education of its real-world relevance. "Always academicize" would amount to "always lobotomize."

Fish is not, it is important to realize, arguing for requiring that competing views be balanced in the classroom, an argument he sensibly rejects. He is instead proposing abstract philosophical and rhetorical analysis as the universal and exclusive model for everything we do in higher education. Values as such have no place in higher education except as objects of analysis. To his credit, he follows this logic through and applies it to the campus as a whole. It is at that point that we realize Fish's brief for disinterested, detached, intellectual neutrality is not simply designed to declare the university classroom a place designed for one and only one kind of intellectual activity. Fish's classroom is intended to advocate for political disengagement as an ideal and a lifestyle. It is itself a political position.

A key moment is when Fish turns to higher education employment practices and endorses an amoral neoliberalism. Should a university commit itself as a matter of principle to assuring its employees a living wage and health care? His answer: no. A university should only do so if the prevailing practices in the industry compel it to do so. "The goal," he writes, "should be to employ the best workers at the lowest possible wages. The goal should not be to redress economic disparities by unilaterally paying more than the market demands" (31). With that administrative advice, the classroom has become the campus as a whole, teaching wage slavery and exploitation to students by example. One can agree with Fish that the business of higher education is education, while taking a more comprehensive view of the ways a campus educates. By exemplifying unfair employment practices, the university sends a clear message to students, faculty, staff, and community members. If Fish really believes a message endorsing employee exploitation is apolitical, he is a fool.

Universities, Fish summarizes, should enforce "the principles appropriate to their mission and not principles that belong to other enterprises" (33). Trying "to improve the lot of the laboring class . . . has everything to do with politics. . . . It is not an intention appropriate to an educational institution" (32). Of course, denying employees a living wage is also a political act. What began as an argument against advocacy in the classroom—"agendas imported into the classroom from foreign venues" (169), presumably Berkeley or Moscow—quickly becomes an argument freeing universities from any moral or social responsibility in any of their affairs. Apparently an employer devoted to disinterested rhetorical analysis is not an employer at all. Yet the truth is that in many communities universities set the prevailing wages and benefits. They have nowhere to look for guidance except to themselves and to the history of arguments for and against workplace justice. Fish urges us to study those arguments but refrain from applying them on campus. If a university acts on such values, it is "using the power it has to impose a moral vision on those who do not share it, and that is indoctrination if anything is" (68). Perhaps Fish should ask cafeteria workers what values they and their unions share before worrying about imposing health care and retirement benefits on them.

Fish's self-congratulatory amorality partly reflects the quixotic imperialism of making rhetorical analysis central to everything the university does. Part of what is wrong with *Save the World on Your Own Time* is thus an exceptional degree of disciplinary blindness. In trying to capture higher education's core mission, he writes, "An unconcern with any usefulness to the world is the key to its distinctiveness" (56–57). Although a philosophy professor with a particular ideological take on the right subspecialization might agree, it is not likely that an anthropology, engineering, immunology, microbiology, climatology, or geography professor would. Having housebroken the humanities and social sciences, Fish extends the rhetorical regime he prefers for them to disciplines that would find it rather puzzling. Sometimes changing world conditions and ongoing research results lead to fundamentally new disciplinary paradigms and broader social responsibilities, as with climatology. Sometimes, as with geography, disciplines evolve and redefine themselves to have greater relevance to social life. Since Fish has written a book about the centrality of rhetoric, it is fitting that he suffers its perils so grandly. In what Kenneth Burke would have identified as the lust to perfect his own logic, Fish concludes by urging us to deny all arguments for higher education's utility, even such basic claims as its contribution to upward mobility, the common good, and the earning potential of its graduates. Thankfully, we are not likely to have to test the political consequences of this advice.

But Fish's model presents problems for individual humanities and social science disciplines as well. Thus, when he asserts that "the judgment of whether a policy is the right one for the country is not appropriate in the classroom" (26), he has weakened debate in history, education, law, medicine, sociology, and political science classrooms. Not all law faculty would agree with Fish that law schools should ignore the "tasks and problems" graduates will encounter as working lawyers (22). Indeed, Fish's narrow goal of introducing students to new materials and equipping them with new skills would, for many disciplines, involve real-world applications. Fish avows in addition that he has not "the slightest idea of how to help students become creative individuals" (119), but many painting, music, dance, and poetry teachers believe they know something about encouraging creativity and drawing it out of their students. "Citizen building," he adds, "is a legitimate democratic activity, but it is not an academic activity" (120), but many disciplines make crucial—if indirect— contributions to citizen building. One can incorporate such indirection into a curriculum. That is a right that academic freedom protects.

Fish's contention throughout his book that poetry makes no fundamental claims on us as human beings or social agents is one that I have spent much of my career disproving. "The exploration of problems, not their solution, and certainly not a program of political action," he writes, "is what poetry offers" (52). But thousands of poems literally urge us to go to war, just as thousands urge the reverse. Poems promote racial equality and debunk it. Poems issued during election campaigns endorse some political candidates and mock others. Does Fish really imagine that such exercises have no claims on how we might vote? Some poems reinforce the existing social order, while others urge that it be overturned. Poems interrogate and revise our notions of gender, urge us to revise our attitudes toward immigration, promote union membership, promote abortion rights, and so forth. Fish is right that poems can provide "oases of reflection" but quite wrong that "poems don't ask you to do anything except read them" (52). If poetry, as he asserts, "is the liberal arts activity par excellence" (52), then the example of poetry disproves his thesis that "the liberal arts are like poetry because they make no claim to benefits beyond the pleasure of engaging them" (59). Where Fish is right is in acknowledging that neither poetry nor teaching comes with any guarantees, but their pressure to change our lives is nonetheless real. Fish would deny me the academic freedom to teach my view of the history of poetry, despite my long history of publishing in the field.

Given that any effort actually to impose Fish's immensely constrained vision of what is appropriate to higher education would violate academic freedom, he is thus effectively compelled to redefine academic freedom to fit his model. He begins, fairly enough, by characterizing it as "a matter of guild protectionism": "it is the freedom to do one's academic job without interference from external constituencies" (80). But of course, he has already defined the "job" very narrowly indeed, and thus he is able to offer a uniquely restrictive brief for what academic freedom must protect: "Academic freedom, correctly (and modestly) understood, is not a challenge to the imperative always to academicize; it is the *name* of that imperative" (80). "One violates academic freedom," he adds, offering broad warrant for faculty dismissals, "by deciding to set aside academic purposes for others thought to be more noble or urgent" (81). He then severs his radical redefinition of academic freedom from all the activities he wants to prohibit: "The moment a teacher tries to promote a political or social agenda, mold the character of students, produce civic virtue, or institute a regime of tolerance, he or she has stepped away from the immanent rationality of the enterprise and performed an action in relation to which there is no academic freedom protection because there's nothing academic going on" (81). "Those magic phrases—academic freedom and free speech," he adds, "are what provide an alibi for professors who cannot tell the difference between a soapbox and a teacher's podium" (96).

Although elsewhere in the book Fish is careful to reject a number of arguments from right-wing organizations, in this fundamental claim he takes the conservative effort to housebreak higher education further, perhaps, than anyone has before. Imagine the regimes of classroom surveillance and review necessary to police the line between "academicizing" and the very broad definition of advocacy Fish assails. Imagine trying to guard against that "moment" when you cease merely analyzing the rhetoric of an argument and allow a moment of affirmation. Then ask yourself this question: since Fish does not always explicitly distinguish between teaching and publication, to what degree does his narrow concept of academic freedom apply to scholarly writing as well?

Although Fish is apparently unaware of the fact, his restraints on academic freedom intersect with a series of well-publicized attacks on individual faculty—and with an argument the AAUP rejects, that collegiality is a valid independent criterion in evaluating a candidate for tenure. "In partisan politics," he remarks at the end of the book, "ad hominem attacks are within the pale; in academic politics, they are not" (173). The problem is that passionate attacks on people's ideas inevitably implicate their powers of reasoning and sometimes their political motivations for advancing certain positions. Unsurprisingly, the rhetorical maneuvers universities have considered excessive have been in the service of leftist politics. Thus, the longest faculty report on Ward Churchill's work faulted him for a "pattern of failure to understand the difference between scholarship and polemic, or at least of behaving as though that difference doesn't matter" (Standing Committee), exactly the core argument of Fish's book and for him sufficient grounds in itself for termination. Similarly, Dean Charles Suchar at DePaul University, in his official evaluation of Norman Finkelstein's tenure case, recommended denying the political scientist tenure in part because he found "the personal attacks in many of Dr. Finkelstein's published books to border on character assassination." University president Dennis Holtschneider then seconded the dean's letter, citing Finkelstein's failure to "show due respect for the opinions of others." But as I suggested earlier, not all ideas merit respect.

As a position paper about one faculty member's vision of higher education, *Save the World on Its Own Time* is useful in its very monomaniacal consistency, as a portrait of Fish pursuing his white whale of classroom politics. Like Fish's online *New York Times* columns, where he drafted most of these arguments, one can readily take issue with him. Indeed, the best thing about his columns is often the articulate comments that readers make. Fish has never, one might add, been noted for having deep convictions. He takes up opportunities for rhetorical intervention and pursues them relentlessly. Yet he is also more than willing to enforce his point of view, and he has offered administrators, trustees, and politicians a series of weapons they can use to police the academy.

Fish's book opens with a charming account of the restless crankiness that, on his report, took over his life when he stepped down as a dean at the University of Illinois at Chicago. If my colleagues there are to be believed, the crankiness was in evidence earlier. Fish considered himself qualified to defund faculty research when it did not match his own sense of intellectual priorities. I am not certain that is the best use of administrative power when the research agendas in question encompass substantial constituencies and active, ongoing publishing activity worldwide. Those faculty members who had research agendas and a sense of mission that Fish endorsed loved him. If the dean's rejection of your funding request concluded with the admonition to "save the world on your own time," you were less likely to be an enthusiast. Not that Fish was precisely consistent in applying his favorite standard. Among the faculty members who worked under him whom I interviewed, a director of women's studies found him unvaryingly supportive, whereas a faculty member specializing in Marxist theory found him dismissive and unwilling to provide resources.

Does the AAUP's defense of classroom political reference mean there are no excessively opinionated, overly politicized faculty in the United States, even in beginning courses? Certainly there are. Horowitz will now ritually bring some brainwashed waif to his public performances, trained to testify to recovered memory of instructional abuse. On-the-spot verification is hardly possible, but I assume that a tiny minority of faculty behave themselves badly. Certainly, given that some faculty, like some people in all occupations, are less than sane, I expect that unacceptable behavior does occur. But there is no widespread, national, systemic problem and thus no necessity for a new reporting, surveillance, and punishment system. The AAUP does strongly endorse structures for students to seek redress for unfair grading, including politically based grading, but a system that would monitor political speech in the classroom would be repressive and destructive.

There are no doubt faculty members who abuse their students politically, just as there are faculty who abuse their students sexually. At some point it becomes a discipline problem. Indeed, schools that cannot address the political mistreatment of students are most likely to be unable to deal with their sexual mistreatment either. Those institutions are typically poorly administered and thus dysfunctional in a whole series of areas. Horowitz prefers to isolate the issues he focuses on because that suits his political agenda, but the solution for an institution incompetently administered is a comprehensive overhaul, not a system to monitor political speech in the classroom.

After my 2007 debate with Horowitz, one of the people in attendance contacted me with a story: "In a course on the Arab-Israeli conflict, the academic had her students, as part of the course work, establish pen pal relations with Palestinians and only Palestinians, not Israeli Jews. This is an abuse and misuse of academic freedom. This, I hate to say, was not uncommon in all of the courses taught by this one professor, yet none of her courses were about the Arab perspective on the Middle East. Had those courses been on the latter topic, then I would say the course was as advertised. But this was not the case." I agree that the course description should have been clear, including the professor's precise expectations for student performance. If she penalizes students for taking opposing views, she should be sanctioned. Aside from that, the pen-pal exercise seems rather interesting. But should this instructor be required to present both sides of the issue? Would anyone trust her to do so? How exactly could she be reformed? Death threats? Cambodian-style reeducation camp? Salary cuts? What are the odds she could be convincingly evenhanded? Students would be better served by experiencing her convictions for what they are, it being hardly likely that hers would be the only perspective they would encounter on campus or elsewhere in their lives.

It is true that many Jewish students who are sympathetic to Israel feel their views about the Middle East are unwelcome on campus; in the wake of September 11, many Arab students feel the same way. Certainly there are Middle East studies programs—typically with faculty specialization spread across a number of area countries—in which pro-Israeli sentiments are not kindly treated. On the other hand, there is a well-organized lobby for pro-Israeli opinion. As I suggested in chapter 4, few people on either side of this issue seem ready to admit that pro-Palestinian political correctness and pro-Israeli opinion—wielded in different ways—compete constantly for student attention. A March 2007 report issued by the Israel on Campus Coalition implicitly suggests universities negotiate with outside "stakeholders" to reach consensus on how controversies over the Arab-Israeli conflict should be taught and represented on campus. Good luck. A number of world leaders have entered that terrain with minimal success. Campus groups should instead simply schedule speakers and seminars to assure their particular views are represented. Meanwhile, we need to accept that many faculty with deep convictions about this subject will share them with students.

It is useful, however, for faculty to let their colleagues know what their pedagogical philosophy and personal guidelines are, including their position on political speech in the classroom. It is essentially a set of personal guidelines that Michael Bérubé offers in his contribution to *Advocacy in the Classroom* when he suggests he would only advocate for specific legislation should it "materially *and immediately* affect the students" in his classroom, but that some subject matter would compel him to advocate "for one form of social organization over another" ("Professional Advocates" 189). The campus certainly needs to be a place where faculty can articulate, debate over, and advocate for a particular professional and pedagogical ethic. But that is quite different from succumbing to an impulse to impose any given pedagogy on one another, let alone ceding such authority either to administrators or to outside stakeholders. Academic freedom requires that faculty have wide latitude in conducting their classes.

Despite Horowitz's claims to the contrary, I believe American students do possess and exercise their intellectual freedom. His claim that leftist faculty routinely deny this right has not been demonstrated. Horowitz's first effort to stigmatize progressive faculty involved efforts to get state-by-state "Academic Bill of Rights" legislation passed mandating political balance in faculty appointments. Ordinarily one does not learn about faculty members' politics during the appointment process, and it would be immensely destructive to interrogate people about them. It is true that faculty in some disciplines are more likely to be either Democratic or Republican, English being an example of the former, business being an example of the latter. But that hardly makes them campus radicals. The Yale English department fought the effort to organize graduate employees for collective bargaining with a vengeance, not exactly standard liberal behavior, though I expect most of these same faculty vote Democratic. Party identification clearly does not indicate what a person's campus politics will be like.

The legislative hearings aimed at considering Horowitz's Academic Bill of Rights in more than a dozen states were occasions for organized AAUP testimony, and Horowitz's efforts failed. The most extraordinary bill was one proposed in the Arizona state legislature, instituting a five-hundred-dollar fine for each verified instance of a faculty member making political comments in a classroom. Horowitz wrote the language but claims he intended it for K–12 education, not for colleges and universities. His decision to disavow the bill and deny responsibility bears comparison with a pilot dropping a bomb on a city from ten thousand feet and claiming he had no idea there were people there. The Arizona bill was fruit of the poisoned Horowitz tree. Although the Horowitz/ACTA effort to provoke legislative interventions has failed, it would be a mistake to conclude that the Right presents no threat to academic freedom.

Where Horowitz has had some direct success is in getting universities to institute procedures for students to complain about political speech in the classroom and trigger investigations. Temple University and Pennsylvania State University both already had on the books overly restrictive policies limiting classroom speech. Penn State's policy (HR64), on the books for some years, is especially bad:

> The faculty member is entitled to freedom in the classroom in discussing his/her subject. The faculty member is, however, responsible for the maintenance of appropriate standards of scholarship and teaching ability. It is not the function of a faculty member in a democracy to indoctrinate his/her students with ready-made conclusions on controversial subjects. The faculty member is expected to train students to think for themselves, and to provide them access to those materials which they need if they are to think intelligently. Hence, in giving instruction upon controversial matters the faculty member is expected to be of a fair and judicial mind, and to set forth justly, without supersession or innuendo, the divergent opinions of other investigators. No faculty member may claim as a right the privilege of discussing in the classroom controversial topics outside his/her own field of study. The faculty member is normally bound not to take advantage of his/her position by introducing into the classroom provocative discussions of irrelevant subjects not within the field of his/her study.

Although the nonsexist language was added in the 1980s, the policy itself dates from the 1950s. It is thus McCarthy-era rhetoric, taking passages from the 1915 AAUP Declaration out of context and ignoring subsequent clarifications. Like Horowitz, Penn State failed at the time to conceptualize the sense in which all teaching and research is fundamentally and deeply political. Humanities and social science teaching and research is more explicitly political, being in dialogue with cultural values and norms that undergo continual change and that are sites of struggle, linked to assumptions about identity that are socially and politically constructed, engaged with social life and the public sphere and thus with the politics of culture, constrained and encouraged by discourses embedded in politics. Academic freedom entails the right to discuss all these relationships in any course whatsoever. Many of them are entangled with the political activities of state and national governments.

Both Horowitz and Penn State argue, in effect, that overt political remarks (and for Penn State, covert ones) can be strictly separated from the intricate web of connections between the academy and the politics of culture. I disagree. The Penn State statement also illustrates the dangers of faculty at one institution—who lack sufficient background and historical knowledge—attempting to write nuanced policy. The AAUP's drafting process is infinitely more elaborate. What Penn State ended up with is nothing less than thought control. You are to remain even tempered at all times; echoing AAUP standards from a more genteel age in higher education, the policy insists that you are to avoid even "innuendo" of an opinion on controversial matters. Although this might fall within the range of ethical advice, rather than enforceable regulation, it certainly could be brought to bear at time of contract renewal or tenure decisions and thus poses substantial risks to academic freedom.

In 2006, however, in the wake of legislative hearings in Pennsylvania, both Penn State and Temple added reporting and investigative procedures for what students perceive as one-sided classroom advocacy. Having failed at getting legislators to act, Horowitz now disingenuously argues that his real purpose all along was to get postsecondary institutions to reform themselves. Although the overwhelming majority of such complaints received may well be dismissed—because it is very difficult for people outside a class to judge context, because students are not likely to know what faculty will or will not find acceptable, and because the entire process will quickly be seen as invasive—once such procedures are activated, they are likely to promote self-censorship. It also certainly gives Horowitz's allies a chance to harass selected faculty with multiple complaints. Moreover, it sets a bad precedent for group surveillance of and intrusion into the classroom, making raids on academic freedom culturally and institutionally acceptable.

Horowitz has made a major effort to personalize his campaign, to tell and retell the story of his conversion from Left to Right activist, since personalizing his story helps him get free publicity, including a full page in *USA Today* in 2006. Lately, despite his own highly personal attacks on over a hundred individual faculty members, he has begun to protest that the Left attacks him, rather than dealing with the issues he raises. His feigned outrage bids fair to turn him into a new breed of attack dog: the pit bull that feels sorry for itself. These apparently contradictory tactics are actually two sides of the same coin, designed to work together to distract us from focusing on the true nature of his enterprise: a well-funded collective project of the far Right. In the power dynamics of contemporary culture, Horowitz is only a pawn in their game.

There is, however, one poignant element to the Horowitz conversion narrative. He habitually tells audiences that his parents were communists but typically receives no reaction from conservative listeners to this repeated revelation. As it happens, the only people capable of understanding the relevant social, generational, and political history are the very people on the Left whom Horowitz vilifies. He has sold himself out to people who will never understand him.

The organized Right has successfully taken on a series of American institutions. First they red-baited the judicial system: "Liberal judges are trying to reinterpret the Constitution. Conservative judges just apply it." No doubt the founding fathers intended us to own assault rifles. Over time, the U.S. Senate rolled over and handed the Right the federal judiciary. Then the Right red-baited the so-called liberal press. A component of that campaign was the attack on "liberal bias" on PBS television, a campaign Horowitz helped to orchestrate (Brock 107). The press was then relentlessly accused of liberal bias, and it eventually went belly-up and failed to do its job in the lead-up to the Iraq war. The Bush administration's claims about Iraq's weapons of mass destruction and its Al

Qaeda connections went uninvestigated and uncontested. Bush, Cheney, and Powell got a free pass on every lie they wanted to tell the American people. Now higher education is being red-baited in the same way, with hyperbolic accusations of left-wing bias. The aim is the same: to house-break yet another independent democratic institution. Anne Neal and David Horowitz are spokespersons for a cultural struggle over the heart and soul of American education.

We are now, to be sure, on the terrain of unpredictable cultural and political struggle. I would not, for example, pretend to predict the strategies the Right may employ in future efforts to limit academic freedom. The Bush administration was aggressive in barring scholars whose views were unwelcome from entering the United States, a particularly brutal and chilling aggression against the ability of American students and faculty members to participate in an international conversation. Both independently and in cooperation with the ACLU and other groups, the AAUP was diligent in fighting these actions. With a new political party occupying the White House as of January 2009, restrictions on foreign scholars entering the United States could well be lifted. But the rhetoric of an international war against terror has spread across the world and encouraged assaults on international communication elsewhere. We cannot know how it will play out everywhere.

The political and cultural climate for academic freedom—especially the level of public tolerance for political dissent on campus—could easily change; indeed, it could change rapidly. In 2006 and 2007, growing public disenchantment with the Iraq war opened space for more dissent in all quarters of American life. Yet at least one plausible series of events has significant potential to curtail tolerance for the loyal opposition on campus. I refer to the possibility of a fresh series of terrorist attacks on American soil. It would not require anything so ambitious as we saw on September 11. A series of bombs placed in airplane cargo holds—even something so relatively low tech as a series of suicide bombings in public places—could be enough to fuel multiple repressive responses from Congress and local authorities. The nature of the response would depend, of course, on the nature of the aggression and the character of the people in power, but some action would be almost inevitable. Campus criticism of such measures would not be welcomed in all communities. Imagine some version of Ward Churchill's "little Eichmanns" remarks about a new series of American victims. Place them in the mouths of those vulnerable part-time faculty invoked throughout this book, and one can see how the weakened institutional ground for academic freedom could lead to its curtailment where it is most vulnerable.

Could academic freedom—grounded as it is now in either an increasingly contingent labor force or a fragmented tenured professoriate—survive the perfect cultural and political storm? In a sense, the question has been unexpectedly asked and answered. The respect that the managerial class of administrators now widely in control of higher education has for faculty rights has been tested and demonstrated and found wanting. The capacity of faculty to resist the perfect institutional storm has also been tested—and found wanting. Because if administrators lose their patience with progressive pedagogy, the only system in place to protect pedagogical freedoms is the weakened one discussed in chapter 1, shared governance.

Let me close this chapter, then, with an instructional riddle for higher education's new millennium. What would a university president do if all existing institutional restraints, all rules and regulations, all checks and balances structured into shared governance, all moral limits besides those imposed by common law, were suddenly and decisively removed? Since this is a riddle for the new millennium, the president in question is not likely to be a philosopher-king. He or she is probably not among the most eloquent defenders of academic freedom on campus. He or she admires faculty who keep their mouths shut and bring in revenue, but he or she does not admire faculty who are the source of inconvenient ethical, political, and professional challenges. You do not look to such a president for intellectual leadership. You may live in fear that such a person would actually *acquire a vision* of the university's mission.

So how would such an administrator behave given complete freedom of operation? How would such an administrator restructure a college or university to meet popular and corporate interests if he or she could do so without any meaningful consultation? How would he or she treat dissident faculty in a political crisis? What if nineteenth-century-style at-will faculty employment returned and swept aside faculty control not only over hiring but also over the curriculum and institutional mission?

Now, instead of a single corporate-style administrator given near absolute power, let us carve off a whole region of the United States. Say that a whole city separates itself from fifty years of shared governance and academic freedom. Say that the tenure system is tossed aside. Say that all human decency is abandoned. Say that administrators begin to lie in public without hesitation. Say that they rule by decree and that every university employee becomes expendable.

Unfortunately, in New Orleans, a perfect educational storm was among Hurricane Katrina's aftereffects. Organized by a series of college presidents—at Tulane University, Loyola University, the University of New Orleans, Southern University at New Orleans, the Louisiana State University Health Sciences Center, and Xavier University—this educational hurricane swept aside academic freedom, shared governance, due process, and tenure. The administration at the University of Texas Medical Branch in Galveston, Texas, did much the same in the aftermath of Hurricane Ike in 2008, terminating 125 faculty, among them 42 with tenure, despite the existence of several other branches in the Texas system that might have offered alternative employment. Everything I described in my worst-case scenario has already taken place. And it has established a precedent that other presidents will apply in comparable disasters— freak storms, earthquakes, fires, and terrorist attacks—or on a lesser scale in other crises and reorganization projects. Indeed, presidents across the country began to do exactly that during the 2008–9 academic year in response to resource reductions during the recession. We have seen the future, and the faculty is not there.

In New Orleans, tenured faculty were fired with scant notice, no due process, no stated reasons, and no appeal except to the very administrators who terminated them. Some were given a couple months' notice. Others were told that they had been taken off payroll and off health care the previous week. Departments and programs were closed down without appropriate review and without regard for shared governance or academic freedom. The schools used the excuse of Hurricane Katrina, but it is clear that no level of emergency existed that required the elimination of due process. Loyola suffered losses of about thirty million dollars, but its three-hundred-million-dollar endowment remains intact.

Faculty senates in New Orleans voted against the actions, proposed alternatives, and in some cases offered votes of no confidence in the administration. Boards of trustees supported the presidents. The faculty were ignored. By then it was too late. One other key fact gives us all warning: most of these schools had excellent guarantees of academic freedom, governance procedures, due process regulations, and appropriate emergency guidelines on the books. All these rules and regulations— everything approved in the faculty handbooks, the faculty senate rules, and governing statutes—were dismissed out of hand. One might say the levees shoring up academic freedom, shared governance, and tenure needed to be reinforced *before* the storm hit. The national AAUP published a detailed report on New Orleans in its May–June 2007 issue of *Academe*. Five administrations were censured in June 2007. As I write, the AAUP is in the midst of negotiating with them about reversing these actions. It has so far been successful with one of them (Southern University at New Orleans) and is negotiating with Tulane.

By the time the academic levees crumbled in New Orleans, it was too late for some proactive solutions, though I would have recommended that faculty return to classes the following semester, earn a first salary check, and then initiate job actions designed to close these universities down temporarily. It was certainly too late for the public institutions to organize rapidly for collective bargaining, a considerable challenge in Louisiana in any case. Nonetheless, the clearest lesson to be gleaned from New Orleans is this: the academic freedom defined in your faculty handbook may well mean nothing in the right context. Your written rules for tenure and due process may mean nothing, although the contractual status of faculty handbooks varies from state to state. That leaves faculty in many states with only one sure option: shared governance, due process, and tenure regulations need to be mirrored in legally enforceable contracts. You have to have a sound basis for taking the administration to court. It may well be that getting these regulations into signed contracts may be far more important than any salary or benefits a union can negotiate. A strong local AAUP chapter that can consistently speak truth to power and help educate the faculty is the first step.

In many states, a faculty that is strong enough and sufficiently united can compel even a conservative administration to negotiate. That will require new faculty identities that embrace greater faculty solidarity and activism. We also need a broad, well-funded program to educate both faculty and the general public about the nature and value of academic freedom. To deny that university freedoms are at risk is to cede the future to corporatization and a form of higher education with little ability to encourage cultural critique. And it is to put academic freedom substantially at risk. It is not too late to act.

8

No Campus Is an Island

Reflections on the AAUP Presidency

Academic freedom is not simply a kind of bonus enjoyed by workers within the system, a philosophical luxury universities could function just as effectively, and much more efficiently, without. It is the key legitimating concept of the entire enterprise.
— Louis Menand, "The Limits of Academic Freedom" (4)

There is only one organization whose primary mission is to promote vigilance in the name of academic freedom. It is the AAUP.
— Stanley Katz, testimonial for AAUP brochure

I used to say that you have to be in the national AAUP leadership for a decade before you understand how the organization works. That was then. After fifteen years on its governing National Council, six of those years as a vice president and four of them as AAUP president, I am still learning things that are absolutely central to how the AAUP operates. Certainly many council members and members of the AAUP's appointed committees, including the members of Committee A, have no clue. Some realize they can only see through a glass darkly; others are blissfully comfortable in the self-confidence that is often a faculty birthright. Thus, even those inside the AAUP factory may not know how its sausage is made. Needless to say, the level of awareness of how the AAUP operates among the faculty at large is barely measurable.

I cannot therefore claim that I knew what I was getting into when people asked me to run for president and I agreed. I had some specific goals: to rebuild what the organization informally calls "advocacy" membership—meaning members outside collective bargaining, both on campuses with and without AAUP chapters—and to encourage new policy initiatives on Committee A. In June 2006, just a few days before becoming president I announced two policy priorities: developing a full statement on politics in the classroom and developing more detailed due process rights for graduate-student employees. I quickly learned I would meet challenges. The chair of Committee A, the committee that deals with academic freedom policy, asked me if I would agree not to do anything on behalf of either graduate students or part-time faculty during my presidency, reasoning that that would help us recruit conservative faculty. I refused, and he soon resigned, frustrated on several grounds. That made it easier to move my agenda. Thus, the first of these goals was fulfilled in 2007 with "Freedom in the Classroom"; the second was achieved with the publication of "Graduate Student Employees." Rebuilding membership has proved more elusive. The organization has made progress, but it will be a long haul.

My opponent in the 2006 and 2008 presidential contests was the same person. Indeed, he had run against my predecessor, Jane Buck, in 2004. He celebrated that first loss by filing an election complaint with a federal agency, the upshot of which was that American taxpayers paid to have the ballots recounted (thereby giving him a few less votes), and the AAUP absorbed forty thousand dollars of legal costs and staff time. His perennial platform had but one plank: "Throw the bums out!" He had two groups of bums in mind: the entire national staff and most of the elected leadership, though as a council member and former head of the AAUP's Assembly of State Conferences (the advocacy group for both CB and non-CB chapters in many states), he could hardly characterize himself as a true outsider to anyone attentive to his history. After an earlier unsuccessful bid to head the Oklahoma Republican Party, he apparently fell to ground on the way to class and discovered he was a Democrat. Declaring that the AAUP would be his route to the Oklahoma governorship, he rose in the ranks of its state leadership and then set his sights on the presidency. In 2008, the AAUP and the country as a whole were both in the midst of presidential campaigns advocating change; indeed, it was a promise both I and my opponent made. Though not a major scholar, he had enough of a national constituency to win about 40 percent of the vote in each of his campaigns, a chastening lesson, since it meant that many of our members were angry. After his third defeat, he let his AAUP membership lapse. If my characterization of my opponent seems unkind, I make no apologies. The election results demonstrate that the AAUP was hovering on the edge of a dangerous member revolt that had no affirmative content—no goals, no plans, no proposals.

It is easy for disenchanted members and leaders to fall into the trap of venting frustration with the national staff tout court. As I try to show in what follows, rather intense resistance to many new ideas and occasional simple rejection of leadership directives have long been widespread features of staff culture in the AAUP's national office. But they are not universal. Rather, they typify certain departments or certain staff members. There are moments—following a mix of staff resistance and complaints that they are not sufficiently praised and respected—when one feels the national office is organized as a terrorist cell within a kindergarten. Yet the only way I have been able to accomplish things has been through working with those inventive, witty, and accomplished staff members who are willing to collaborate. That was my problem with my opponent's broad-brush call for revolution. His contempt for the leadership, which he called "the in-crowd," was equally misplaced. To take the most obvious example, most members of the AAUP Executive Committee are wise, worldly, and completely dedicated to the organization. Without their continuous political advice I would not be able to function effectively.

Much more than I feared or imagined, my time as president has been occupied with helping to repair the national office: removing incompetent staff, reorganizing departments, restructuring the AAUP's tax status, reasserting the constitutional authority of the elected leadership. That means dealing with about twenty phone calls and over a hundred emails a day, sandwiched between about twenty trips annually to the AAUP's national office, local chapters, and various academic conferences, some trips lasting as little as four or five days, some lasting two weeks or more. There have been low points when I thought giving up might be the best course, perhaps the worst being a six-week stretch working all day long, every day, with dedicated lawyers trying to resolve a recalcitrant staff problem. Second worst on my list was another month of the same. Then something would happen to keep me going, either the completion of a project or the experience of important policy development. Few things are more gratifying than talking through an important issue with one of our active committees.

I almost always consult widely before acting. When my university in the midst of the 2008 national election issued a prohibition against faculty and staff attending political rallies on campus (even in the evening), wearing political buttons on campus, or having endorsement bumper stickers on cars parked in university lots, I needed to protest the new rules quickly. I sent draft statements on a Thursday to several constitutional law and academic freedom authorities among long-time AAUP faculty and to several staff members. Our chief staff lawyer, Rachel Levinson, wrote me a wonderfully detailed response on a plane trip that weekend. By Monday, I had the advice I needed to revise the two memos and have the staff email them to all faculty members on the three University of Illinois campuses. With additional pressure from the ACLU and the Foundation for Individual Rights in Education (FIRE), the university withdrew most of the rules.

On other occasions, I have had to act independently, mostly following my own counsel. The trick in these cases is to guess right; otherwise your political capital will disappear overnight. After a series of very negative stories about the AAUP appeared in the *Chronicle of Higher Education*, stories "balanced" by laudatory treatment of Anne Neal and ACTA, I took advantage of communication scholar Cat Warren's offer to write an essay for the AAUP publication *Academe* evaluating the *Chronicle*'s news coverage. *Academe*'s faculty-member editor approved of her essay, but, with only one exception, the staff members in the national office urged that the article not be published. They cautioned that it could backfire, make the *Chronicle* take reprisals against us, and asked instead that I have yet one more conversation with the *Chronicle* requesting fairness. I knew that the only way to make headway was to shame the *Chronicle* by publicly demanding that they honor their responsibility for journalistic objectivity. Warren's essay was published, and since then, the *Chronicle*'s coverage has been fair.

Faced with the need to build the AAUP's modest endowment, there was general agreement that the organization should mount a capital campaign, but there was absolutely no agreement on how to proceed. The general secretary built a distinguished roster of people who agreed to serve on a national advisory board, but, unfortunately, without clearing this plan with anyone, he assured each of them that they would not be asked to do any fund raising. Standard advice for a capital campaign is to ask your regular donors to give more. Unfortunately, most of our twenty-five to fifty annual donors give twenty-five to fifty dollars a year. The closest we could get to a consensus was to ask all our members to give what they could. I realized we would all meet our maker long before that technique would bring us anywhere near our ten-million-dollar goal.

The challenge, I felt, was to find a way of turning regular AAUP members into donors. So I came up with a plan: launch a campaign in which everyone would be urged to donate at least one thousand dollars. Build a sense of commitment, solidarity, and momentum around one-thousand-dollar contributions. That is more than most faculty members have ever donated to anything, but I proposed setting it up so people could pay by way of automatic monthly credit card or bank debit payments if they chose. Over, say, four years that comes to $20.83 a month for a thousand-dollar, tax-deductible donation. The relevant committee was entirely against my plan. I offered an initial target of a hundred pledges, and everyone said we would never get there. But they agreed I could go ahead, and then they would say, "We told you so," when I failed. Before long, we passed our goal of a hundred donors. I discovered that I really do not mind asking people for money. Then I met my match. The finance department was incapable of billing people accurately. Some were billed not at all, while others were dunned who had already paid. Taking phone calls from people in these categories was another low point in my presidency. I decided to slow the capital campaign until the finance department was rebuilt. Yet thousand-dollar donations have continued to arrive, and the campaign received a major boost when former AAUP president Jim Richardson negotiated a challenge grant from Jim Rogers, chancellor of Nevada's higher education system; Rogers would match two twenty-five-thousand-dollar donations a year, and several of our CB chapters came through with that amount.

When it became clear that the finance and membership offices would need not only to be restaffed but also to be reorganized, I made a confidential request to two staff members and an outside consultant to develop a detailed plan for how this could be done. We knew that the plan could not survive staff meddling and protest unless it was drafted in secret. Only when the plan was drafted did I share it with others. At that point, the department heads were given a chance to suggest revisions. Indeed, the chief financial officer only learned about the plan then. The Executive Committee approved it, and it was distributed to the rest of the staff. I realized that this kind of process could be castigated as high-handed, but I also knew the plan would otherwise fail. And I knew the office could not function unless a generation's accumulation of patchwork, inconsistent, ad hoc assignment of membership and finance responsibilities was rationalized. In 2008, I went further, requesting a series of confidential white papers evaluating the major national office departments. I went not to the people obviously responsible for those departments but, rather, to well-informed staff members and leaders who could offer a fresh perspective. The reports were shared only with the Executive Committee and the incoming general secretary.

Some examples of staff conservatism are the subject of substantive frustration on the part of the leadership, but others simply provoke sadness at missed opportunities. In June 2006, I met with a dozen staff members to say we could build respect for and appreciation of what the staff does if they were each willing, every few years, to write up a little story about themselves—describing a project, a special service, or a typical day's work—and let me email it to members, most of whom have no idea what staff members do. I gave as an example a story I wrote and published in *Inside Higher Education* about staff assistance to the AAUP's Eastern Michigan University chapter during a 2006 strike ("Solidarity"). They all endorsed the idea, but a typically frank department head told me privately that they would never do it unless ordered to do so by the general secretary. So I asked two council members, Larry Gerber and Sheila Teahan, to write up stories they had told me about exceptional help their chapters had received from staff members. I emailed those to the membership as a whole. Then I asked the general secretary to promote the idea. When that failed, I approached several staff members individually with a request to write stories. No results. Then I wrote about the idea in one of my *Academe* columns. Then I approached the general secretary again. No results. This modest effort could have gone a long way toward limiting the anger at the staff that some people in the organization capitalize on.

Now and again, staff attitudes seem grounded in nothing more than habitual resistance to any leadership initiatives. The members of Committee A spend long hours talking with one another in meetings. Unlike the elected officers and council members, who distribute capsule biographies during elections, Committee A members never receive any information about their colleagues except name, institution, and departmental affiliation, the AAUP's version of protocols for prisoners of war. They often have no idea what the other members' accomplishments or intellectual interests are, knowledge that might increase understanding of one another's arguments. Shortly after assuming office, I suggested to the head of the Department of Academic Freedom that we gather brief bios for the committee members and distribute them. He rejected the idea vehemently: "They know each other's university departments. That's all they need to know." Rather than turn my suggestion into a major political battle, I simply gave up.

In all of this, one central question is how much authority the AAUP president and the elected leadership have. Knowing I would inherit a fundamentally passive leadership and a long tradition of a presidency more often seen than heard, I began acting more forcefully six months before being elected, both to test the possibilities for action and to acclimate everyone to the experience of more activist leadership. Theoretically, the leaders set policy, and the staff carries it out. But staff members have always been willing literally to ignore leadership directives, to delay carrying them out indefinitely, or to implement them in such a weak way that they collapse of their own weight. So regular monitoring and dialogue are essential. Even so, if the general secretary is intermittently unwilling either to compel or cajole staff compliance, there are few realistic options. You cannot fire staff members every week. One route I chose from time to time was to take formal charge of supervising a key program. Most of the members of the Executive Committee tolerated that, though one or two were usually uneasy with that model. As the organization moved into terminal mode late in 2006, however, the Executive Committee realized that extraordinary measures were necessary. It became clear then that the AAUP was faced with an impending crisis of finance and responsibility that might compel us to close our doors. Did I have the authority on my own to order the locks changed to guarantee that an employee could not gain access to the office? I issued such orders without knowing for certain whether anyone would listen. As it happened, they did.

To fully understand the current pressures on the AAUP and the necessity of getting both staff and leaders to address them, it is necessary to set the organization's recent history in a broader national context, then return to the AAUP's special story. When the University of Minnesota Board of Regents launched its infamous assault on tenure in 1996 (Honan), faculty all across the country soon realized it put them at risk as well. The national AAUP joined with local leaders to win that battle. In the course of the struggle, membership in the University of Minnesota AAUP chapter quadrupled, from roughly two hundred members to about eight hundred. Two years later, chapter membership was back where it had started. So, too, around the country faculty seemed to feel the battle had been won for everyone. And perhaps it was. Direct assaults on tenure mostly disappeared. Instead, universities went full steam ahead with the steady and inexorable erosion of the percentage of tenured faculty in higher education.

Despite success in the tenure battle, University of Minnesota faculty failed to win collective bargaining for themselves. Disputes among campus constituencies erupted at the last moment, and a vote to unionize lost by a very small margin. If the AAUP could have organized a major Big Ten research campus, it might have opened possibilities elsewhere as well. There too a potential lasting impact dissolved. There were numerous lessons to be learned, some heartening, some depressing. Good news was certainly built into the fact that a local victory could have national impact. Bad news was evident in the lesson that attracting and holding the attention of faculty on one campus, let alone throughout the country, was more than a daunting goal. And yet the need to maintain an adaptive form of national vigilance was readily apparent.

On issues of academic freedom and shared governance, on the effort to guarantee that the people making educational decisions are the ones most qualified to do so, national vigilance has one venue: it is embodied in the AAUP. As the only effective voice for all the faculty that speaks comprehensively on matters of principle and policy, the AAUP is an organization we all have a vested interest in strengthening. There is otherwise little hope of reversing the most insidious trends in higher education and shaping our future for the common good.

Nothing we take for granted in higher education is protected from historical pressures for change. Academic freedom is not guaranteed when new conditions emerge and new employment realities are established. New arguments have to be made. New policy has to be written. The wide range of policy documents the AAUP disseminates could not be produced by any one campus. The organization involves people from a wide variety of colleges and universities in crafting statements. It has a professional staff devoted to researching issues. It is the only game in town, and it does this work very well indeed. The strongest advocacy chapter, the strongest union local, the strongest faculty senate, could not build the necessary support for academic freedom into its rules or contracts without *Academe* and the AAUP's three-hundred-page *Redbook* as sources.

Over the past decade alone, the AAUP has published over thirty policy statements and an equal number of investigative reports. Recent policy statements range from "The Faculty Role in the Reform of Intercollegiate Athletics" to "Academic Freedom and National Security in a Time of Crisis," from "Academic Freedom and Electronic Communications" to "Academic Freedom and Outside Speakers," along with statements on the rights of graduate students, part-time faculty, and academic professionals. These statements offer campuses detailed language they can incorporate directly into their regulations.

AAUP membership is often described as an insurance policy for the professoriate. It is that and more. The dues of individual members collectively pay for this elaborate process of researching and writing policy about emerging—and often unanticipated—matters that are critical to the survival of an effective professoriate. These policies are necessary if faculty members are to do their jobs. Our academic disciplines need them; we need them in our daily lives. The most powerful and the most vulnerable faculty members benefit from them every day. Without them, the academy would be a chaos of conflicting policy established by administrative fiat.

What would the academy be like today without the 1940 statement on academic freedom and tenure? At-will employment and summary dismissal without cause or due process would rule the day. There would be hundreds of wildly different employment policies across the country, many of them concealed from the faculty. Take scores of

AAUP policies off the books, eliminate the organization's history of censuring rogue institutions, withdraw the legal briefs it has sponsored for dozens of court cases, cancel thousands of individual academic freedom cases negotiated over decades, erase the AAUP's assistance to local chapters, and virtually all colleges and universities would be outlaw institutions.

Despite this history, many faculty today—with the frequent exception of AAUP activists—fail to recognize when local events have systemic implications or that national trends threaten everyone. When they do, they may feel there is little or nothing they can do about them. It is time to reverse both forms of defeatism. Now as in the past, faculties have sufficient power to enforce the principles that guide their profession.

In some respects, of course, faculty at different institutions are in competition with one another. Certainly we compete for students and staff. Yet in the areas of academic freedom and tenure, we have and must hold common cause. To be sure, the potential for universal professional solidarity is not helped by the increasing disparity in disciplinary salaries and career support at some institutions. How much solidarity should an assistant professor of art feel with an assistant professor of business earning more than twice as much? How much solidarity should a part-time faculty member earning fifteen hundred dollars a course feel with a faculty member earning hundreds of thousands of dollars a year, let alone with a million-dollar university president?

The inequities that divide us call out for redress, the sooner the better. Yet we need to recognize and act on common interests. In our national capital, of course, legislators can be opponents on one issue, allies on another. It is a strategy faculty members increasingly need to adopt. A diminishing commitment to humanities, arts, and interpretive social science disciplines is an international trend. So too is increasing reliance on contingent labor throughout the academy. Contempt for shared governance is embedded in the bones of far too many administrators. In this context, a victory for one campus faculty is a victory for all. And a defeat sends shock waves across the whole academic ocean.

We also need to be concerned with the strength and resolve of local faculty and their organizations everywhere. Collective bargaining chapters (CBs) certainly know that good contract provisions on one campus make for good models elsewhere. Indeed, it is time for faculty unable to obtain collective bargaining to examine CB contracts and work to adopt some of those gains in their handbooks. All members at unionized chapters should care deeply about the health and fate of their brother and sister chapters. Although AAUP-style unionization means that each local chapter sets its own goals and priorities, all CB locals benefit from local strength elsewhere. Faculty victories for AAUP principles—as well as improvements in working conditions, benefits, and salaries—raise boats everywhere. CB victories even benefit faculty in states where public-employee collective bargaining is prohibited. All of us gain nationally every time good local patterns and practices are enhanced. So it is in our interest to care about all our brothers and sisters.

In the same way, local advocacy chapters and faculty senates can help not only themselves but also one another by proving themselves decisive in promoting due process, shared governance, and academic freedom on their individual campuses. Even those elite university faculties who see themselves as wholly self-sufficient are subject to national and international pressures. Think how much good could be done by effective, newsworthy AAUP chapters at Columbia, Duke, Harvard, Princeton, and Yale, among others. They need not hold monthly bake sales, but they need to be organized as activists in reserve to meet challenges to academic freedom and shared governance.

I sometimes meet faculty at all sorts of schools—private universities, state universities, liberal arts colleges—who are confident they could make it on their own, as if the last local faculty on earth endorsing academic freedom could stand alone. Perhaps we would be better off not testing this thesis. We are not all in the same boat across the whole range of issues that confront us, but our fates are deeply interconnected nonetheless. No campus is an island unto itself.

Despite all this, AAUP membership is well less than half of what it was in 1970. Although it has remained roughly stable since 1990 and gained several thousand members as a result of a 2007–9 email campaign, the AAUP should be part of every faculty member's identity, and it is not. Reasons are multiple. The organization lost members in the 1970s when faculties at a number of schools organized for collective bargaining with the National Education Association (NEA) or the American Federation of Teachers (AFT) and let their AAUP memberships lapse.

The AAUP became involved in collective bargaining itself in the 1970s because it wanted to provide faculty with an alternative. NEA and AFT had large memberships among and primary loyalties to K–12 faculty. The AAUP thought faculty should have the option of an organization focused on higher education, one in which academic freedom and shared governance would have equal status with bread-and-butter issues, a difference that is often apparent in the sort of contracts AAUP collective bargaining locals negotiate. The AAUP also sought a union model offering chapters much greater autonomy and self-determination, so it adopted a model in which it would help faculty organize and give advice and assistance thereafter, but not formally represent them.

Whether this was the best decision politically is now arguably irrelevant. It happened. Had the national educational unions had different value systems, alternative arrangements might have been possible, including joint AAUP affiliations nationwide or mandated AAUP memberships as part of AFT and NEA union contracts. The price the AAUP paid for involving itself in collective bargaining was offering its critics the opportunity to dismiss it as "just another union," antagonizing antiunion faculty, and leaving some faculty in private universities and right-to-work states feeling alienated. Yet as I argued in chapter 5, collective bargaining for faculty in the neoliberal academy is more important now than ever before. Not having the AAUP involved in defining and shaping collective bargaining is no longer a good option.

The organization does, however, recognize the need to separate its collective bargaining organizing efforts from its more universal academic freedom and professional advocacy activities. Restructuring will establish three separate tax entities and organizational efforts under one AAUP umbrella: (1) a 501(c)3 foundation focused on academic freedom; (2) a 501(c)6 professional organization, which would include all individual AAUP members; (3) and a 501(c)5 labor union, composed of collective bargaining chapters. There will no doubt be some way of becoming a "friend of academic freedom" and affiliating with the foundation; contributors to its programs would know their donations would never be used to support collective bargaining.

Whether the AAUP actually lost members in response to its decision to move into collective bargaining is now impossible to say. Certainly there are also many thousands of faculty members sympathetic to collective bargaining who are not AAUP members. The key issue is a fundamental change in faculty identity. Widespread emphasis on disciplinary identification and competitive careerism over two generations has curtailed young faculty members' identification with the professoriate as a whole. The organization regularly confronts two chastening questions: "What is the AAUP?" and "What has the AAUP done for me today?"

The consequence of these attitudes is not only a serious loss of individual members but also a perilous aging of AAUP membership. I have now spent years visiting AAUP local chapters and AAUP state conferences, the latter being state organizations for AAUP chapters. The standard joke at these meetings is, "Is this the AAUP or the AARP?" It is more than unnerving to find only one or two people in the room under the age of sixty, but it happens regularly. Some chapters have settled into comfortable clubs with older leaders not eager to expand membership and potentially lose control. But for the most part, long-term members have no idea how to reach out to their much younger colleagues. With help from Gwen Bradley and Pat Shaw from the national office and Glenn Howze from the national leadership, I have placed extensive recruitment aids on my personal website (www.cary-nelson.org) to help solve this problem, meanwhile working steadily to make the national AAUP more visible. There is, of course, every reason for faculty members to join a national organization doing vital work for higher education, but campuses need their own local AAUP chapters as well. In the end, there is no way to organize and sustain a local chapter from Washington, DC. People have to visit their colleagues and urge them to join. If they do, they will find that 75 percent of those they ask will do just that.

The other troubling fact about AAUP membership is that fully 75 percent of its members are now in chapters organized for collective bargaining, most under the AAUP banner. Although I have supported collective bargaining throughout my career—ever since organizing a University of Illinois card drive in 1971 (Nelson and Watt, *Academic Keywords*)—I also know that it is not in the AAUP's best interest politically for collective bargaining so fully to dominate the organization's member profile.

Academic freedom benefits the country as a whole, not just the professoriate; AAUP principles do not travel best if they are seen exclusively as products of collective bargaining. The AAUP needs to speak for all faculty and to have all faculty involved in the organization. In 1970, none of the organization's one hundred thousand plus members was in AAUP-facilitated collective bargaining. That means the large-scale disengagement with the national professoriate among non-CB faculty is even more serious than one might have estimated. Some faculty members in AAUP collective bargaining, moreover, know little or nothing about the national organization. In that, they replicate faculty knowledge on nonunion campuses. When the *Chronicle of Higher Education* in 2007 bluntly asked whether the "venerable" organization could remain "relevant," I was more than a little offended (Wilson, "The AAUP"). For the reasons enumerated earlier and at the end of this chapter, I had no doubt about either the value of the AAUP or the quality of the work it did. But if relevance was a matter of *perception,* the AAUP was in serious trouble. If the organization issues cutting-edge policy recommendations on matters of great importance, but most faculty are too preoccupied with their own affairs to read them, then it is simultaneously relevant and irrelevant.

In the 1960s, the AAUP's membership growth was described as inexorable. As postwar universities grew in size and number, AAUP membership expanded with them. Little recruitment effort was required. Literally scores of older faculty tell the same story: they completed their dissertation, and their adviser told them, "Now it's time you joined the AAUP." Or they arrived at their first job and heard the same message. Founded as an elitist (and male) organization in which prospective members had to be nominated and approved, the organization switched to open membership when it literally could no longer vet the volume of new members. On the Champaign-Urbana campus of the University of Illinois, AAUP membership reached 708 by 1953 and then grew larger; today, with a much larger faculty, chapter membership hovers at 120.

One minor fact may illustrate a deeper change in faculty culture. The AAUP does not distinguish between members and nonmembers when responding to faculty requests for assistance. Indeed 80 to 90 percent of those the AAUP helps are nonmembers. What is notable—and what tells us something about contemporary faculty culture and its self-interested sense of entitlement—is that though the people assisted offer thanks, very few of them actually join the organization. They cannot extract any general lessons from their personal situations.

The wholesale transformation of professorial culture cannot be laid at the AAUP's doorstep. Nor is it clear the organization could have anticipated and fought it. But in significant ways the organization's conduct of its daily affairs made matters worse. I do not refer to its products. Legal briefs remained of high quality and of critical importance. Policy documents were (and continue to be) both timely and of extremely high quality. Committee A investigative reports have remained thorough, careful, and persuasive; at times they are riveting. But in other respects, the organization has been blind to a changing world and run its affairs with wanton incompetence.

One may begin with the most unwelcome piece of information: like most disciplinary organizations, the AAUP has—with two key exceptions, editing *Academe* and writing policy documents—been largely staff run for decades. Many of the disciplinary organizations run that way because their members prefer it. They want paid staff to do the daily work. But the more important difference is that many disciplinary organizations have no more than three major functions: running a job fair, raising money, and creating opportunities for members to add lines to their vitas. The AAUP, in contrast, crafts national policy across a whole range of issues and investigates institutions that violate those policies. Given that the AAUP is not dedicated to enhancing members' personal careers, it also lacks the narrow self-interested hook that gets people to join a disciplinary society.

Having served on two 501(c)3 (charitable organization) governing boards before joining the AAUP's, I can make some comparisons. The Modern Language Association's Executive Council, at least when I was serving on it, received the same useless, generic budgets as does the AAUP's Executive Committee and National Council. Such budgets collapse expenditures into broad categories such as "publication costs" and "travel" that make it impossible to judge what programs money is actually being spent for; you cannot tell what a given department is spending or what a given program costs. Did that special conference earn money or lose money? Best consult a fortune teller. The AAUP's staff is now pledged to begin doing departmental budgeting and to reform its budget tracking so that the council can exercise full, responsible oversight and fulfill its constitutional task of assuring that expenditures match policy obligations. Because many AAUP staff members have multiple responsibilities, apportioning their labor to different projects is challenging, but it can be done. Suffice it to say that impenetrable, generic budgets are a great way for the staff to maintain control of an organization. The MLA certainly operated that way, but the AAUP should not. By the time this book is published, full-scale departmental budgeting should be in place at the AAUP.

But the AAUP had more elaborate ways of managing its elected leaders. When I was elected as AAUP vice president, in which capacity I served for six years, I joined the AAUP's eleven-member Executive Committee (EC), which acts on behalf of the thirty-nine-member National Council (NC) when the latter is not in session. I was thus introduced to the AAUP's practice of silencing by report. The heads of the AAUP's various departments—Academic Freedom, Membership, Communications, Finance, Organizing, Government Relations, Research—would read long, self-congratulatory reports on their activities at each meeting of the EC (four times a year). With luck, the reports would take up enough time so that little space was left for EC members to say anything. In June and November, EC meetings were immediately followed by meetings of the full National Council. On those occasions, EC members had the great pleasure of listening to exactly the same reports read in exactly the same order two days in a row. It would take hours. Then, in what amounted nearly to a mortal blow, in June the reports would be read a third time to all the members attending the national meeting. Eventually, over strenuous staff objections, the reports began to be distributed in advance so the meetings could be devoted to discussion, though at least one department persists in delivering oral reports nonetheless.

More than one general secretary used another standard, manipulative technique for gaining EC and NC approval for new programs. Instead of presenting proposals in writing in advance of a meeting, they were regularly laid out without warning in the briefest of oral presentations. That meant there really was no time to think about, evaluate, and discuss proposals in advance. Moreover, it was always made clear that a decision to approve or disapprove was really a matter of whether the leadership did or did not personally support the general secretary. In 2006, I proposed—and the EC adopted—a policy that new program initiatives had to be distributed in advance in writing.

After briefly introducing the idea that professors could repair their national image by becoming poll watchers during elections, general secretary Roger Bowen went ahead and announced it as a major initiative. Like other EC members, I had suggested it was a bad idea. The public needs to learn to value what faculty members actually do: teach and do research. We could not win respect for those roles indirectly, either by adopting a local highway for faculty cleanup, by counting bird populations, or becoming poll watchers. But Bowen went ahead and filed a grant application without our approval. "Professors at the Polls" had a brief life in Maryland, then disappeared. Luckily no reporters asked my opinion of the project.

Other mad projects died before they could get off the ground. Bowen excitedly showed me a proposal he planned to present to the EC for the AAUP to buy two small buildings a block apart from each other. The staff would walk back and forth between them no matter what the weather. The organization had no way to pay for this convenient arrangement, but Bowen was convinced the AAUP could approach Venezuela's Hugo Chávez, who would buy the buildings as a way of showing his support for academic freedom and embarrassing the U.S. government. The proposal never left his office.

All this might be tolerable for a time if the national office were working well across all its priorities, but it was not and could not. The professional and political issues the AAUP must deal with require input, advice, and policy formation from its elected leadership. The staff for the most part spend little time on campuses and need to rely on a flow of information and insight from leadership. But these long-term issues were not the core of the AAUP's problems. More central still were two critical weaknesses: the organization was out of touch with its members, and the national office had been poorly managed for well more than a decade.

For years the model of member relations in the national office was simple: we send you *Academe* every other month, and you love us for what we do. When the organization set about to redesign its website a decade ago, a debate ensued in the national office about whether the AAUP should add photographs to what was then a text-only site. Happily, those staff members who argued that photographs would demean the organization lost the battle, but efforts to add video have so far failed, though I expect that will change by the time this book is published. Meanwhile, other member-based organizations were ramping up their communication models, increasing member contact by adding regular electronic communication to occasional print mailings and establishing a presence on YouTube. My proposal to create an AAUP recruitment documentary online and on DVD was endorsed by the EC but died in the office.

When I became president in June 2006, the AAUP had only about seven thousand of its forty-four thousand members' email addresses and no plans to collect more. The office stance was, "If the members wanted us to communicate, they'd send their email addresses to us on their own." My reply: "Why would they do that since you show no interest in communicating with them?" This stalemate had persisted for years, with the staff simply ignoring leadership's requests for reform. Luckily, Martin Snyder, the head of the AAUP's Department of External Relations, agreed with me, treated my suggestion as a presidential "order," and directed his staff to collect member emails and establish all the technical protocols for such an effort. Within a year, the national office had most of its members' email addresses and began to communicate twice a month. In the summer of 2007, the AAUP took on a larger project: collecting email addresses from nonmember faculty. I reasoned that if the AAUP did not educate faculty members nationally about what it is and what it does, they would never join. Though a number of staff members disliked the project, I had strong support from the other elected leaders, eager cooperation from the Department of External Relations, and enough grant money to fund a mass email-acquisition project. In September 2007, the AAUP began regularly emailing four hundred thousand faculty members about AAUP work and pressing issues in higher education. Robin Burns did the technical work superbly. The office expects to increase the scope of its email outreach still further. Whether the AAUP can really succeed in rebuilding non-CB membership remains to be seen. Years of neglecting the need to communicate broadly with the professoriate and years of faculty across the country failing to socialize new colleagues will not be repaired overnight, but the organization needs to make the effort.

The failure to communicate extended to organizational elements of AAUP culture as well. Assured in 2007 that the national office's Department of Organizing and Services (DOS) kept impeccable and up-to-date records of chapter leaders and contact information for both CB and non-CB campuses, I sent a membership recruitment offer to all non-CB chapter officers. It was immediately clear that the contact list was deeply flawed. The staff member responsible for doing the work, who has since resigned, had not been supervised by the department head, who in turn had not been supervised by the general secretary. We had no idea whether many of our purported non-CB chapters even existed, let alone who their officers were. For years, the AAUP had casually claimed anywhere from four hundred to eight hundred non-CB chapters. I began making selective calls to campuses. It was clear we actually had no more than 150 living and breathing non-CB chapters, even counting those on fluctuating life support.

Contact with CB chapters was much better but still uneven. There were a few AAUP CB chapters where we had not actually talked to anyone in years and several others where we only talked to one person, a dangerous pattern, since loss of that chapter leader meant the chapter was essentially cut loose. In 2009, the new general secretary, Gary Rhoades, made fixing all this a priority, establishing a contact schedule and a spreadsheet that keeps track of contract negotiations in all AAUP CB chapters. All it took was competent management and a willingness to confront diverse departmental cultures in the national office. If the Committee A staff is unvaryingly bureaucratic, necessarily preoccupied with its files, DOS is entrepreneurial and thus indifferent to mere record keeping.

Meanwhile, by 2005 relations with individual AAUP members had deteriorated as well. A cascade of bad management decisions by more than one general secretary had begun to produce near catastrophic consequences. One general secretary had forced through a decision to hire permanent staff with short-term revenue, thereby building likely overruns into future budgets. A chief financial officer was hired without thoroughly examining his knowledge or qualifications; he proved unable to do the job. When, curious about just how perilous things were, I asked him to specify the difference between petty cash and an endowment fund, he could not do so. An expensive membership processing and billing software program was ordered from an unreliable company over Executive Committee objections. When a new general secretary came on board, the problems only compounded. Personal conflicts between him and the membership director led to a resignation, and the position was not filled as a way to save money. The flawed membership software was never properly tested during installation and eventually proved literally incapable of accurately printing out data that had been entered into it.

By the fall of 2005, the entire membership and finance departments in the national office had disintegrated. Not that the leadership really knew. Members were complaining that their dues payments were not being processed, but the staff assured us this was not true. In fact, staff in the membership office were routinely tossing new membership applications into a large plastic bin, rather than processing them. When they did process them, little care was taken to type in addresses accurately. Chapters complained that they could not obtain current membership rosters, and again their allegations were vigorously denied. Financial record keeping seemed unreliable, but the leadership was unable to prove that until a huge discrepancy between receivables and income (think Enron) surfaced in 2006, outlandish projections for anticipated investment income were budgeted, and outside consultants who ordinarily reported to the general secretary broke routine and contacted the leadership directly to communicate their grave concerns about financial record keeping and reporting. Management claimed that the AAUP had a budget surplus, when it was actually running a deficit. Careful auditing later confirmed there was no fraud, but there was certainly misleading representation of the organization's finances. What this factual account cannot communicate, I should add, was how stressful this period was.

It was not until the end of 2006 that the full scope of the chaos in the office began to become clear. An experienced interim general secretary, Ernst Benjamin, was rapidly brought in then to take charge of the association's finances. The entire staff of both the finance and membership departments was replaced. By fall 2008, both departments were well staffed, and the association's operations were back on track. With the staff members who had bullied the leadership into a bad software purchase no longer employed by the organization, new staff conducted an exceptionally careful and thorough review of software alternatives and selected a new system for purchase. Yet it will not be in place by the time this book is published.

Widespread public recognition that something was wrong with the AAUP did not materialize until the collapse of a planned 2006 conference on academic boycotts, to be held at a retreat in Bellagio, Italy. Leadership had approved the event without being given many details. It was billed simply as a way of broadening international discussion of the AAUP's position against any and all boycotts of academic institutions. The leadership saw the actual funding applications to the Ford Foundation and two other foundations only long after the event imploded. In fact, the grant application had made a specific promise: to hold a conference designed to win international signatories to the AAUP's antiboycott statement. But then the general secretary decided it would be more interesting to turn the event into a debate pitting a number of proboycott Palestinians against an equal number of antiboycott Israelis. Getting endorsements for the AAUP's policy would now be impossible. Neither the leadership nor the foundations were told of the change in plans. The elected leaders learned later that staff were told and that they warned that this new plan could produce a disaster, but their views were swept aside.

The AAUP's elected leaders learned that the conference was disintegrating only from newspaper reports and reporters' phone calls. Public embarrassment escalated when news broke that an essay by a Holocaust denier had been included among background essays distributed to conference attendees. Presented with a pile of essays—some recommended by attendees, some culled from key-word Internet searches, but with their sources unrecorded—the general secretary leafed through the pile and selected background essays without actually reading them, not that it would have required reading beyond the first page to recognize that the essay in question was inappropriate. Indeed the essay's title—"The Jewish Declaration of War on Nazi Germany"—might have prompted a little more curiosity than he manifested.

At that point, the three foundations (Ford, Rockefeller, and Nathan Cummings) asked that the conference be postponed until its purpose could be clarified, hardly an inappropriate request. Choosing not to inform the elected leaders of the foundations' request, the general secretary simply announced on the AAUP's website that the conference would go forward anyway. Again, the AAUP's officers learned about all this from the press. We were not just out of the loop; there was no loop. Acting as vice president, I called a special phone meeting of the Executive Committee; we directed that the conference would be postponed and so informed the foundations. What if any impact the pro-Israeli lobby may have had on the foundations themselves I cannot say. In any case, the Executive Committee was neither concerned about nor interested in those views. We were confronted by an event that had become incoherent. Shortly thereafter, the Italian government decided it could not provide security for a conference that had blossomed into an international scandal and withdrew the right to use the Bellagio retreat. Later, the staff on its own decided to cancel the conference entirely, choosing instead to publish the papers written for it in *Academe,* though the antiboycott participants withdrew their papers, thus compounding the fiasco.

It was clear that the imbalance in the authority of the elected leadership and the staff had to be repaired. We had been informed early in 2006 that the AAUP president had no inherent right to attend any AAUP event; the staff would decide whether to grant permission. During the conflict over the Bellagio conference, the general secretary asserted his right to submit grant applications for new programs without leadership approval. Then he suggested all contacts between elected leaders and staff members should require his prior approval; I observed that the job title appropriate to such responsibilities was "receptionist." *Academe* carried a column by the general secretary each issue, but the previous president had been informed there was no space for her to have one. For years, the president's regular "report" to the National Council was restricted to an account of his or her travel schedule. The president, who had no way whatsoever of addressing AAUP members, was also to make no substantive remarks to the leadership. All that has now been changed.

I also insisted that the Executive Committee renew an older practice of meeting regularly for a day without staff present. This was regarded by several members of the senior professional staff as nothing less than a human rights violation, but the EC had no chance of reasserting its constitutional authority without talking through problems in confidence, building consensus, and gradually bonding as a group. Over a period of half a dozen years, poor management had cost the organization an unnecessary loss of two million dollars. That included roughly five hundred thousand dollars spent on the bad software purchase, interest on the purchase loan, and subsequent payments to the same company seeking software corrections. A still larger sum, over eight hundred thousand dollars, was spent on consultant accountants who helped us gain control over disorganized and unreliable financial records. Proper oversight had to be restored. Other serious issues remain, but I am confident they can be addressed. The culture that dominates the national office and shapes the psychology of some (though not all) key senior staff remains one dedicated to withholding as much information from the elected leaders as possible. That means backsliding remains a possibility if key staff members remain convinced they can wait out the current crop of leaders. There is no common sense of mission in the office, and a number of staff members are routinely exceptionally rude to one another, but in 2009 a new general secretary with the management skills to address these matters began working.

What is remarkable is that through this whole series of trials—and I have by no means described them all—the association for the most part continued to serve the professoriate well. That is partly because most departments in the national office simply ignored bad management and continued to do their jobs despite the meltdown in membership and finance. The AAUP's national, state, and local divisions worked together effectively in defeating conservative efforts to destroy academic freedom in the classroom. The association conducted a powerful investigation of multiple institutions in New Orleans. It regularly joined with other organizations in fighting the Bush administration's efforts to keep foreign scholars out of the country. Faced with academic spillover from the Arab-Israeli conflict, the AAUP fought the effort to boycott Israeli universities and fought for Palestinian students' rights to attend U.S. colleges and universities, displaying a principled evenhandedness unimaginable in many quarters. It crafted special notices supporting the right of faculty and student groups to invite controversial speakers to campus and distributed them in advance of the typically volatile national election season. The AAUP produced its widely read annual survey of faculty salaries on time. It issued new policy documents as needed. It kept up its pressure on the courts to preserve academic freedom and shared governance. It has managed a major project of revising the AAUP's tax status so as to enhance its ability to perform its whole range of activities. This continuing activism is due in part to the presence of a number of very bright, talented, and dedicated people on the national staff and in part to a substantial cadre of member volunteers who work selflessly year after year without remuneration or any reward beyond personal satisfaction. Some of the best staff members are shamelessly overworked, to be sure, because the office has been so poorly managed, but the organization's record of major work accomplished is unbroken. Members trying to pay their dues or make financial contributions may have a very different perception of the organization, but the AAUP's continuing record of impressive accomplishments needs to be recognized nonetheless. Like it or not, there is not one but two rather different stories to be told about the national AAUP: a story about occasional incompetence and a story about impeccable, highly principled professionalism. It is now moving more of its activities from the first to the second category. Major progress is being achieved on all fronts.

Many of the organization's best projects are based on collaboration between staff and leadership. Although I was in charge of basic policy for the large email project, I knew I could leave the many necessary technical decisions to the several hardworking and creative staff members engaged in the effort. When I mandated a confidential review of and recommendations for the restructuring of the AAUP's membership and finance operations, I relied on skilled staff to conduct the review and craft recommendations. A critical core of staff members agree that the organization's long dominance by senior staff needs to be remedied. That process, under way since 2006, is beginning to bear fruit. One of its next challenges will be to review how the AAUP's historic Committee A on Academic Freedom and Tenure and the Department of Academic Freedom, Tenure, and Governance do their work. That is the subject of the next chapter.

[9]

Evolution or Devolution

The Future of the AAUP's Committee A on Academic Freedom and Tenure

If . . . [Beverly Enterprises] had succeeded in its efforts to silence me or gain access to my data, the impact on scholars in every field would have been devastating. That is why AAUP's support for my case was so important not just for me but for academics in general.
—Kate Bronfenbrenner, testimonial for AAUP brochure

When the AAUP was founded by a group of faculty in 1915, there was every expectation that inquiries into violations of academic freedom would be relatively rare. The AAUP's founders were largely from elite universities, including a large number from Johns Hopkins, and by and large they were comfortable with their jobs. They were, to be sure, aware of many general threats to faculty independence, among them the influence of big business on secular higher education that had been growing for decades. Arthur Lovejoy, the association's first president, on the other hand, was well aware that more individually targeted incidents could occur; Lovejoy himself was among the Stanford faculty who resigned in protest when Edward Ross was fired in 1900. Nonetheless, the first priority was to issue a basic statement of principle about the role of the faculty. As I have pointed out earlier, like all such documents that aim to speak to the ages, the famous 1915 Declaration is also marked by its historical moment. Its view of college teaching reflects a more innocent—and still significantly rural—student population. But its definition of faculty interests and responsibilities is as eloquent as anything ever written on the subject.

Matthew Finkin and Robert Post provide an exceptionally helpful account of key ways in which AAUP principles evolved after the 1915

Declaration. The very first AAUP investigation took up the case of a University of Utah faculty member fired after being overheard criticizing the board of trustees. As Finkin and Post point out, "the committee of investigation seized the occasion to expatiate on what it meant for faculty to be 'equal' and 'independent' participants in institutions of higher education" (120). In 1927, a committee investigating the dismissal of a University of Louisville professor who had criticized the president "used the case to develop the rudiments of a theory of intramural speech" (121), that is, speech addressing how the university is run and administered. "By 1933," they add, "the AAUP had come to view intramural expression as a full-fledged form of academic freedom" (123).

Finkin and Post also argue that the 1915 Declaration was "genuinely diffident about extramural speech"—that is, faculty speech in the public arena—giving special warnings to faculty to avoid "unverified or exaggerated statements, and to refrain from intemperate or sensational modes of expression" (128). Even if merely hortatory, this advice sets standards hardly typical of public debate in the United States or elsewhere. Despite years of gradual clarification, it was not until 1970 that the AAUP drew a clear line in the sand: "The controlling principle is that a faculty member's expression of opinion as a citizen cannot constitute grounds for dismissal unless it clearly demonstrates the faculty member's unfitness for the position," namely, by displaying incompetence in the field of his or her teaching and research. Prohibiting punishment for extramural speech, the AAUP now recognizes, is an essential part of preserving independent teaching and research. Once again, investigative reports helped the organization reach this point of clarity.

Exactly how and when the new organization would draw the lines between acceptable and unacceptable faculty and administration behavior and how it would develop rationales for doing this also remained to be seen. That would require more detailed explanation; the concept of academic freedom itself would have to be elaborated and tested against specific practices. An unanticipated series of investigations provided the occasion for that critical process of clarification. There was no staff to speak of in the AAUP's first years. Indeed, as late as the mid-1950s, the AAUP had only three people in its national office, though at that point members themselves were clamoring to increase staff so that the organization could take on more work (Hutcheson). So the AAUP's early investigations were faculty conceived, faculty run, and faculty written. Through the end of the 1940s, in fact, AAUP policy was largely developed by way of investigations. Then for six years in the midst of the McCarthy period, fearful of reprisals and understaffed, the association conducted no investigations at all (Hutcheson; Schrecker, *No Ivory Tower*). Thereafter, it began to enlarge the staff, growth further facilitated by steady increases in membership through the 1960s. By the 1970s, the AAUP had accumulated enough investigative reports to set a pattern of which sorts of violations of academic freedom and tenure it would pursue, if necessary, all the way to censure. Less and less was the organization feeling its way toward its priorities. Increasingly, the operative logic was that of precedent: the AAUP would emphasize doing largely what it had done before. At the same time, the enlarged staff began to handle a large number of faculty inquiries that could be resolved by letter and phone call. There was thus a natural evolution toward the staff's deciding which of the unresolvable complaints should develop into full-blown cases and formal investigations. Faculty would still form investigative teams, but much of the hard work was by then already accomplished, and the staff had already drawn the key conclusions. Indeed, there have been periodic complaints when the views of the faculty investigative team have been overruled by staff.

As investigations became staff controlled, faculty retained a major role in shaping association policy, but they did so by reversing their documentary priorities. The faculty appointees to the organization's Committee A on Academic Freedom and Tenure, selected from AAUP members around the country by the president after receiving staff and leadership input, would identify emerging problems and appoint subcommittees to draft new policy statements in response. In other words, policy documents became the leading edge of evolving association principles. Some members began to perceive investigative priorities as inflexible as a result. Indeed, reading through the AAUP's distinguished set of policy statements—popularly known as the *Redbook*—would not give the uninitiated reader much of a hint about which violations the AAUP would and would not seek to police. The only way to make such an analysis would be to read through the recent history of investigative reports and to assume that the organization would doggedly continue doing what it already had been doing. Since all specific violations were treated as potential cases and investigations—even though barely half a dozen of the hundreds of inquiries received each year actually reached that point—the staff became by default responsible for the organization's public statements on incidents of wide professional interest. On occasion, the staff gives the members of Committee A the opportunity to review and comment on news releases addressing controversial issues. But appropriate statements are often never issued. One of my aims in running for AAUP president was to find ways of making the association more responsive to events in real time. Too many faculty members compare the AAUP unfavorably to FIRE (the Foundation for Individual Rights in Education), which has a legal staff focused on gathering information and reacting quickly, a terrain in which the AAUP will never be able to compete fully but in which it should do better than it does. FIRE has, for example, done very fine work in publicizing campus speech codes that violate constitutional rights.

As many faculty members know, I preinaugurated my presidency of the American Association of University Professors when the then-current president, Jane Buck, and I were arrested at New York University in April 2006 as part of a demonstration on behalf of NYU's graduate-student employees. Some staff members in the AAUP's national office in Washington, DC, strongly endorsed the action, while a few others were fearful the organization would lose thousands of members in protest. That anxiety proved unwarranted. But a more serious objection was also raised: would the AAUP's ability to conduct an impartial Committee A investigation of NYU be imperiled if two AUUP presidents dramatically signaled where they stood as individuals? Although I made it clear at the time that I would recuse myself from any decision about an NYU investigation, some staff nonetheless still felt that the AAUP's quasi-judicial stance of investigative objectivity would be compromised.

The issue is fundamental: when and how will the AAUP speak out about challenges to its principles? When staff members dealing with a case conclude that an exceptionally clear violation of AAUP rules has occurred, they often themselves announce the organization's "concern" (a decorous term designed to fall far short of explicit condemnation) about the alleged offense, typically in very measured language and in a letter to the campus parties involved. The language the staff uses, it is worth recognizing, may vary according both to the nature of the offense and the style of the staff member handling the case. Some staff members write more forceful letters than others, but staff members, as employees, have reason to be cautious in their public statements. Often this "concern" becomes public when one of the recipients exercises his or her right to make the staff letter public, sometimes by placing it on a website or by distributing it to the press.

Oddly enough, the staff will typically not publicize such a case letter—say, by placing it on the national AAUP website or by emailing it to AAUP members or other faculty—even if it has already been made public by its recipients. In the staff's view, the organization has thereby maintained its neutrality and objectivity. But faculty members nationwide have no idea that the national office operates with such a protocol. The main effect of this policy is that faculty members often think the AAUP has not done anything in a case even if it has acted. In my view, the national office should be able to say, "The recipients have elected to make this letter public; we are therefore distributing it to other interested parties." The national office does, however, issue statements on public matters that are not the subject of complaints or case files, though it does so far less frequently than I believe it should.

Even with complaints that have become cases, however, it should be possible to make public statements on a selective basis. Making strong public statements is a role more typically taken on by elected leaders in membership-based organizations, though many AAUP presidents have deferred to the staff. My own view is that an AAUP leader can legitimately make a still stronger statement about a violation of AAUP principles so long as a strict firewall is maintained—on a case-by-case basis—between the leader making the statement and the staff members directly responsible for handling a case, so long as the leader does not participate in making key decisions about that particular case, and so long as the faculty member or graduate student involved does not object.

It is also important to realize that long-term AAUP staff develop areas of expertise, significant national constituencies, and expectations for public advocacy that also make it difficult and politically counterproductive for them to remain silent about particular campus incidents. So staff, in consultation with the general secretary, who is the employee responsible for supervising the national office, also need to be able to speak forthrightly when violations of academic freedom touch their areas of responsibility. Simply listing the titles of some AAUP committees suggests how the employees staffing them might be expected to respond to grievances in those areas: Academic Professionals; College and University Governance; Community Colleges; Contingent Faculty; Graduate and Professional Students; Historically Black Institutions and Scholars of Color; Sexual Diversity and Gender Identity; Women in the Academic Profession.

Grievances about academic freedom, shared governance, and employment relevant to these constituencies and all others are handled by the staff members in the AAUP's historic Department of Academic Freedom, Tenure, and Governance (its name hereafter shortened). That department officially staffs Committee A, which is composed of association members appointed by the president, but the in-house staff has for many years so efficiently managed the entire investigation process that a conventional, if confusing, shorthand has come to refer to the staff itself as Committee A. As a 2008 confidential internal report about the operations of the department, quoted here with permission, noted, "While it is possible to see the blurring of member and staff designations in this instance as a sort of benign shorthand, it can also be seen as symptomatic of a failure to understand and honor the separate and appropriate roles of the two groups." Although I take note of the recent evolution of Committee A, this chapter is not a history of it or an account of its many accomplishments. It is rather an account of how its talented staff operates now and a series of suggestions about how its departmental practices might be revised to better serve the profession. At no point, therefore, am I concerned with or seeking to evaluate the performance of individual staff members, all of whom are genuinely dedicated to their work. My focus is on the culture of the office and of the department at issue. My aim is thus not only to help faculty members across the country become better informed about how Committee A and its staff make decisions but also to initiate wide discussion of how that process might be updated and adapted to a changing world.

Returning to my opening example will help demonstrate, however, that these decisions can be quite complicated. Adjudicating the relative roles for staff and leadership action in response to events at NYU involved issues of timing, impact, authority, and organizational politics. I was convinced the AAUP would never formally investigate NYU, either for its withdrawal of graduate employees' bargaining rights or its threats to fire those who went on strike. Although the AAUP's National Council had affirmed the right of all employee groups, including graduate-student employees, to engage in collective bargaining in 1998—and although the United Nations recognizes such action as a basic human right—the AAUP has never actually censured an institution for refusing bargaining rights to an employee group. The AAUP's Recommended Institutional Regulations (RIRs), a set of fundamental practices that the organization seeks to advocate and enforce, which are distinguished from AAUP statements that are primarily advisory, were not clear and detailed enough on graduate-employee due process rights and protection against retaliation for job actions. I made it a priority to encourage updating RIR number 14, the one dealing with graduate-student employees, and *Academe* has now published a revised RIR 14 for comments ("Graduate Student Employees"). Formal adoption will follow. It lays out more detailed due process rights for graduate-student employees, explicitly protects those on strike, and shifts the burden of proof to the administration in cases of dismissal midcontract, all matters relevant to NYU's conduct.

Had Jane Buck and I chosen to do nothing, then, the AAUP as a national organization would effectively have remained silent on NYU's distinctive abridgement of AAUP principles, distinctive in part because NYU's president used a new National Labor Relations Board ruling to justify withdrawing bargaining rights after first granting them and then negotiating a first contract. The Executive Committee of the AAUP's Collective Bargaining Congress might have issued a statement criticizing the NYU administration, but that would have had less force on its own, since it might have been seen as one union simply supporting another (NYU graduate students are represented by the United Auto Workers). The AAUP presidency likewise would have remained a mute and irrelevant office. That was precisely what some members of the national staff considered appropriate and necessary; they viewed it as their exclusive right to make public statements on such events as those at NYU. Buck and

I disagreed with that view. And so did the staff members who strongly endorsed our action.

Those staff members who objected to our actions generally made the argument that organizational silence about potential cases is the price the AAUP pays for the high regard in which its final published investigative reports are held. If, however, one reads through a number of investigative reports, all of which are published in *Academe* and all of which are now available from the national office on a searchable CD-ROM, an alternative explanation readily comes to mind: that these reports are respected because they are incredibly thorough and persuasive. In other words, the superb staff work that goes into them pays off in the way they are received. Predictably, readers of AAUP reports are more focused on content than on process. That tendency is enhanced by a tradition of looking beyond the immediate facts of a violation to ask broader questions: How have the incidents reported affected both the individuals directly involved and the general character of campus life? How characteristic are they of the campus administrative style? The result can be a report that becomes a compelling narrative.

One could argue, on the other hand, that it is the quasi-judicial detachment characteristic of the process that brings some administrations to the table and makes them willing to negotiate changes in campus practices. Again, it may instead be more to the point to say that the care and accuracy with which evidence is presented has more of a role in carrying the day. Moreover, no matter what procedures the staff adopts, there is little they can do to alter the fact and perception that the organization is an advocacy group. When the AAUP's tax status changes from being a public charity to being a professional organization, that perception will be reinforced, though it will at the same time be putting further distance between Committee A's professional activities and the AAUP's collective bargaining efforts. In the end, however, the effectiveness of the threat of censure is partly a function of how much power the organization is perceived as wielding. If AAUP membership were to be dramatically expanded, it is likely that still more administrations would be willing to negotiate to avoid censure. The cultural authority the organization embodies has always exceeded its size, but the two are not unrelated. There is, of course, another issue at stake in the decision about when and how to act: who should shape the AAUP's public face, the members and their elected representatives, the staff, or all these groups together?

A more recent case suggests other complications concerning staff and leadership roles. When in June 2007 Antioch University's board of trustees announced the closure of Antioch College in Yellow Springs, Ohio, the only residential campus among the university's six campuses, the college faculty asked the AAUP for assistance. Antioch faculty members asserted, and the AAUP's report confirms, that, contrary to AAUP rules, financial exigency had been declared with no faculty consultation and no opportunity for faculty to propose less drastic alternatives ("Report—College and University Government: Antioch University and the Closing of Antioch College"). As an Antioch College graduate and the spouse of a dissenting member of the Antioch University board of trustees, I was obviously an interested party. This time also I recused myself from any decision about whether an investigation should be initiated. I wrote two brief essays about Antioch, one for the *Chronicle of Higher Education* and one for *Inside Higher Education*. Studiously avoiding criticism of the university's board of trustees or the university administration, I wrote about my undergraduate educational experience there and about the significance of Antioch to the liberal arts tradition. Months later, after the AAUP staff wrote a letter urging the board of trustees to give full consideration to offers to help save the college, I published an open letter in *Inside Higher Education* reinforcing that position in my own words. After the decision to launch an investigation was announced, I wrote a short, requested comment for *Teacher's College Record* addressing the significance of the loss of the college. In October 2008, I gave a public lecture about higher education in Yellow Springs during a festival week organized by former Antioch faculty and students. The following month, I keynoted an Antioch-alumni-sponsored symposium at Harvard University entitled "Reinventing Liberal Arts Education for the 21st Century: Promising Directions." No one at Harvard addressed Antioch's actions in closing the college. Indeed, several speakers made it clear they were not familiar with events at Antioch; they were there to present their research on the future of liberal arts institutions. Others at the symposium summarized the efforts by former Antioch faculty to create a new enterprise in Yellow Springs, the "Nonstop Liberal Arts Institute."

I spoke about threats to academic freedom nationwide and about how liberal arts traditions and ideals provide a model for resisting them. It is something I have talked about across the country. Yet the Committee A staff became intensely concerned, feeling that my being associated with Nonstop in any way undermined the appearance of AAUP objectivity. Antioch University, I might note, denied Nonstop the right to use college property or the Antioch name but otherwise lodged no objections to the enterprise, preferring to pretend it did not exist. The president of the AAUP chapter at nearby Wright State University in Dayton, Ohio, had already written a letter to Wright State's president urging him to offer Nonstop temporary accreditation. Committee A staff members, however, argued that, since the thirty-dollar conference registration fee would go to support Nonstop faculty salaries, it could present the appearance of bias. I argued that these faculty members, many of them tenured, had lost their jobs after the AAUP's principles and procedures were not followed. They were now conducting a courageous and impressive, community-based educational experiment in the best traditions of liberal arts education. The AAUP should be proud to support them. If the AAUP cannot support an innovative educational experiment and help faculty who have unjustly lost their jobs, it is hard to see why faculty nationwide should support the organization.

Again, while my Antioch-related activities caused consternation among some staff members, others supported me. Some remain convinced that I should have remained silent about both NYU and Antioch. I often respond—only partly in jest—that I did not run for AAUP president either in order to lose my academic freedom or to cede my presidential responsibility to represent faculty interests and AAUP values. Yet I realize I am not a free agent, and I try to gauge my actions accordingly.

In both the NYU and Antioch incidents, I was frequently responding to faculty and student requests for action on my part (not only by those directly concerned). In both instances—because I am AAUP president—I evaluated requests and turned down more than I accepted. My public statements about NYU were blunt, because I knew the AAUP would not open an investigation. About Antioch, I was obviously very active, but I was also more circumspect. In contrast, Paula Treichler's essay in *Inside Higher Education*, "Antioch: Report from Ground Zero," is detailed and explicit in reporting on and evaluating the actions of Antioch University's chancellor and board of trustees. In response to the AAUP staff's concern about my Antioch roles, I agreed to expand the range of my recusal. I had already remained mute on the basic decision to investigate; I agreed that I would not see any Antioch-related memoranda or reports until drafts were distributed to Antioch faculty and administrators. The whole incident may now demonstrate the AAUP's ability to combine measured leadership advocacy with a full investigation.

These examples raise a more general concern about how the AAUP can balance its dual identities as both a quasi-judicial body and an advocacy organization. That question bears regularly on Committee A investigations. The staff for Committee A largely believes the AAUP's judicial work must be rigorously isolated from (and have priority over) its advocacy activities. I contend that it is not quite that simple. Although the staff should not be repeatedly pestered by AAUP members to pursue a particular case, members do need to be able to make a case for action, elected leaders do need ways of obtaining input, and staff do need direction about the profession's most urgent needs. Not all Committee A staff members have recent experience as faculty members or of daily life on today's campuses. Occasional visits cannot equal the knowledge of the contemporary university held by the AAUP's leaders and members. A dialogue with actively engaged members and leaders is critical if the AAUP is to remain relevant and effective.

That dialogue can take several different forms. As president, I regularly exchange information with Committee A staff, and I review case files when matters gain national attention or when specific faculty ask me for assistance. But I do not argue with individual Committee A staff for the investigation or resolution of particular cases. I do have detailed conversations with the general secretary, which is a necessary and appropriate way for me to represent faculty interests to the Committee A staff. Recently, when two nationally publicized incidents gained public attention—events surrounding Ward Churchill at the University of Colorado and Norman Finkelstein at DePaul University in Chicago—I argued to the general secretary that it was important for the AAUP to address them.

Actions taken against both were politically inflected, and faculty across the country needed to hear the AAUP express concern about political interference with academic freedom. Staff members themselves certainly recognized that they should protest Colorado politicians' early efforts to bully the university into punishing Churchill, and they issued an effective February 2005 statement to that effect. In doing so, the staff were not situated "above politics," to cite one common claim about AAUP work; they were appropriately engaged in politics in defense of academic freedom. Nor was the staff exhibiting transcendent agency when it issued yet another Churchill case letter in March 2005, congratulating the university for not initiating a politically guided investigation into Churchill's extramural statements. I consider that letter ill conceived and misguided, even if it was designed to be cautionary, since it gives the university credit it did not deserve and provides advance cover for the politically motivated investigation to follow. Indeed, it suggests that the AAUP is more than ready to endorse sham due process if it has the formal appearance the organization demands.

Once the University of Colorado initiated its own inquiry into Churchill's scholarship and selected a faculty review committee, however, the issues did become more complicated. The AAUP then probably had to await the result of the faculty investigation. Conversely, most of the issues remained clear in Finkelstein's case, among them the DePaul University administration's inappropriate decision to apply an independent criterion of collegiality to his writing, the belated demand that he display Vincentian standards for interaction, and the denial of his appeal rights.

According to the Committee A department head at the time, only Finkelstein, not Churchill, actually asked us to investigate, though Churchill disputes that account. What is absolutely clear from communications sent by Natsu Taylor Saito, who is Churchill's wife and an attorney who was serving as his legal representative to the national office, is that both Churchills believed they were requesting an investigation every time they sent letters and documents to the AAUP office in Washington, DC. Thus, a September 5, 2006, letter from Saito to general secretary Roger Bowen and Department of Academic Freedom head Jonathan Knight, quoted here with Saito's permission, concludes, "As noted in our previous communication, we appreciate the statement issued by the AAUP early

in this process, as well as your longstanding defense of academic freedom, and hope that you will be willing to investigate the many breaches
of faculty rights, due process, and academic freedom involved in this
case." The national office never requested anything more explicit from
the Churchills, but then their wishes were entirely clear. Alan Jones, vice
president and dean of faculty at Pitzer College in California, who was also
assisting Churchill with his case, participated in phone conferences with
the general secretary and the head of the Department of Academic Freedom; he has told me clearly that he believed the staff was moving toward
an investigation. Certainly in Saito's communications with Jones as well,
which have been shared with me, she urged him to stress the Churchills'
desire to see a full investigation take place when he talked with the general secretary. The issue also arose in a group phone conference between
the Churchills, Jones, and the AAUP staff. The record is clear. There is
no way either the general secretary or the staff member handling the case
could not have realized the Churchills were requesting an investigation.
Committee A was misled.

What is less clear is *why* the faculty members on Committee A were
told Churchill had never requested an investigation. Some detail about
how the Churchill case proceeded does help contextualize the matter.
Ordinarily, the full committee receives only brief updates about cases
that may lead to investigations. The actual decision to investigate is made
during a staff conference, with the chair of Committee A (a faculty member appointed by the president) and the AAUP president participating by
phone. Because the Churchill case was a national issue, however, the full
committee discussed it at length, both in face-to-face conversations and
by email. After the first detailed report was issued in Colorado, the committee became deeply divided. Reasonable people can and do consider
some of the evidence against Churchill persuasive. Thus, even those who
do not consider plagiarism an appropriate term for what he did may well
find that ghostwriting an essay and then citing it later as if it were scholarship by others supporting your own position is completely unacceptable.
The committee was not, moreover, in possession of the usual clear recommendation from the staff, until a detailed August 2007 staff memo was
distributed, arguing that there was no reason to act on Churchill's behalf.
That memo did not fully silence debate. Thus, I believe the decision was

made to misrepresent the facts to the committee so as to settle the issue by making the question of investigation moot. Presumably it was an ends-justify-means decision, but it is disturbing nonetheless.

Except in very rare instances, as when Angela Davis was a fugitive and could not be reached (she later read the draft report from jail), the AAUP staff does not intervene directly in an individual faculty member's situation unless he or she asks for help, though national press coverage can, in effect, mandate public expressions of the AAUP's concern and certainly can justify the AAUP's writing to an administration. It is worth noting that, unlike the AAUP, the Canadian Association of University Teachers will grieve an injustice whether or not a faculty member asks it to; it views such interventions as protecting rights and principles for everyone. The national AAUP, unfortunately, in my view did not fully engage with the issues in Finkelstein's case once it did intervene, addressing only the denial of his appeal rights; the statewide AAUP organization in Illinois issued a more effective letter. And once Committee A was told that Churchill had not requested an investigation, the issue of a traditional investigation was settled.

But there are actions available short of a full investigation. Though, for example, the AAUP should ordinarily not launch a formal investigation into an unresolved matter against a faculty member's wishes—a situation that often occurs when a faculty member is represented in collective bargaining and the union wants to grieve the case—the AAUP can comment publicly on those factual elements of a case that are not in dispute. It can also comment on the general issues that are at stake and that reflect fundamental AAUP policies. That is what I sought to do in speaking very briefly about the 2009 case of University of California at Santa Barbara sociology professor William Robinson when *Inside Higher Education* interviewed me about it (Jaschik, "Crossing"). Robinson, who was eventually cleared by the university, had been accused by the Santa Barbara chapter of the Anti-Defamation League of intimidating his students in a Globalization course by sending them an email offering "parallel images of Nazis and Israelis." I pointed out that "historical comparisons are protected by academic freedom, whether or not they are endorsed by a majority of other scholars, even if the analogies are debatable, provocative, or reprehensible." There are times when AAUP silence reflects procedural schizophrenia, as when Committee A members or staff argue that we should remain forever mute on a case that involves fundamental principles and has been fully resolved. The idea that the AAUP should not speak about a case it was not involved in—even if the case has had (or may have) an impact on national standards for academic freedom—is both irresponsible and irrational. The organization is the major source of principled standards on academic freedom; it has a responsibility to address prominent cases.

The Churchill affair took yet another turn in April 2009, when a Colorado jury in a civil case decided the university had fired him for political reasons. In the immediate aftermath of the verdict, I did not hear any mandarin contempt for this jury of six Americans from my faculty contacts, though I assumed correctly it would be safe to hold my breath while waiting. What the verdict suggests, at the very least, is that when all the academic rationalizations, self-justifications, and self-congratulations are stripped away, the political character of the case stands bare. Given that the university president was always determined to fire him—and thus that Churchill's termination was unequivocally fruit of the poisoned tree of political outrage that prompted the whole process—the jury's verdict was sound. At the same time, the monetary award for damages, merely one dollar, may well represent the jury's own punishment for Churchill's "little Eichmanns" analogy, as well as their recognition that he sought vindication, not money.

The day before the jury verdict, former general secretary Roger Bowen published a letter in the *Wall Street Journal* acknowledging his contacts with Saito but offering his own opinion that "portions of Mr. Churchill's scholarship were dishonest." Not that Bowen ever had the courage to say that to the Churchills. Stanley Fish, on the other hand, published a witty and pointed column in the *New York Times* on April 5 that endorsed the jury's decision and argued, in my view correctly, that the rhetoric and accusations in the case were typical of scholarly disputes and should have continued to be addressed in scholarly debates, not referred to a disciplinary committee. The disciplinary process was, he concludes, "a circus that should have never come to town" ("Ward Churchill Redux"). Asked to comment, I said much the same that day and urged that Churchill be reappointed. The NAS predictably issued a press release decrying the jury verdict. On April 7, the AAUP's National Council approved the following resolution, which I had issued in the first person but which the National Council then revised by using "we" instead of "I": "We believe the disputes over Ward Churchill's publications should have been allowed to work themselves out in traditional scholarly venues, not referred to disciplinary hearings. We believe Churchill should be reinstated to his faculty position at the University of Colorado."

Actual admiration for Churchill was in very short supply in the substantial online National Council discussion about the resolution, but there was frequent distress at the political triggering of the process and its elements of bias. The council was persuaded that Churchill had not received adequate due process. Questions about the conclusions reached by the University of Colorado committees were also raised, such as whether "plagiarism" was an appropriate designation for citing an essay you had ghost-written yourself. Many Committee A members explicitly distanced themselves from his "little Eichmanns" remark but reiterated that the AAUP defends faculty members' rights whether or not they exercise them in ways people admire. The National Council was also aware that this could well be the AAUP's last opportunity to intervene in the case before the issue of his reinstatement was decided.

Some of the more senior consultants to Committee A could not understand why the press of external events should influence the AAUP's actions. They felt the National Council should not have spoken. Most of the Committee A staff in the national office agreed, believing also that Committee A, intricately guided by staff, should be the final arbiter of all academic freedom issues. But the AAUP's constitution gives the National Council the authority to act if it chooses. From time to time, in fact, it has chosen to send Committee A a message. Thus, after the president of the University of South Florida (USF) announced at a board of trustees meeting that she was planning to fire pro-Palestinian professor Sami Al-Arian without a hearing, the AAUP sent a committee there immediately and convinced her to place him on paid leave. Committee A issued a detailed and compelling investigative report but declined to recommend censure or any other formal action to the National Council and the annual meeting. Committee A did "condemn" USF's actions in a different document, its overall annual report, and the National Council then on its own recommended that the USF administration instead be formally condemned; the annual meeting proceeded to do so ("Report of Committee A").

Certainly the AAUP's debates about a particular case are often contentious. At the June 2004, 2005, and 2006 annual AAUP meetings, there was strong sentiment for censuring Medaille College, a small, career-oriented liberal arts college in Buffalo, New York. Faculty there had been dismissed without sufficient cause and without appropriate due process. A detailed published report had helped fuel anger in the New York State Conference of AAUP chapters. Once the individual faculty cases were settled, a clear majority of the Medaille faculty preferred to withhold censure and to use the threat of censure to win better protections in their faculty handbook. Both the members of Committee A and the staff agreed, but some of those attending the meeting argued vigorously for censure. The elected leadership supported the Committee A stand, and censure action was postponed.

Despite this kind of evidence of leadership support for sound staff judgments, for some years, certainly predating my presidency, candidates for the general secretary position have been asked a significant question by one or two staff members in the national office: "Can you protect us from the elected leadership?" Now and again, a staff member has suggested that this is the general secretary's main responsibility. My strong preference, in contrast, is for a working partnership with the staff, a partnership that should include thinking together about Committee A's priorities.

Many active AAUP leaders and members are haunted by cases that the AAUP failed to pursue. For me, it is the case of a contingent faculty member with more than twenty years of full-time service at the University of Kansas, Fred Whitehead. There were no complaints about his work, which included major student advising responsibilities, and he had a distinguished publication record. He was fired in June 2000—just five years before he would have been eligible for retirement—without cause or due process, and the AAUP did not adequately defend him, despite the organization's official objections to long-term full-time faculty service off the tenure track. The staff did write letters on his behalf, one of which produced an insulting offer from the University of Kansas to provide him with what amounted to a clerk's job. To add additional humiliation to this "offer," he was prohibited from having any papers pertaining to his scholarly research on his new desk. Whitehead refused and asked the AAUP to pursue the case further. My own view is that the AAUP had sufficient warrant to launch a full investigation and pursue it to censure if necessary. The staff differed. Contingent faculty were not a priority. The historic RIR number 13 that the AAUP's Committee A approved in November 2006 has remedied this flaw for part-time faculty, but as long as I live I will never rest easy about Fred Whitehead's case. He will never receive justice. The AAUP will never publicly address his case. And despite the organization's historic convictions about peer review, it was not faculty members but AAUP staffers who decided his fate. Although I was not yet AAUP president, I was in contact with Whitehead because he had edited two books for my American Poetry Recovery Series at the University of Illinois Press. His case was an opportunity for the AAUP to defend those full-time contingent faculty who spend their careers without any job security, and it was an opportunity to do so at a flagship state university. It was a clear case where an individual injustice meshed perfectly with a broad professional priority. But the staff did not see it, and the general secretary was nowhere to be found. Understanding that telling his story was the only way to get the truth on record, Whitehead has summarized it in a *Workplace* essay and given a detailed account in a self-published book, *KU Confidential*.

A case with deeper historical resonance came up in 2004. That year Native American faculty at Bacone College in Oklahoma contacted the national office alleging a pattern of academic freedom and shared governance violations by the president, the dean of faculty, and the president's special assistant. The papers filed with the national office, however, focused on the stories of two individual Native American faculty, both of whom either had settled with Bacone by then or were about to do so. It is a little-known Committee A staff practice not to take up individual faculty grievances that have been settled; if a complaint is settled in medias res, the AAUP drops it, since there is no additional remedy available for the faculty member involved. Since the "remedies" the AAUP obtains are often negligible, this policy should probably be revised. Although there were indications in the Bacone file that additional faculty were at risk and that shared governance issues were involved, the staff was viewing the file through its preferred lens of violations against individual faculty who seek redress. Communications among all parties fell short of the clarity needed. Staff requests for more information went unanswered. Unknown to the staff, a broad overview of patterns at Bacone, nearly seven thousand words in length ("A Resolution for Condemnation of Bacone College's Senior Administrators and Board of Trustees"), had been written by Native American faculty and submitted to the Oklahoma State Conference of AAUP chapters with the understanding that it would be forwarded to the AAUP office in Washington, DC. It never arrived. I do not believe it was ever sent. Full documentation to support the wider faculty allegations in the report thus also never arrived, but the report itself is now available online at http://cary-nelson.org/nelson/Academic-FreedomIssues/bacone-college-faculty-report.pdf.

Although not every department in the AAUP's national office can boast flawless record keeping, the Department of Academic Freedom is invariably efficient and bureaucratic. It has no choice. There is no other way to manage the hundreds of new requests for assistance received each year, along with those files from past years that are still active. It is inconceivable that the department would have misplaced the Bacone report. The staff member in charge first saw it after I sent it to him in 2008. What appears to have happened, based on interviews I conducted in 2008, is that the Oklahoma state conference official responsible for mailing the 2004 report was getting cold feet about supporting the Bacone faculty allegations—for fear, so my Oklahoma colleagues suggested, that the litigious Bacone president would sue the state conference if it became involved. We will never know for certain. Nor will we ever know how large a role another local motivation played: keeping the national office uninformed so that an ambitious Oklahoma AAUP member could build a power base around complaints about national AAUP "inaction." There were certainly current Native American Bacone faculty whose jobs were in peril in 2004. Yet even if the AAUP had received documentation about their cases, the price of investigating them individually would have been high. Bacone faculty were convinced the president would have fired them immediately. The only real option for Bacone was a governance investigation, something that could have kept the names of both current and former Bacone faculty confidential, but the staff is reluctant to do governance investigations. From June 2007 to May 2008, AAUP staff acted on only one governance complaint—from faculty at Antioch College.

Except for occasional vague references to Bacone from members elsewhere in Oklahoma, including some serving on the AAUP's National Council, I knew little about the Bacone case. I became involved when I was scheduled to visit Oklahoma in February 2008. In preparation, I asked Oklahoma leaders for background information and received the detailed report I have mentioned. It was then that I found to my surprise that staff in DC had never seen it. I spent some hours with Native American faculty that winter and invited them to update the AAUP's files with events since 2004. They have done so. By the time I arrived in Oklahoma, some forty-seven Native American faculty and staff had been dismissed or driven to resign. Numerous Native American students have also withdrawn, sometimes because the Bacone administration was billing them for fees they were never told about. The assault on Native American students, faculty, and staff amounts to another historic example of Native American removal. Founded in 1885, Bacone is the oldest Native American institution of higher education in continuous operation in the state. It is being stripped of its historic mission. Though former Bacone faculty members are now dispersed and fact gathering is thus even more daunting, I nonetheless await the possibility of AAUP action before the last Cherokee at Bacone is gone.

As the Kansas and Oklahoma examples make clear, cases can have many complications. Decisions about whether to launch an investigation are by no means simple. Respecting that, I nonetheless argue that what Committee A needs is sunlight and policy revision. By sunlight, I mean that these decisions should not be insulated but should take place in dialogue with other staff in the national office and with leaders who are elected to represent members' interests. Committee A staff conduct too much work in seclusion, deaf to alternative views. Over time, the Committee A staff is trained to conform to a single ideology. But there are other reasons why these decisions need wider input. It is fundamentally unfair to the staff members themselves to expect so few of them to make decisions with broad repercussions. Moreover, it is often the general secretary and the elected leaders who end up defending those decisions.

Policy revision can make it much clearer to all parties what AAUP policy enforcement responsibilities should be.

The important revisions of RIRs 13 and 14 do exactly that. They were initiated, respectively, by the Contingent and Graduate committees and then negotiated with the Committee A staff and members. One could imagine a version of the "can you protect us" stance that would lead staff to conclude that both RIR revisions constituted "intrusions" into the work of the staff, since each revision had implications for the daily work that staff members do and the kinds of cases that the organization might pursue to a full investigation. Yet each revised RIR represents an evolution of existing AAUP policies and priorities, not a revolutionary change. They are further specifications of how due process and academic freedom are to be secured for contingent faculty and graduate-student employees. Though initiated by members, both revised RIRs eventually reflected staff-leadership collaboration; at some point in the process, the staff role is facilitation, not resistance, and staff must accept the regulations and act on them. The revised RIRs are also fundamentally responses to a changing profession, one that has massively shifted teaching from tenure-track to contingent employees.

Some staff, as I suggested earlier, argue that they must be insulated from politics, indeed be *above* politics, as though lodged in an Olympian world of changeless conditions and principles. But though the principle of academic freedom may remain unchanged, the real-world challenges it faces change all the time. These changes confront the AAUP with political necessities—not political in a narrow or partisan sense but in the broad sense of the social forces and institutions that shape faculty lives. Neither Committee A staff nor anyone else can be protected from politics thus construed. Attention to the political pressures that can transform, improve, or undermine higher education is a good and necessary thing.

As I mentioned earlier, the AAUP is often criticized for being slow in responding to events. In truth, its very careful and thorough policy development and investigative practices are about as efficient as they can be if they are to maintain their quality. But there are also occasions when rapid and public response or intervention is appropriate, as with the Churchill and Finkelstein examples and, I believe, with the situation with Antioch, though what the AAUP could say in each of these instances was very different. Sometimes the AAUP may need to opt for aggressive advocacy and forgo an investigation. On other occasions, some negotiated balance between the two alternatives may be possible.

Rapid real-time public advocacy requires the facts to be clear. In many individual faculty complaints, they are not. The AAUP has learned from long experience that individual narratives of events can be misleading. Some faculty members do not understand their own campus regulations, let alone AAUP policies. Like all human beings, faculty may also give accounts that exclusively embody their own perceptions and interests; thus, the AAUP requests input from all parties.

At the same time, cases sometimes hinge not on individual testimony but on documents. In the Finkelstein case, the key documents were publicly available early on. In the Churchill case, it took months for the AAUP to obtain the final faculty report; that delayed what response the organization could make. Antioch may present a unique example: an immense archive of public and confidential documents relevant to the closure decision (over five thousand pages) is online and publicly available on a series of websites, most notably The Antioch Papers (www.theantiochpapers.org). When the major evidence is widely available and the case has national implications, it would seem that the voice of the AAUP could be heard promptly.

Can the AAUP take firm stands on such occasions without the appearance of bias? Obviously the organization does have a preexisting stance in favor of its carefully articulated, published principles. Applying them is not evidence of bias. The cases of unambiguous violations are more likely to result in the AAUP's version of conviction and sentencing, which is the publication of an investigative report and a vote to censure by those faculty members attending the June annual meeting. One thing the AAUP does do to preserve objectivity is to separate directly involved political leadership from investigative committees. As president, I could not possibly serve on an NYU or Antioch investigating committee. Nor are the members of an investigation committee—typically tenured faculty from different institutions—likely to live in fear of AAUP leaders who have expressed an opinion about a case. In fact, by the time a faculty investigative team visits a campus, a thorough and careful staff investigation has already occurred. The staff have gathered documents and testimony and written a case overview. The faculty investigating the campus receive that overview, along with detailed, annotated appointment schedules. Often they are there largely to test what amount to provisional conclusions.

Formal investigations of violations of academic freedom and tenure are thus fundamentally staff supervised and structured. That is not the case with AAUP policy statements, which are typically initiated by faculty members and written by ad hoc faculty committees or subcommittees. Such committees are usually staffed by a member of the national staff, and the policy statement will eventually be widely discussed (and modified as necessary) by additional faculty and staff, but the document itself is largely the work product of faculty members appointed to the committee. Within Committee A, therefore, there are two fundamentally different activities—investigation and policy creation—with two different groups (staff or faculty) in charge. Because policy documents may be supported by staff research and are modified through discussion and debate, they end up being excellent examples of collaboration between staff and members. A third kind of document—reports on issues of interest—can be jointly authored from the outset. But investigative reports that lead to censure, far more than most faculty realize, are staff projects, often, though not always, with more limited faculty input.

The two efforts—producing policy recommendations and investigating institutions that fail to honor those policies the AAUP considers enforceable—are obviously interrelated, but they are not altogether interdependent. Most policy enforcement takes place on individual campuses, once AAUP policies are incorporated into faculty handbooks, university statutes, or faculty union contracts. Hundreds of faculty handbooks and contracts, notably, incorporate language from the AAUP's 1940 statement on academic freedom and tenure. The AAUP has never had (and never will have) enough resources to be the academy's police force. It tries to mark boundaries and issue widely applicable warnings through its investigations, and censured institutions often work with the AAUP staff to reform themselves and get off censure. But as the organization has evolved, the production and approval of the policy documents themselves may now be the more important activity.

If, however, one looks at the recent history of published AAUP investigative reports, it is apparent that they emphasize misconduct toward individual faculty members and give too little attention to broad violations of shared governance. They also give too much weight to small religious institutions and historically black colleges and universities. Although the grievances investigated are consistently appalling and the analysis of them impressive, their potential impact on national trends is increasingly diminished. AAUP activists used to believe that the prevalence of smaller, less prestigious institutions on the censure list meant that top elite schools would not want their names on the same list and would go far to avoid censure. Censure could thus send a double warning about activities the organization would not tolerate. But the neoliberal managerial ideology that increasingly dominates higher education means that administrators are generally less concerned about AAUP censure and faculty disapproval.

One arena where AAUP protection and the threat of censure do, however, remain relevant, even at small and little-known institutions, is on behalf of contingent faculty. The AAUP certainly needs to take up the mistreatment of contingent faculty at major institutions, but small schools, where practices can be monstrous, need to be put on warning that they are not invisible. Although protecting the rights of contingent faculty is a relatively new priority for the AAUP, Committee A staff members are now aware that it is a priority. Once again, this places the AAUP in the world of political change, not above it. Yet contingent faculty are concentrated in community colleges and other institutions without strong AAUP contacts or strong shared governance traditions, and they are thus also far more vulnerable than either tenured or tenure-track faculty. The traditional strategy of selective investigation and censure is likely to be less effective in protecting their rights nationwide. Not only does the AAUP need to invent more strategies to use in protecting their jobs and their academic freedom; it also needs more aggressively to seek out appropriate cases involving contingent faculty and graduate-student employees.

Indeed, although AAUP staff members are not ambulance chasers, both staff and leaders need to keep their eyes open for cases that will help showcase and reinforce appropriate practices nationwide. I believe that at least one well-known federal court operates in somewhat the same way. Staff has implicitly been doing that for years, but it is time to do so more openly, to announce what the AAUP's priorities are. Yet neither staff nor leadership can effectively set these priorities unilaterally. They need to be in conversation with one another and with AAUP members.

An undue emphasis on investigating little-known schools is only one of the more obvious consequences of a long-missing dialogue between staff and faculty leaders. Also glaringly absent, again, are investigations of failures of shared governance, despite the continuing crisis of shared governance in American higher education. Shared governance investigations are complex and require more elaborate investigation and more staff time than, say, an investigation of one fired faculty member. Investigations of individual faculty mistreatment have a clear victim and thus potentially a clear focus. The issues in shared governance cases may often be less clear. Investigating an unambiguous aggression against a single faculty member can in key respects be routine. Indeed, many initial staff letters—written when an inquiry turns into a complaint—consist largely of boilerplate language. In truth, reluctance to take on difficult assignments is one component of the pattern for selecting cases for investigation. A dramatic exception is the AAUP's major, multicampus investigation of the educational aftermath of Hurricane Katrina, the single most ambitious investigation the organization has undertaken in years. Some key staff members were opposed to taking on such a complex investigation. Happily, one immensely experienced staff member insisted on doing so and offered to do the work. Notably, the leadership had no opportunity to be engaged in the conversation and could only stand back and applaud.

The major existing check against staff insularity is a requirement that the general secretary authorize all investigations. That procedure is supposed to open a way for the general secretary to advocate for particular cases, but it has been more honored in the breach. Beginning in 2007, a general secretary with long Committee A experience began to do this part of the job effectively, but for more than a decade Committee A staff operated with only pro forma supervision or input. Several things had worked against a more productive relationship. First, Committee A standards are far from obvious. Few faculty members, for example, are aware that although investigative reports will sometimes critique the conduct of faculty committees, the staff only very rarely argues for actually overturning a decision by a duly constituted faculty committee. Such a recommendation basically requires malfeasance on the part of a campus committee. Years ago, when a faculty member who was denied tenure at the University of Judaism was inadvertently sent copies of letters from outside faculty evaluators, the AAUP was able to show that a faculty committee's representation of the letters as negative was manifestly false. But otherwise the organization does not question the substance of faculty committees' judgments. Though I think this practice is unwise, it is not an altogether unreasonable one, given that the AAUP exists in part to ensure that the faculty has a decisive role in its areas of primary responsibility, among them deciding who will teach and what will be taught. Nonetheless, it still surprises people, including faculty members who serve on Committee A, to learn that the AAUP usually does not seek to reverse a bad decision made by a faculty committee, because it means that the AAUP blocks itself from seeking justice in some cases. Perhaps a notable piece of evidence that might lead the AAUP to rethink this practice is this: the Canadian Association of University Teachers does extremely thorough Committee A–style investigations, produces investigative reports that are even more detailed than the AAUP's, and has no problem disagreeing with the stand taken by a university faculty committee.

The AAUP's reluctance to reverse a faculty committee is a key reason why the AAUP would have had major difficulty doing a full investigation of the Churchill case; at least from the perspective of the majority of the staff members in the Department of Academic Freedom, he had received due process by being reviewed by several faculty committees. Some of the members of Committee A agreed; others did not. For some, therefore, whether the University of Colorado committees made the right decision was beside the point, though in my view the AAUP could have raised questions about the character of the review and the risks to academic freedom it raised nationwide, short of committing itself to a full investigation. I suggested at the time that the AAUP empanel a special committee to report on the implications of the Churchill case, but there was not enough support among the committee members and consultants to do so. In this instance, therefore, my difference is with them, many of whom I appointed, rather than with the staff. Since then, I have asked the committee—and it has agreed—to study several politically influenced faculty reviews and evaluations, including Churchill's, so as to offer general advice to the profession.

This special committee will issue a detailed report on the threats posed by political interventions in university affairs and recommend ways of dealing with them. Censure of the University of Colorado will not be an option, and the committee might well not rehearse the facts in the case against Churchill. In other words, the AAUP would not be aiming to retry the case. An effort to retry the case might be undertaken by a disciplinary organization if it were willing to organize a panel of experts in the field, though in Churchill's case that would require considerable thought. Not, one might add, that the experience that disciplinary organizations have had in investigating actual plagiarism cases has been a happy one. The AAUP special committee will instead address the many concerns raised by the University of Colorado investigation as a way of establishing standards for future such actions. Ward Churchill's 2009 account of his case and Eric Cheyfitz's essay on it alone raise basic professional issues that the AAUP should address. And other scholars have work on the Churchill affair in progress (Schrecker, "Ward Churchill"). Among the issues needing clarification are these: What distinguishes professional disputes, differences of opinion, and claims of error or misjudgment that are best handled within the scholarly community from those that should be heard by a campus disciplinary committee? How should such a disciplinary committee establish the norms and practices of a scholarly field? How are such norms complicated by interdisciplinary work? What level of expertise in a given academic field is required of committee members conducting detailed review of a faculty member's scholarship? Is disciplinary expertise more necessary on a panel considering removing a tenured faculty member than it is for a faculty committee reviewing an initial award of tenure? What criteria should be used to disqualify someone from service on such a panel? Should the members of a review committee be held to an oath of silence if they are attacked in the press? Should administrators be entitled to distribute unsolicited materials about a case? Should investigation of specific accusations about issues in a faculty member's publications be supplemented by a more thorough review of all his or her scholarship? Does it matter to the AAUP if more than one faculty committee is involved and if their judgments differ? Can an independent, impartial review be conducted no matter what level of criticism by politicians and members of the press is present? Should politically charged investigations be delayed until more disinterested evaluation is possible? Can the AAUP take issue with an administration's choice of a specific disciplinary action if it differs from what a majority of the members of a faculty review committee recommends, whether or not there are flaws in the process?

Among the many reasons to believe that the Churchill review was flawed, one may cite the fact that law professor Marianne Wesson, the chair of the panel appointed by the University of Colorado's Standing Committee on Research Misconduct to investigate the charges against Churchill, had early in 2005 circulated an email linking him with "other charismatic male celebrity wrongdoers" (Churchill 154). Incredibly enough, the two hundred University of Colorado faculty members who signed a petition supporting Churchill were disqualified from serving on the panel, whereas Wesson was counted as unbiased. I must say that I cannot comprehend Robert O'Neil's dismissal of this matter as "a passing claim that one member of the review panel or committee could be said to have brought a predisposition to the task" (O'Neil, "Post-9/11 University" 523). Nor, given that the panel only investigated a handful of passages from a score of Churchill's books, can I endorse O'Neil's assertion that "a prolonged and careful review of his publications and papers" was conducted (ibid.). As things developed, the only two well-qualified members of the panel—the only two panelists in Native American studies, Bruce Johansen of the University of Nebraska and Robert Williams of the University of Arizona—both resigned under a press onslaught, being prevented from defending themselves by a university gag order (Churchill 154–55); their resignation established further evidence of outside interference and additional grounds for Cheyfitz's describing the whole affair as "the political construction of research misconduct" (231).

On these and other matters the AAUP remained silent, once again waiting for the formal decision to launch a complete investigation. The staff no doubt solemnly agrees that I should carry my own views with me to the grave. I refrained from speaking out for three years, but I am now removing the gag. Thousands of pages were accumulated in the Churchill file. Conversations were held with key parties. The general secretary pledged his deep devotion to the case. And it was all a dumb show. Once the final faculty report arrived in the negative, the AAUP closed its doors.

It never intended to do anything else if that was the result, even though the University of Colorado dropped most of the charges by the end.

The Colorado state conference of AAUP chapters did come to Churchill's defense, as did the local University of Colorado chapter. In person, Churchill little resembles the polemicist from whom so many American academics have distanced themselves. Although he takes no prisoners in print, and although he can be confrontational in contentious settings, he often displays a disarming, affable, distinctly Western persona. It unfailingly wins audiences over to his cause. Even after months of living under assault, the accounts he provides of his difficulties lack any real suggestion that the experience has distorted his character. I am not saying there is no tension in him. He will sometimes draw a deep breath and pause, reassembling his affability, before answering a question that hits home. It is a communicative breath, not simply an invisible adjustment, but it is also as close as we will get to knowing what it is like to be Ward Churchill. He will not otherwise impose his pain on colleagues. Ordinarily it is almost axiomatic that an academic who has gone through anything like Churchill has will behave like the ancient mariner. Yet he does not.

Does this matter? Is it pertinent? Yes. It helps make it clear why—in addition to a distrust of investigations triggered by political witch hunts and the desire to defend unpopular speech on principle—many University of Colorado faculty members rallied to his side. They were not harboring private doubts about him. They were not defending someone they would rather not meet in a department hallway. To put it another way, with how many other recently fired academics would you be willing to spend a day? And it helps locate him as a writer with different evidentiary and argumentative standards, one playing to the beat of a different drummer, not a rogue with no standards at all. For many of his fellow Americans, steeped in the ideology of American exceptionalism, every violence against Indians is a divergence from fundamental decency and goodness. For them, every accusation needs to be proven beyond a shadow of a doubt. For Churchill, our history is fundamentally genocidal. That colors a willingness to draw conclusions based on a pattern of behavior.

The AAUP has, of course, defended radical faculty members in the past, Angela Davis and Bertell Ollman being the most well known examples and Sami Al-Arian and Mohamed Yousry being among the most recent. That does not mean we have had or ever will have the power to win their jobs back. The AAUP does not have an army. Our last resort is censure, which we employed on behalf of both Davis and Ollman. In Ollman's case, interestingly enough, Committee A was divided, and the National Council made one of its rare interventions into an investigation and made the censure recommendation. What censure can do is clear a faculty member's name, establishing from the judgment of an independent group that he or she is a victim, not a villain. In a number of cases, this has helped make it possible for a fired faculty member to get a job elsewhere. Fired from UCLA, Angela Davis later got a job at UC Santa Cruz, and the AAUP did not remove censure until the California board of regents approved that new position. I do not believe the University of Colorado would have reappointed Ward Churchill no matter what the AAUP might have said or done. If the faculty at the University of Colorado had mounted a strike on Churchill's behalf, I believe it would have failed. If the entire university community—students, faculty, and staff— had acted in unison and withdrawn all their resources from local businesses in company with a strike, that might have worked.

In any case, the AAUP was trumped by flawed due process at the University of Colorado. Whether or not faculty at large would agree with Committee A's unwillingness to second-guess a faculty committee, they should at least be aware that is how the AAUP operates. Faculty members nationwide who have voiced distress at Committee A's work would be less likely to resent AAUP inaction if they understood such criteria. Second, for a general secretary to advocate for a case effectively, he or she must if anything be even more familiar with it than the staff are. That can mean mastering a dossier containing several hundred pages of material. And finally, the Committee A staff has been very adept both at maintaining an unbroken wall of solidarity and at mustering key faculty allies in defense of its positions. Most general secretaries have simply quit the field and turned their attention to other matters. The AAUP's investigative procedures, enforced for several decades, have become somewhat inflexible and even outdated.

In the organizational maneuvering of Committee A staff, they are embedded in an officewide staff culture that has ruled the association for decades. With the exception of the creation of policy statements and the editing of *Academe*, the national AAUP is fundamentally a staff-run organization. If it were reliably running well, that would be less of a problem, but as I outlined in the previous chapter, with the substantial decline in non-collective-bargaining membership, the 2005 collapse of the organization's membership and finance departments, the installation of nonfunctional software in the national office, the long-term problems in communicating with members, the consistently inadequate contact with local chapters, and the marginal relevance of too many Committee A investigations, fundamental reform of the AAUP's power relationships is necessary.

Despite these problems, it must be said that the national staff is dedicated, highly intelligent, and very talented. They just cannot right the ship independently. The culture of the office, indeed the culture of the entire organization, must change. Staff and leaders must work together in genuine collaboration. One product of that reformed relationship should be to rethink the goals, priorities, and procedures of Committee A. It many ways it *is* the organization, but practices put in place decades ago no longer adequately match the changing higher education landscape. Campus crises often explode on the Internet and across the news days or hours after they break. Overly ponderous responses from the national office get little press play. And an investigative report appearing a year or two after events unfold is not necessarily better late than never. The last thing the AAUP should do is to abandon its careful practices. But the organization needs ways to have major national impact in real time and then follow it up with reports, investigations, and policies that can stand the test of time. To sustain its long-term goals and fund its deliberative products, the AAUP needs to be a time-sensitive advocacy organization.

Being an advocacy organization also means concentrating on how all AAUP statements—both those issued rapidly and those issued after long research and investigation—are disseminated and received. The Hurricane Katrina investigative report is among the most important and impressive AAUP texts ever issued. It is a testament to the quality of work that an experienced and knowledgeable staff can do when they take up the right tasks and work more closely with an investigative committee. Sadly, the anecdotal evidence I gather in speaking on many campuses suggests that most faculty members nationwide are still unaware of what happened at and to Louisiana universities after Hurricane Katrina. It did not help that the *Chronicle of Higher Education* leaked stories about draft versions of the report and thereby reduced the newsworthiness of the final product. But the real problem is that the AAUP does not seek to maximize the impact of its work. Its news releases are too often designed to preserve the organization's dignity rather than to attract coverage. Every document the AAUP produces needs to be disseminated in advocacy mode, framed to maximize visibility and impact in the press. One National Council member regularly suggests that the AAUP hire a professional publicist when the right issue comes along. In retrospect, the Katrina report may have been such an occasion.

The AAUP has an obvious opportunity to rethink how it operates. The Department of Academic Freedom saw its head retire in 2007. A new department head from outside began working in the fall of 2008. A new general secretary came on board in January 2009. If Committee A's work is to evolve to become more, not less, influential, then the AAUP's elected leaders must now join forces with staff who share these goals—and there are many in the national office who do—and make it a more effective, more responsive, and less secretive operation. The criteria for pursuing cases need to be made more explicit, both to the leadership and to the profession as a whole. Although the staff has, in effect, promoted itself as the profession's grievance committee, it has always been highly selective in choosing which cases to pursue to a full investigation; this disjunction between self-characterization and reality has left many faculty disillusioned with the committee and with the AAUP as a whole.

Yet it is worth noting that, measured by the faculty complaints the Committee A staff handles, a grievance committee (mostly for faculty without collective bargaining) is exactly what it is. The staff receives a large number of inquiries each year by email, letter, or telephone; these include simple requests for information, as well as faculty requests for assistance. If a request for assistance involves a substantive grievance that meets AAUP criteria, the staff typically asks for relevant documentation. Once documentation is received, the matter is classified as a "complaint." An analysis of the complaints open from May 2007 through June 2008 shows that 74 percent of them fall into the categories of tenure or promotion problems, nonrenewal, dismissal, termination, and suspension. Another 21 percent are accounted for by accusations of discrimination or harassment and problems with salary, posttenure review, grading, disciplinary action, collegiality, reprimands, furloughs, laboratory removal or transfer, sabbatical awards, and retirement arrangements. The staff coded 3 percent of the complaints open that year as focused specifically on issues of academic freedom. If a staff member acts on a complaint by writing a letter, it becomes a "case."

Complaints, it should be noted, often remain "open" for many years, even though no action takes place in regard to them. At some point, they are marked "closed," though that does not necessarily signal a resolution. It often simply represents an acknowledgment that the matter is dead. Thus, for example, neither a complaint about "termination for cause" that has a file established in 2002 and is finally closed in 2007 nor a complaint about "termination for 'grave misconduct'" that is opened in 2002 and closed in 2008 nor a "grading dispute" that is opened in 2001 and closed in 2007 nor a dispute over "nonpayment for overload" that opened in 2004 and closed in 2007—to cite actual examples—is likely to have been a subject of real work all that time. Staff opened 163 new complaint files from June 2007 through May 2008. One staff member planning to retire did some appropriate housekeeping and closed 141 of his complaint files that year. One may suggest that there has been an unnecessary tendency to overstate the actual number of genuinely active cases in any given year. It would be better to promote more transparency.

Of course, the Committee A staff does other things as well. It staffs numerous committees; it fields questions from the press; it gives highly detailed recommendations to faculty facing handbook revisions. And it gives advice to faculty, including faculty in collective bargaining, on a whole range of issues. Moreover, any time the AAUP successfully defends its principles for a nonunionized faculty member, it strengthens those principles for unionized faculty as well, just as good union contracts, conversely, help set standards for nonunionized faculty. Since 1997, there have typically been from 150 to 200 "cases" handled per year. The character of the cases pursued to full investigation is, of course, set by the nature of the complaints addressed. The AAUP takes on no more than about half a dozen full investigations each year. In 1980, *Academe* published a piece about how staff in the Department of Academic Freedom proceed from an initial request for assistance to a full-blown investigation (Kurland), but that essay remains somewhat misleading, since it admits no political and administrative triage in the process. Finkin and Post notably echo that account, most probably because they believe it (49–52). Even long-term Committee A members have no access to the process of case triage. Kurland's essay suggests an inexorable progression from level to level, with no meritorious complaint left behind, and that less-than-accurate picture has left many faculty members unhappy with the real-world results of the AAUP's efforts. It is certainly possible to account for why the AAUP has pursued the investigations it *has* taken up—indeed faculty members are in the midst of such a study—but accounting for why the AAUP *did not* pursue most grievances so aggressively over the years would be impossible for anyone not on the staff. Yet some increased openness about the principles and standards the staff uses would help. The AAUP has created expectations it cannot meet, and that does the organization no good; hundreds of frustrated and alienated faculty members are among the consequences it has faced for decades.

The legalistic model for Committee A operations comes into play the minute a staff member begins to handle an inquiry from a faculty member. "Do our regulations and policy statements apply to this grievance?" is a key opening question. Staff members may consult with one another early on if the issue is not clear, but more intense discussion and dispute may precede a decision to do the considerable research and fact finding that must take place before an investigation can be launched. The quasi-legal model takes the *Redbook* as the pertinent body of AAUP jurisprudence and the history of investigative reports as the relevant case law. Staff may disagree both about which AAUP regulation is most relevant and about whether a given regulation is applicable at all. Some differences of opinion are strategic—and thus, once again, fundamentally political in the broader sense. By the time an investigative report is published, typically little trace of these debates remains.

Like any set of laws or regulations, despite the best efforts of the original draftees to be clear and to anticipate circumstances and events, the AAUP's *Redbook* documents end up requiring interpretation. In 2008, I presented a long-term staff member in the national office and a long-term

Committee A member with the same hypothetical grievance and asked if the relevant regulation would apply. Their opinions were diametrically opposed, with the staff member convinced the AAUP would not pursue the grievance and the Committee A member convinced it should. Both were coauthors of the very regulation in question. The Committee A member went on to say the regulation would be rendered worthless were the AAUP to refuse such a complaint, and I agreed. The issue at stake was how RIR 13 on contingent appointments should be interpreted. The staff member insisted a long-term and broadly qualified part-time faculty member could be terminated if an institution asserted that the precise courses the faculty member happened to have taught recently were no longer needed. Moreover, the staff member added, it would always be acceptable to dispose of a highly qualified part-timer in order to hire a considerably less accomplished tenure-track faculty member. Sometimes the staff operates like a Republican-appointed judiciary, offering extremely narrow interpretations of congressional legislation.

If Committee A operated with a genuinely legalistic model, faculty members should see continuing debate and scholarship about the meaning and applicability of AAUP policies. But Committee A staff operations are actually more like a court staffed by a priesthood. It wants its investigative reports to appear like inexorable applications of platonic principles, not as an evolving intellectual and political tradition. Few faculty members anywhere have any idea that substantial debates take place within the staff, let alone how intricate the negotiations over the application of AAUP law actually are. Faculty members who want to see a grievance pursued are motivated by a sense of injustice. A staff refusal based on technicalities appears heartless or indifferent. In the end, however, this problem may not be solvable simply by explaining why the staff does not act, though that is a role I often take on. It may be that the whole process needs to be opened up, that faculty members nationally need to have more of a stake in how AAUP policy evolves and how it is applied to individual grievances.

The *Academe* account also omits directly addressing another fundamental problem with AAUP procedures. A case develops out of a complaint. Lacking an actual grievance—most often by a faculty member who claims to have been harmed—the staff will not open a complaint file or launch an investigation. Broad issues will sometimes be taken up in reports coauthored by faculty members, as in the example of the major 2003 report "Academic Freedom and National Security in a Time of Crisis," but inquiries into most campus-based infractions have to be triggered by a formal request for assistance. That is essentially a staff restriction instituted and maintained without ongoing discussion and evaluation by the actual members of Committee A. In informal office parlance, the question often posed when a potential case arises is, "Where's the body?" For example, early faculty settlements at Bacone appeared to eliminate the relevant bodies from consideration, thus leaving the wider issues unresolved. As a 2008 AAUP confidential internal report observes, occasionally "a staff member will contact a highly publicized victim of administrative abuse to offer AAUP assistance, but most of the staff's work is passive and reactive. If a dead body does not appear on the doorstep, nothing happens. This quasi-prosecutorial procedure indiscriminately winnows out large numbers of possible cases which a more aggressive, proactive approach might discover."

The staff's focus on the relevant body also brings us back to the issues that opened this chapter. When University of California at San Diego (UCSD) graduate teaching assistants Benjamin Balthaser and Scott Boehm were not rehired to teach in the "Dimensions of Culture" program in 2007, and the evidence suggested they were being punished for being outspoken critics of how the curriculum had been politically compromised, a national firestorm erupted. *Inside Higher Education* covered the story (Redden, "Inquiry"), the Foundation for Individual Rights in Education (FIRE) issued a strong statement (Creeley), and comments appeared on weblogs across the country. The Committee A staff wrote a typically restrained letter to the graduate employees involved as a way of giving notice of their concern; posted online by its California recipients, it amounted to the most ineffective statement any major national organization issued on the matter. Asked not to comment so as to avoid compromising the potential investigation, I unhappily agreed. Then the staff, in its standard fashion, concentrated on whether the graduate employees were eventually offered alternative employment, which would render the search for individual "remedies" moot; when they were, the case was dropped. This was a fundamental case about academic freedom—on behalf of the vulnerable class of graduate employees—and the AAUP's response, hampered by the way the Committee A staff does business, was completely inadequate. A staff member did encourage the two students to see if the UCSD faculty senate might adopt a statement affirming graduate-student academic freedom, but that modest behind-the-scenes advice let the violation stand. In my view, the AAUP still should have launched an investigation of the original incident. The remedy would have been for UCSD to build more effective guarantees of academic freedom into its regulations. The absence of remaining victims should not have prevented us from pursuing the principles at stake.

Although I believe the UCSD example shows a need for finding what one staff member has described as "another arrow in our quiver," another way to proceed, it should be made clear that not every well-publicized case merits AAUP intervention. Some complaints, including some that receive national publicity, are not pursued because the evidence to support a faculty member's contentions either has never been provided or simply does not exist. Faculty members nationwide may write letters in support of a colleague at another school, sign petitions, and denounce the AAUP for inaction, but the organization cannot simply act on the basis of a faculty member's uncorroborated account of events. People may well suspect that either a given administrator or a given committee had unacceptable motives for refusing to grant tenure to a faculty member, but one may never find out for certain. The AAUP had more than sufficient grounds for acting in the Finkelstein case because of the actions and written rationales of DePaul administrators, but even a full-scale investigation might not have revealed whether (or how much) outside interventions such as those of Harvard University's Alan Dershowitz influenced the DePaul decision. Short of direct testimony or an indicative email or letter, one may always be in doubt. Most complaints, moreover, need to remain confidential, but some very much in the public domain give the AAUP an opportunity for revealing its operating principles.

Yet a full investigation of Finkelstein's case might well have clarified a great deal. Absent a settlement agreement, Finkelstein would have been able to talk freely with the AAUP, and that could have provided numerous matters to discuss with others on campus. The AAUP could have inquired into claims that DePaul administrators expressed grave concerns about the potential impact of Finkelstein's notoriety on donors long before his tenure was under consideration. The surprising endorsements of his collegiality in all DePaul documents might have benefited from further discussion. Reports that this most polemical of writers is uniformly nonpolemical in class are supported not only by Finkelstein's own Horowitzian advocacy of pedagogical "balance" (Finkelstein 296) but also by his ability to adopt an eerily neutral, almost willfully affectless style. That certainly helps explain student reports that he does not try to impose his own political views on them. On the other hand, he can also be relentless, driven, and virtually unstoppable in extemporaneous debate with his peers. I would not be surprised to learn that the absence of any official concern about his collegiality, a criterion the AAUP rejects, masked its relevance to his case.

The Committee A staff has long operated on the basis of twin logics for selecting cases for investigation that essentially cancel one another. On one hand, AAUP activists privately assert that the organization defends principles, not people, meaning that it investigates when a critical principle whose defense would benefit many is at stake. Yet the AAUP investigates to defend principles only when they are embodied in aggrieved individuals. Then, in a gesture that deftly jettisons principle, the staff typically abandons a case if an individual settles with his or her institution, unless a report has been written, in which case staff will demand that an institution adopt appropriate permanent general remedies. Although some people worry that AAUP reluctance to stand down after a settlement would jeopardize an institution's willingness to make an individual whole, in truth the organization often tolerates (and even recommends) minimal settlements for aggrieved faculty that have little more than symbolic value. The organization also tends to place a much higher priority on gaining handbook revisions than on compensating faculty members who have been seriously harmed. I would argue that it is time to consider decoupling principles from people more often—on a case-by-case basis, because the truth is that this nest of conflicting logics has only one core result: leaving the staff in full control of investigative decisions.

The practice of the AAUP's recommending minimal financial settlements can be genuinely destructive. For the first few decades of its existence, to be sure, as the association confirmed in a detailed report in the

May 1965 issue of what was then called the *AAUP Bulletin*, redress for injured faculty members was not commonly sought as a condition for removal of censure ("Report of the Self-Survey" 157–59). But that practice has continued to trouble both leaders and members, and it needs to be more broadly rethought. Imagine the following scenario: a tenured faculty member has been fired without cause and sues the university for damages. The AAUP censures the institution, then agrees to take it off censure if it revises its policies and offers the faculty member, say, twelve thousand dollars in compensation for the loss of lifetime employment. The Committee A staff makes the offer to the university without even informing the faculty member about it. Since the civil suit meanwhile is still pending, does the university go into court and testify that the AAUP believes that twelve thousand dollars is fair and reasonable compensation? The faculty member, who is seeking several years' salary, has just had his or her case undermined by the very organization dedicated to defending faculty rights. We are now in the surreal world of the remedy that remedies nothing, whose sole reason for existence is to promote the illusion that the AAUP is administering justice. I have no problem with such symbolic settlements when the faculty member at issue prefers such an option or has found alternative employment or when time has passed and the faculty member no longer seeks substantial redress or is no longer alive. But I do not believe an AAUP staff member in Washington, DC, should otherwise have this kind of unilateral power to set policy or to undermine a faculty case that is actually still in the courts. When, on the other hand, the national staff is not occupied with trying to make such arrangements with administrators but instead advising faculty members who have sued censured administrations, the results can be quite different. Katrina-related settlements to Loyola University faculty members in 2009 have included amounts of $120,000, $160,000, and $350,000, plus attorney's fees. There are also reports of one major settlement from Tulane.

The internal operations of Committee A's staff, long distinctly secretive and hierarchical, need to be more democratic, with no senior professional staff in the department excluded from regular meetings, as they have been for many years, and with Committee A members and leaders better informed about the staff's ongoing work. The socialization of new Committee A staff, long based largely on an exceedingly slow mentoring process that maintains them in what amounts to an unofficial apprenticeship for years, needs to be accelerated and supplemented by a self-directed reading program focused on key case files and representative staff letters. Although the work of the department that staffs Committee A is rather specialized—nothing else in the world quite prepares an employee for it—and thus an apprenticeship of a year or two is appropriate, extending an apprenticeship for a decade or more is not. There is absolutely no question, moreover, that the Committee A staff works very hard and that the quality of their work is most often very high, but their priorities need to be set collaboratively. That is a leadership responsibility. Discussion of the impact of investigative reports in a changing world needs to be the subject of frank, ongoing, and open interchanges between staff and leaders, not treated as a betrayal of AAUP values. These goals and the others I have outlined earlier are all subject to debate and discussion. But that conversation has to be based on more transparent committee operations. This chapter, which includes a number of clarifications and procedural details not typical of the AAUP's norms for disclosure, is a step in that direction.

No doubt, both some AAUP staff and some of the organization's elected leaders would prefer that this conversation only take place internally. But I believe the cult of secrecy has ruled too long for any reforms of AAUP methods for handling complaints to become sufficiently apparent either to the organization's members or to the faculty at large. More aggressive advocacy, conversely, is visible, but ignorance about AAUP investigative standards cannot easily be replaced by knowledge of new standards and procedures without public disclosure of the issues at stake.

The AAUP has no cause for pride greater than the pride all its members can take in the statements of principle in the *Redbook* and in the compelling history of investigative reports, which date back to the reports Arthur Lovejoy wrote in 1915 (Pollitt and Kurland). Those of us who have had a hand in writing some of those documents—both staff and members—know that what we have done will outlast us in a way that little personal scholarship can. The AAUP is the major vehicle for faculty to have a nationwide voice in the future of the profession. My firm belief is that increased openness about how the AAUP operates—and willingness to modify its practices—will enhance both that history and its potential. Because nothing about the future of academic freedom is guaranteed. I thus cannot answer this book's opening question—Does academic freedom have a future?—with any certainty. But what I do believe is that it cannot survive in a form that will serve us well without the AAUP. And the AAUP cannot preserve academic freedom unless Committee A continues to adapt. Although the decision-making process that identifies cases for investigation cannot operate as a democracy, neither should it continue to function as a secret society, a society that issues intermittent reports from an invisible elsewhere, reports that are read only by a small minority of faculty members nationwide.

There are signs that change has some support. Key staff members from other departments in the national office have voiced sentiments similar to my own, as have members of the AAUP's Executive Committee. Meanwhile, there are broader signs of increased interest in academic freedom across the country. One positive sign is a sudden increase in conferences devoted to academic freedom in the new millennium. They have been held at the University of California at Berkeley, Loyola Marymount University, New York University, Columbia University, Cornell University, and Indiana University of Pennsylvania. Books or special issues of journals edited or coedited by Beshara Doumani, Evan Gerstmann, Edward Carvalho, and Evan Watkins followed, reviving a tradition exemplified earlier by Edmund Pincoffs and William Van Alstyne. The massive issue of *Works and Days* edited by Carvalho and David Downing is of special note. Most of the conferences included speakers well versed in AAUP policy. Two did not, which is a troubling disconnect. All these conferences came about in part because Bush administration policies led many academics to recognize that their worlds were not secure. That has opened an opportunity to engage more faculty members in the intellectual and political work of defining and protecting academic freedom. The AAUP needs to give them opportunities to do so.

As the NAS analysis of "Freedom in the Classroom" demonstrates, wider discussion of academic freedom and close analysis of AAUP documents will clearly produce mixed results. At a 2008 NYU conference, Roger Bowen oddly advocated an end to the struggle for national academic freedom standards and instead urged the academy to take up individual battles to define academic freedom in all fifty-one state legislatures ("A Faustian Bargain"). Bowen, a man of notably fallible judgment, was unwittingly offering Horowitz and his allies new opportunities for mischief, as well as a guarantee that national principle would degenerate into local chaos. No better was a proposal for "people's academic freedom" offered with utopian flourishes by Cathy Prendergast and Sam Nelson at a 2009 Cornell University academic freedom conference. Heralded as "an expansive view of academic freedom, one even more expansive than the AAUP embraces," the paper this duo presented proposed that all American citizens deserve academic freedom, thereby severing the concept from academic credentials, from college and university appointments, from peer review, and from its fundamental link to higher education. If academic freedom is grounded either in an employment relationship— or, in the case of independent scholars, in the scholar's participation in peer review for publication—then academic freedom is precisely *not* universalizable. Believing that a definitive example would clinch the deal with the audience, they argued at length that universal academic freedom would entitle all Americans to pursue research in the Unabomber papers. I suppose we may all be relieved that no one directed Sarah Palin to offer the winning entitlement of universal academic freedom to the American public as a campaign pledge.

The Prendergast-Nelson proposal may well have legs for some Left enthusiasts, since it has a certain unreflective egalitarian flair. Indeed, Jeff Schmidt, author of *Disciplined Minds*, perhaps the fiercest book-length denunciation of faculty cowardice, endorsed the same idea at NYU's April 2009 conference on academic freedom. But this plan has a somewhat longer history, dating at least to Mark Bauerlein's 2004 call to dilute the influence of leftist professors by expanding academic freedom "to all constituencies of the campus." This kind of false populism is politically reversible. It dilutes professionalism and makes academic freedom a vehicle for majority opinion, a danger the AAUP has understood since 1915. And—as a minor objection—I would point out that opening fragile archival materials to casual use by nonprofessionals is not likely to promote historical preservation.

The need to counter misguided proposals is a price worth paying if academic freedom gets more attention as a result. The alternatives are likely to be more bleak than we realize. In support of that contention, it is worth contemplating a connection that I did not make explicit in chapter 2 and that should not be dismissed as coincidental: it was the very same University of Illinois vice chancellor who argued that the university should prioritize funding and rewarding product-oriented "translational" faculty research and who bullied a graduate student into shutting down a website critical of the Singapore government. Financial expediency motivated both actions. Academic freedom was implicated in both incidents—the freedom of faculty to choose their own research goals without coercion in the first case and the freedom to speak and publish in the second. Combining the two stories can give us some indication of how the neoliberal university will evolve in years to come.

It is also clear that, though Horowitz and Neal have failed completely in their attempts to obtain legislative oversight of curriculum and hiring, they have helped turn the university into an available and acceptable political target. That is one thing that the public interventions into tenure cases and the public efforts to block campus speakers have in common. One of the stunning lessons of public drives to disinvite campus speakers from 2007 to 2009 is their political diversity. Not only have both the Right and, to a lesser degree, the Left been hard at work; a whole series of political groups and constituencies have mounted both successful and unsuccessful campaigns to demolish academic freedom by depriving faculty and student groups of the right to invite speakers of their choice. Consider the range of political views and the different cultural and political constituencies involved in the successful campaigns to cancel Larry Summers's private job talk at UC Berkeley and William Ayers's lectures at the University of Nebraska and Boston College, in the initial announcement that Norman Finkelstein's presentation at Clark University was canceled, in the efforts to block Archbishop Desmond Tutu's commencement talks at Michigan State University and the University of North Carolina, or in the unsuccessful drives to get biologist Richard Dawkins and U.S. president Barack Obama disinvited, respectively, at the University of Oklahoma and Notre Dame: right-wing patriots, profeminist faculty, pro-Israeli lobbies, antiabortion groups, and antievolution zealots, along with legislators, donors, editorial writers, citizens both ordinary and deranged, and talk-show hosts.

Of course, there is another lesson in this story: the only thing that will stop such trends is for colleges and universities to develop the spine required to stand up for academic freedom. That will not happen without a stronger and more influential AAUP promoting academic freedom nationwide. There is no other organization to play that role. The survival of academic freedom as we know it depends both on faculty nationwide and on the AAUP.

I often tell audiences that I have been summarizing trends and predicting outcomes in higher education for twenty years but that I have always gotten things wrong. When the inevitable laughter subsides, I add, "That means things have always turned out worse than I expected." This time the laughter is more nervous, because the remark touches on fears, often unvoiced, that most faculty share. Yet we also share intelligence and the capacity to act simultaneously in our own interests and in the interests of a worldwide community that needs our core values and our services. There is common ground where the common good and the fundamental needs of the professoriate intersect. That point of intersection is where academic freedom has been articulated since the 1915 Declaration. Though academic freedom is sometimes disparaged or coopted by our opponents, it is nonetheless a rallying cry we have underused for nearly two generations. It is time faculty members take full possession of it again and begin promoting it as colleagues and as citizens.

There is an inevitable elegiac tone in a great deal that those of us committed to a broad notion of academic freedom now write about higher education. It is apparent even in titles, from Stanley Aronowitz's *The Last Good Job in America* to Frank Donoghue's *The Last Professors*. Of course, higher education is not literally a dying industry, one being historically and economically erased. The last professor will not quite be the equivalent of the last blacksmith, since there will still be hundreds of thousands of teachers performing the educational equivalent of shoeing horses. Yet the job is becoming less appealing for many faculty, and the character of the work risks being diminished. Higher education is being dramatically transformed and, for the most part, not for the better. The intellectual freedom of the faculty is being undermined, and the gains made in equal access for students are being replaced by a system that gives rich and poor students different caliber educations. We may in some respects

be watching the last days of an industry that seemed intellectually revital-
ized in the 1970s and 1980s, when disciplines transformed and reformed
themselves, took on a degree of reflexivity, interrogated earlier blind-
nesses, and seemed to foresee unlimited intellectual horizons. Then economic contraction joined forces with conservative counterreaction and
neoliberal conviction. Yet intellectual expansion was already paradoxically accompanied by a depressed academic job market. Meanwhile, even
as the culture wars began to metastasize, new opportunities for promoting change appeared. Building coalitions with email and on websites,
listservs, wikis, and blogs makes achieving a critical mass of progressive
activists far more realistic than it had been before. Higher education as an
industry has taken advantage of remarkable technological advances over
the past thirty years to enhance both communication and research. Now
it is time to enlist those resources in a great cultural struggle for our own
renewed commitment and our fellow citizens' better-informed loyalties.

Always a contradictory cultural formation, American higher education
has evolved through new forms of paradoxicality. Now hope and despair
about its future alternate. These mixed impulses are woven into my prose.
They are best confronted. But work in the end is better than passivity. We
need to face our demons and move on. Those faculty members who have
given up need to wake up instead, because higher education's governing
principles of academic freedom and shared governance need not be lost
if we are willing to fight. Resistance is not futile, especially if we have an
alternative vision to offer, if we can promote community and citizenship
in place of the ruthless economic philosophy that is increasingly shaping our fate. *No University Is an Island* has moved in a series of chapters
through the various terrains where academic freedom is at risk in order
to demonstrate both their practical autonomy and their pervasive inter-
dependence. Shaped alike by forces such as corporatization, they nonetheless offer distinct arenas for intervention. That gives all of us opportunities for focused work and action that simultaneously contributes to
a larger cause—be it through shared governance, organizational activism, or progressive unionization on behalf of contingent teachers, graduate-student employees, and tenured faculty. Part of higher education's
distinctive appeal and cultural capacity is its ability to fuse elitism with
democratic populism, intellectual appeal with broad outreach. We need

both. And we can win. We have the numbers *and* the heights on our side, the thousands of students and faculty who can be galvanized and the ideals that can inspire them.

The opposition has nothing but bad faith and economic or political opportunism to offer, though those are powerful weapons. *No University Is an Island* has sought to be unsparing in its account of the challenges higher education faces—from the disempowering of hundreds of thousands of contingent faculty to the proliferation of crass commercial relationships that sabotage research independence, from efforts to police or chill classroom speech to external campaigns seeking to influence tenure decisions, from increasing indulgence in administrative fiat to political assaults by conservative organizations, from unbridled faculty careerism to unionization that has been stripped of its social agendas. Yet I have named and analyzed these forces for a reason: so we can combat them. Even though the causes and effects of these challenges are linked, they can be addressed by committed people working strategically in separate domains. None of us has to take on every task. Yet every success has reverberations elsewhere. Our agency is intertwined. Every local struggle for academic freedom, shared governance, and workplace justice is an inspiration for every other beleaguered community. Intellectuals need to abandon their guilt about principled activism on behalf of their peers. Just as no university is an island, so too does no university senate, no faculty or graduate-employee union, and no AAUP chapter stand alone in its potential impact.

BIBLIOGRAPHY

Altbach, Philip G. "Academic Freedom and the International Perspective." Paper presented at the Academic Freedom conference, New York University, April 2009.

American Association of University Professors (AAUP). "Academic Freedom and National Security in a Time of Crisis." *Academe*, November–December 2003, 34–59.

———. "College and University Academic and Professional Appointments" (2002). In AAUP, *Policy Documents and Reports*, 93–97.

———. "Faculty Participation in the Selection, Evaluation, and Retention of Administrators" (1974). In AAUP, *Policy Documents and Reports*, 145–46.

———. "Freedom in the Classroom." *Academe*, September–October 2007, 54–61. Revised version published online in November 2008; available at http://www.aaup.org/AAUP/comm/rep/A/class.htm.

———. "Graduate Student Employees." *Academe*, September–October 2009, forthcoming.

———. "Hurricane Katrina and New Orleans Universities." Report of an AAUP Special Committee. *Academe*, May–June 2007, 59–126.

———. "Joint Statement on Rights and Freedoms of Students" (1967). In AAUP, *Policy Documents and Reports*, 273–279.

———. "1915 Declaration of Principles on Academic Freedom and Tenure." In AAUP, *Policy Documents and Reports*, 291–301.

———. "On the Relationship of Faculty Governance to Academic Freedom" (1994). In AAUP, *Policy Documents and Reports*, 141–44.

———. *Policy Documents and Reports*, 10th ed. Baltimore: Johns Hopkins University Press, 2006. (Popularly known as the *Redbook*; includes all policy statements cited in this book.)

———. "Recommended Institutional Regulations on Academic Freedom and Tenure." Available at http://www.aaup.org/AAUP/pubsres/policydocs/contents/RIR.htm.

———. "Report—Academic Freedom and Tenure: University of South Florida." *Academe*, May–June 2003, 59–73.

———. "Report: Brigham Young University." *Academe,* September–October 1997, 52–71.

———. "Report—College and University Government: Antioch University and the Closing of Antioch College." *Academe,* November–December 2009, forthcoming.

———. "Report—College and University Government: Elmira College." *Academe,* September–October 1993, 42–52.

———. "Report—College and University Government: Francis Marion University." *Academe,* May–June 1997, 72–84.

———. "Report—College and University Government: Lindenwood College." *Academe,* May–June 1994, 60–68.

———. "Report—College and University Government: Miami-Dade Community College." *Academe,* May–June 2000, 73–88.

———. "Report of Committee A, 2002–2003." *Academe,* September–October 2003, 77–83.

———. "Report: The Ohio State University." *AAUP Bulletin,* Autumn 1972, 306–21.

———. "Report of the Self-Survey Committee of the AAUP." *AAUP Bulletin,* May 1965, 99–209.

———. "The Role of the Faculty in Budgetary and Salary Matters" (1972). In AAUP, *Policy Documents and Reports,* 149–52.

———. "Statement on Government of Colleges and Universities" (1966). In AAUP, *Policy Documents and Reports,* 135–40.

———. "Statement on Graduate Students" (1999). In AAUP, *Policy Documents and Reports,* 280–82.

———. "Statement of Principles on Academic Freedom and Tenure" (1940). In AAUP, *Policy Documents and Reports,* 3–11.

———. "Trends in Faculty Status, 1975–2007." Table compiled from U.S. Department of Education, IPEDS Fall Staff Survey. Available at http://www.aaup.org/NR/rdonlyres/7D01E0C7-C255-41F1-9F11-E27D0028CB2A/0/TrendsinFacultyStatus2007.pdf.

American Association of University Professors and Canadian Association of University Teachers (AAUP and CAUT). "On Conditions of Employment at Overseas Campuses." Available at http://www.aaup.org/AAUP/comm/rep/A/overseas.htm.

American Council of Trustees and Alumni (ACTA). "How Many Ward Churchills?" Washington, DC: ACTA, May 2006.

Areen, Judith. "Government as Educator: A New Understanding of First Amendment Protection of Academic Freedom and Governance." *Georgetown Law Journal* 97:4 (April 2009): 945–1000.

Aronowitz, Stanley. "Academic Unionism and the Future of Higher Education." In Nelson, *Will Teach for Food,* 181–214.

———. *The Knowledge Factory: Dismantling the Corporate University and Creating True Higher Learning.* Boston: Beacon, 2000.

———. *The Last Good Job in America: Work and Education in the New Global Technoculture.* Lanham, Md.: Roman and Littlefield, 2001.

———. "Should Academic Unions Get Involved in Governance?" *Liberal Education* 92:4 (Fall 2006): 22–27.

Bauerlein, Mark. "Securing Academic Freedom on Campus." *Front Page Magazine,* March 2004. Available at http://www.frontpagemag.com/Articles/Read.aspx?GUID=680C1AAA-6163-4509-A263-72BB58FAA36E.

Beinin, Joel. "The New McCarthyism: Policing Thought about the Middle East." In Beshara Doumani, ed., *Academic Freedom after September 11,* 237–66. New York: Zone Books, 2006.

Benjamin, Ernst. "Faculty Bargaining." In Benjamin and Mauer, *Academic Collective Bargaining,* 23–51.

———. "Reappraisal and Implications for Policy and Research." In Ernst Benjamin, ed., *Exploring the Role of Contingent Instructional Staff in Undergraduate Learning,* New Directions for Higher Education 123, 79–113. San Francisco: Jossey-Bass, 2003.

———. "Some Implications of the Faculty's Obligation to Encourage Student Academic Freedom for Faculty Advocacy in the Classroom." In Spacks, *Advocacy in the Classroom,* 302–14.

Benjamin, Ernst, and Michael Mauer, eds. *Academic Collective Bargaining.* New York: Modern Language Association, 2006.

Berry, Joe. "Contingent Faculty and Academic Freedom: A Contradiction in Terms." In Carvalho and Downing, "Academic Freedom and Intellectual Activism in the Post-9/11 University," 359–68.

Bérubé, Michael. *The Left at War.* New York: New York University Press, 2009.

———. "Professional Advocates: When is 'Advocacy' Part of One's Vocation." In Spacks, *Advocacy in the Classroom,* 186–97.

Birnbaum, Robert. "The End of Shared Governance: Looking Forward or Looking Back." AAUP archives, unpublished paper, 2003.

Bok, Derek. "Academic Values and the Lure of Profit." *Chronicle of Higher Education,* April 4, 2003, B7–B9.

Bousquet, Marc. *How the University Works: Higher Education and the Low-Wage Nation.* New York: New York University Press, 2008.

Bowen, Roger. "A Faustian Bargain for Academic Freedom." *Chronicle of Higher Education,* October 3, 2008.

———. "Freedom, but for Honest Research. *Wall Street Journal,* April 1, 2009.

Brand, Myles. "The Professional Obligations of Classroom Teachers." In Spacks, *Advocacy in the Classroom,* 3–17.

Brenneman, Richard. "UC-BP Debate Reveals 'Two Cultures' Schism." *Berkeley Daily Planet,* April 13, 2007.

Brock, David. *The Republican Noise Machine: Right-Wing Media and How It Corrupts Democracy.* New York: Crown, 2004.

Brown v. Armenti. 247 F.3d 69 (3rd Cir. 2001).

Burgan, Mary. "Save Tenure Now." *Academe,* September–October 2008, 31–33.

Butler, Judith. "Academic Norms, Contemporary Challenges: A Reply to Robert Post on Academic Freedom." In Beshara Doumani, ed., *Academic Freedom after September 11,* 107–42. New York: Zone Books, 2006.

Carvalho, Edward J., and David B. Downing, eds. "Academic Freedom and Intellectual Activism in the Post-9/11 University." Special issue, *Works and Days* 51–54 (2008–2009).

Chait, Richard, ed. *The Questions of Tenure.* Cambridge, Mass.: Harvard University Press, 2002.

Chait, Richard, and Cathy Trower. "Where Tenure Does Not Reign: Colleges with Contract Systems." Washington, DC: American Association for Higher Education, New Pathways Working Paper Series, 1997.

Challenges for Governance: A National Report. Los Angeles: Center for Higher Education Policy Analysis, 2003.

Cheyfitz, Eric. "Framing Ward Churchill: The Political Construction of Research Misconduct." In Carvalho and Downing, "Academic Freedom and Intellectual Activism in the Post-9/11 University," 231–52.

Churchill, Ward. "The Myth of Academic Freedom: Experiencing the Application of Liberal Principle in a Neoconservative Era." In Carvalho and Downing, "Academic Freedom and Intellectual Activism in the Post-9/11 University," 139–230.

Clements, Kate. "UI Prohibits E-mail Politics: Officials Say New Rule Codifies Old Practice." *News-Gazette,* September 17, 2004, 1, 8.

Connick v. Myers. 461 U.S. 138 (1983).

Creeley, William. "Students Walk Out at UCSD as Dismissal of TAs Raises Academic Freedom Concerns." FIRE's The Torch weblog. May 30, 2007. Available at www.thefire.org/index.php/article/8105.html.

Cross, John C., and Edie N. Goldenberg. *Off-Track Profs: Nontenured Teachers in Higher Education.* Cambridge, MA: MIT Press, 2009.

Delbanco, Andrew. *Melville: His World and Work.* New York: Knopf, 2005.

Des Garennes, Christine. "New UI Research Facility Opens in Singapore." *News-Gazette,* February 13, 2009, A5.

Donoghue, Frank. *The Last Professors: The Corporate University and the Fate of the Humanities.* New York: Fordham University Press, 2008.

Doumani, Beshara. "Between Coercion and Privatization: Academic Freedom in the Twenty-First Century." In Beshara Doumani, ed., *Academic Freedom after September 11,* 11–57. New York: Zone Books, 2006.

Dudzic, Mark, and Adolph Reed, Jr. "Free Higher Ed!" *Nation,* February 2, 2004.

Duncan, Robert. "Up Rising." In *Bending the Bow.* New York: New Directions, 1968.

Duryea, E. D., and Robert S. Fisk, eds. *Faculty Unions and Collective Bargaining.* San Francisco: Jossey-Bass, 1973.

Edwards v. California University of Pennsylvania. 156 F.3d 488 (3rd Cir. 1998).

Eisenberg, Daniel. "United Faculty of Florida." *Journal of Hispanic Philology* 11 (1987): 97–101.

Farrell, Nick. "Singapore Government Attacked for Bullying a Blogster." *Inquirer* (London), May 10, 2005.

Finkelstein, Norman G. "Civility and Academic Life." In Carvalho and Downing, "Academic Freedom and Intellectual Activism in the Post-9/11 University," 291–305.

Finkin, Matthew W. "The Tenure System." In A. L. Deneef, C. D. Goodwin, and E. S. McCrate, eds., *The Academic's Handbook,* 86–100. Durham, N.C.: Duke University Press, 1988.

Finkin, Matthew W., and Emanuel Donchin. "Tenure's Rationale and Results." *Chronicle of Higher Education,* May 30, 2007.

Finkin, Matthew W., and Robert C. Post. *For the Common Good: Principles of American Academic Freedom.* New Haven, Conn.: Yale University Press, 2009.

Fish, Stanley. "George W. Bush and Melville's Ahab: Discuss!" *New York Times,* October 21, 2007. Available at http://fish.blogs.nytimes.com/2007/10/21/george-w-bush-and-melvilles-ahab-discuss/.

———. *Save the World on Your Own Time.* New York: Oxford University Press, 2008.

———. *There's No Such Thing as Free Speech and It's a Good Thing, Too.* New York: Oxford University Press, 1994.

———. "Ward Churchill Redux." *New York Times,* April 5, 2009.

Foster, Andrea L. "U of Illinois Administrators Ask Professor to Remove Web Site about Diploma Mills." *Chronicle of Higher Education,* October 13, 2003.

Friedman, Thomas L. *The World Is Flat: A Brief History of the Twenty-First Century.* New York: Farrar, Straus and Giroux, 2005.

Fukuyama, Francis. "Why We Should Get Rid of Tenure." *Washington Post,* April 19, 2009.

Garbarino, Joseph W. "Emergence of Collective Bargaining." In Duryea and Fisk, *Faculty Unions and Collective Bargaining,* 1–19.

Garcetti v. Ceballos. 126 S.C. 1951 (2006).

Gerber, Larry. "Defending Shared Governance." *Change* 39 (September–October 2007): 5–6.

———. "Inextricably Linked: Shared Governance and Academic Freedom." *Academe,* May–June 2001, 22–24.

Gerstmann, Evan, and Matthew J. Streb, eds. *Academic Freedom at the Dawn of a New Century: How Terrorism, Governments, and Culture Wars Impact Free Speech.* Stanford, Calif.: Stanford University Press, 2006.

Giroux, Henry A., and Susan Searls Giroux. *Take Back Higher Education: Race, Youth, and the Crisis of Democracy in the Post–Civil Rights Era.* New York: Palgrave Macmillan, 2004.

Gomez, Manuel N. "Inquiry, Respect, and Dissent." *Academe,* July–August 2006, 55–57.

Gorenberg, Gershom. "The War to Begin All Wars." *New York Review of Books,* May 28, 2009, 38–41.

Graff, Gerald. *Beyond the Culture Wars: How Teaching the Conflicts Can Revitalize American Education.* New York: Norton, 1993.

Greenhouse, Stephen. *The Big Squeeze: Tough Times for the American Worker.* New York: Knopf, 2008.

Gumport, Patricia J., and Daniel J. Julius. "Graduate Assistants' Bargaining." In Benjamin and Mauer, eds., *Academic Collective Bargaining,* 52–63.

Gurman, Hannah. "Class, Culture, and the University in Decline." *minnesota review* 71–72 (Winter–Spring 2009): 308–18.

Harding, Jeremy. "Call Me Ahab." *London Review of Books* 24:21 (October 31, 2002). Available online at http://www.lrb.co.uk/v24/n21/hard01_html.

Hearn, Alison. "Exploits in the Undercommons." Paper presented at Academic Labor/Freedom conference, Nonstop Liberal Arts Institute, June 2009.

Hess, John ["Contingent"]. Posting to Contingent Academics listserv, February 26, 2009.

Hoeller, Keith. "Adjunct Professors Need Their Own Union." *Seattle Post-Intelligencer,* February 11, 2009.

Hofstadter, Richard, and Walter P. Metzger. *The Development of Academic Freedom in the United States.* New York: Columbia University Press, 1955.

Honan, William H. "University of Minnesota Regents Drop Effort to Modify Tenure." *New York Times,* November 17, 1996.

Hong v. Grant. 516 F.Supp.2d 1158 (S.D. Cal. 2007).

Horowitz, David. *The Professors: The 101 Most Dangerous Academics in America.* Washington, D.C.: Regnery, 2006.

Horowitz, David, and Jacob Laksin. *One-Party Classroom: How Radical Professors at America's Top Colleges Indoctrinate Students and Undermine Our Democracy.* New York: Crown Forum, 2009.

Hulbert, Claude, and Anestine Hector Mason. "Exporting the 'Violence of Literacy': Education According to UNESCO and the World Bank." *Composition Forum* 16 (Fall 2006). Available at http://compositionforum.com/issue/16/.

Human Rights Watch. "Reading between the 'Red Lines': The Repression of Academic Freedom in Egyptian Universities." 2005. Available at http://www.hrw.org/en/reports/2005/06/08/reading-between-red-lines-repression-academic-freedom-egyptian-universities.

Hutcheson, Philo A. *A Professional Professoriate: Unionization, Bureaucratization, and the AAUP.* Nashville: Vanderbilt University Press, 2000.

Jacoby, Dan. "The Effects of Part-Time Faculty Employment upon Community College Graduation Rates." *Journal of Higher Education* 77:6 (November–December 2006): 1081–1103.

Jaeger, Audrey J. "Contingent Faculty and Student Outcomes." *Academe,* November–December 2008.

Jaschik, Scott. "Beware the Button Police." *Inside Higher Education,* September 24, 2008.

———. "Crossing a Line." *Inside Higher Education,* April 23, 2009.

———. "Hoover in the Heartland." *Inside Higher Education,* September 20, 2007.

———. "Michigan Severs Ties to Controversial Publisher." *Inside Higher Education,* June 18, 2008.

———. "A Moderate MLA." *Inside Higher Education,* December 31, 2007.

———. "New Ideas on Grad Students, Unions." *Inside Higher Education,* April 20, 2009.

———. "Return of Grad Union Movement." *Inside Higher Education,* January 28, 2009.

Jones, P. "World Bank Financing of Education: Lending Learning, and Development." *Comparative Education Review* 40:1 (1992): 86–89.

Keyishan v. Board of Regents. 385 U.S. 589 (1967).

Kramer, Jane. "The Petition: Israel, Palestine, and a Tenure Battle at Barnard." *New Yorker,* April 14, 2008, 50–59.

Krause, Monika, Mary Nolan, Michael Palm, and Andrew Ross, eds. *The University against Itself: The NYU Strike and the Future of the Academic Workplace.* Philadelphia: Temple University Press, 2008.

Krieger, Zvika. "The Emir of NYU." *New York,* April 13, 2008. Available at www.nymag.com.

Kuehn, Larry. "The Education World Is Not Flat: Neoliberalism's Global Project and Teacher Unions' Transnational Resistance." In Mary Compton and Lois Weiner, eds., *The Global Assault on Teaching, Teachers, and Their Unions,* 53–72. New York: Palgrave Macmillan, 2008.

Kuh, George. "What We're Learning about Student Engagement from NSSE." *Change* 35:2 (2003): 24–32.

Kurland, Jordan E. "Implementing AAUP Standards." *Academe,* December 1980, 414–18.

Lee, Barbara A. *Collective Bargaining in Four-Year Colleges: Impact on Institutional Practice.* AAHE-ERIC Higher Education Research Report 5. Washington, D.C.: AAHE, 1978.

Lieberwitz, Risa L. "Faculty in the Corporate University: Professional Identity, Law, and Collective Action." *Cornell Journal of Law and Public Policy* 16:2 (Spring 2007): 263–330.

Longmate, Jack, and Frank Cosco. "Part-Time Instructors Deserve Equal Pay for Equal Work." *Chronicle of Higher Education: The Chronicle Review,* May 3, 2002, B14.

Lowell, Robert. *Interviews and Memoirs.* Ed. Jeffrey Meyers. Ann Arbor: University of Michigan Press, 1988.

Maternowski, Kate. "Blago-Style Admissions." *Inside Higher Education,* June 1, 2009.

Mauer, Michael. "Prospects." In Benjamin and Mauer, *Academic Collective Bargaining,* 386–90.

McClennen, Sophia A. "Neoliberalism and the Crisis of Intellectual Engagement." In Carvalho and Downing, "Academic Freedom and Intellectual Activism in the Post-9/11 University," 459–70.

Menand, Louis. "The Limits of Academic Freedom." In Louis Menand, ed., *The Future of Academic Freedom,* 3–20. Chicago: University of Chicago Press, 1996.

Messer-Davidow, Ellen. "Caught in the Crunch." In Carvalho and Downing, "Academic Freedom and Intellectual Activism in the Post-9/11 University," 399–419.

Metzger, Walter. *Academic Freedom in the Age of the University.* New York: Columbia University Press, 1955.

Morris, Benny. "From Dove to Hawk." *Newsweek,* May 8, 2008, 28.

National Center for Education Statistics. Table 20. In *Supplemental Table Update.* Washington, D.C.: NCES, May 2007.

Nealon, Jeffrey. "The Economics of Academic Freedom." Paper presented at the Academic Freedom conference, Cornell University, February 2009.

Nelson, Cary. "Higher Education and September 11." *Cultural Studies–Critical Methodologies,* May 2002, 191–96.

———. *Manifesto of a Tenured Radical.* New York: New York University Press, 1997.

———. "Solidarity." *Inside Higher Education,* September 12, 2006.

———. "Whose Academic Freedom?" *Academe,* July–August 2009, 54–55.

———, ed. *Will Teach for Food: Academic Labor in Crisis.* Minneapolis: University of Minnesota Press, 1997.

Nelson, Cary, and Stephen Watt. *Academic Keywords: A Devil's Dictionary for Higher Education.* New York: Routledge, 1999.

———. *Office Hours: Activism and Change in the Academy.* New York: Routledge, 2004.

Oliver, Cindy. "Globalization." Paper presented at the COCAL VIII conference, San Diego State University, August 2008.

O'Neil, Robert. *Academic Freedom in the Wired World: Political Extremism, Corporate Power, and the University.* Cambridge, Mass.: Harvard University Press, 2008.

———. "The Post-9/11 University: It Could Have Been Much Worse." In Carvalho and Downing, "Academic Freedom and Intellectual Activism in the Post-9/11 University," 519–25.

Pickering v. Board of Education. 391 U.S. 563 (1968).

Pincoffs, Edmund L., ed. *The Concept of Academic Freedom.* Austin: University of Texas Press, 1972.

Pollitt, Daniel H., and Jordan E. Kurland. "Entering the Academic Freedom Arena Running: The AAUP's First Year." *Academe*, July–August 1998, 45–52.

Post, Robert. "The Structure of Academic Freedom." In Beshara Doumani, ed., *Academic Freedom after September 11*, 61–106. New York: Zone Books, 2006.

Prendergast, Cathy, and Sam Nelson. "Murderabilia Inc.: Where the First Amendment Fails Academic Freedom." Paper presented at the Academic Freedom conference, Cornell University, February 2009.

Rabban, David. "A Functional Analysis of 'Individual' and 'Institutional' Academic Freedom under the First Amendment." In William W. Van Alstyne, ed., "Freedom and Tenure in the Academy: The Fiftieth Anniversary of the 1940 Statement of Principles." Special issue of *Law and Contemporary Problems* 53:3 (Summer 1990): 227–301.

Ramos, Arturo. "Globalization." Paper presented at the COCAL VIII conference, San Diego State University, August 2008.

Readings, Bill. *The University in Ruins.* Cambridge, Mass.: Harvard University Press, 1996.

Redden, Elizabeth. "Failures of Leadership." *Inside Higher Education*, April 24, 2008.

——. "Inquiry or Indoctrination?" *Inside Higher Education*, May 3, 2007.

——. "On Israel, Shifted Ground." *Inside Higher Education*, March 6, 2009.

——. "Threats to Rare Resource for Humanists." *Inside Higher Education*, March 15, 2007.

Rhoades, Gary. *Managed Professionals: Unionized Faculty and Restructuring Academic Labor.* Albany: State University of New York Press, 1998.

Robbins, Bruce. "Outside Pressures." In Carvalho and Downing, "Academic Freedom and Intellectual Activism in the Post-9/11 University," 339–45.

Rolfe, Edwin. *Collected Poems.* Ed. Cary Nelson and Jefferson Hendricks. Urbana: University of Illinois Press, 1993.

Rorty, Richard. "Does Academic Freedom Have Philosophical Presuppositions?" In Louis Menand, ed., *The Future of Academic Freedom*, 21–42. Chicago: University of Chicago Press, 1996.

Ross, Andrew. "Global U." *Inside Higher Education*, February 15, 2008.

Rothberg, Michael. *Multidirectional Memory: Remembering the Holocaust in the Age of Decolonization.* Stanford, Calif.: Stanford University Press, 2009.

Rothberg, Michael, and Peter K. Garrett. *Cary Nelson and the Struggle for the University: Poetry, Politics, and the Profession.* Albany: State University of New York Press, 2009.

Rutgers, the State University, Zoran Gijac, Karen Thompson, and Richard Moser. "Teaching at Rutgers:

A Proposal to Convert Part-Time to Full-Time Appointments and Instructional Full-Time Non–Tenure Track Appointments to Tenure Track Appointments." Available at http://senate.rutgers.edu/ContingentFacultyProposal_KThompson090507.pdf.

Schibik, Timothy, and Charles Harrington. "Part-Time Faculty Utilization and Departmental Academic Vitality." *Department Chair* 13:1 (2002): 17–19.

Schmidt, Jeff. *Disciplined Minds: A Critical Look at Salaried Professionals and the Soul-Battering System That Shapes Their Minds.* Lanham, Md.: Roman & Littlefield, 2000.

Scholtz, Greg. "What Is Shared Governance Anyway?" AAUP archives, unpublished paper, 2007.

Schrecker, Ellen. *No Ivory Tower: McCarthyism and the Universities.* New York: Oxford University Press, 1986.

———. "Ward Churchill at the Dalton Trumbo Fountain: Academic Freedom in the Aftermath of 9/11." *AAUP Journal of Academic Freedom,* forthcoming.

Scott, Joan W. "Academic Freedom as an Ethical Practice." In Louis Menand, ed., *The Future of Academic Freedom,* 163–80. Chicago: University of Chicago Press, 1996.

———. "The Critical State of Shared Governance." *Academe,* July–August 2002, 41–48.

Shaull, Richard. Foreword to *Pedagogy of the Oppressed,* by Paulo Freire, 30th anniversary edition. New York: Continuum, 2000. Foreword written in 1994.

Sinder, Janet. "Academic Freedom: A Bibliography." In William W. Van Alstyne, ed., "Freedom and Tenure in the Academy: The Fiftieth Anniversary of the 1940 Statement of Principles." Special issue of *Law and Contemporary Problems* 53:3 (Summer 1990): 381–92.

Smith, Stacy E. "Who Owns Academic Freedom? The Standard for Academic Free Speech at Public Universities." *Washington and Lee Law Review* 59 (2002): 299–360.

Sniderman, Paul M. "Two Theories of Self-Censorship." In Gerstmann and Streb, *Academic Freedom at the Dawn of a New Century,* 157–74.

Spacks, Patricia Meyer, ed. *Advocacy in the Classroom: Problems and Possibilities.* New York: St. Martin's, 1996.

Standing Committee on Research Misconduct. "Report of the Investigative Committee of the Standing Committee on Research Misconduct at the University of Colorado at Boulder Concerning Allegations of Academic Misconduct against Professor Ward Churchill." May 9, 2006. Available at http://www.colorado.edu/news/reports/churchill/download/WardChurchillReport.pdf.

Stork, Joe. "Academic Freedom and the International Perspective." Paper presented at the Academic Freedom conference, New York University, April 2009.

Strossen, Nadine. "First Amendment and Civil Liberties Traditions of

Academic Freedom." In Spacks, ed., *Advocacy in the Classroom,* 71–83.

Strum, Philippa. "Why Academic Freedom? The Theoretical and Constitutional Context." In Beshara Doumani, ed., *Academic Freedom after September 11,* 143–72. New York: Zone Books, 2006.

Tait, Robert. "Iranian President Calls for Purge of Liberal Lecturers." *Guardian,* September 6, 2006, International News Section, p. 14.

Taylor, Mark C. "End the University as We Know It." *New York Times,* April 27, 2009, A23.

Tirelli, Vinnie. "The State of the Profession." Paper presented at the COCAL VIII conference, San Diego State University, August 2008.

Treanor, Paul. "Neoliberalism: Origins, Theory, Definition." 2005. Available at http://web.inter.nl.net/users/Paul.Treanor/neoliberalism.html.

Treichler, Paula. "Antioch: Report from Ground Zero." *Inside Higher Education,* July 10, 2008.

Trentelman, Charles F., and Brooke Nelson. "Adjunct Professors May See Cut in Pay at Weber State." *Standard-Examiner,* March 1, 2009.

Urofsky v. Gilmore. 216 F.3d 401 (4th Cir. 2000).

Van Alstyne, William W. "Academic Freedom and the First Amendment in the Supreme Court of the United States: An Unhurried View." In William W. Van Alstyne, ed., "Freedom and Tenure in the Academy: The Fiftieth Anniversary of the 1940 Statement of Principles."

Special issue of *Law and Contemporary Problems* 53:3 (Summer 1990): 79–154.

Warren, Cat. "The *Chronicle,* the Professoriate, and the AAUP." *Academe,* May–June 2008, 29–32.

Washburn, Jennifer. "Academic Capitalism and the Commodification of Knowledge." Paper presented at the Academic Freedom conference, New York University, April 2009.

Watkins, Evan, ed. *South Atlantic Quarterly* 108:4 (Fall 2009). Special issue on academic freedom.

West, Andrew F. "What Is Academic Freedom?" In Walter P. Metzger, ed., *The American Concept of Academic Freedom in Formation: A Collection of Essays and Reports,* 432–44. New York: Arno, 1977. Reprinted with original pagination from the *North American Review* (1885).

Whitehead, Fred. *KU Confidential.* 2002. Available from the author at fredwh@swbell.net.

———. "'Reallocation' at the University of Kansas School of Medicine: A Pathological Case History." *Workplace* 4:2 (February 2002). Available at http://louisville.edu/journal/workplace/whitehead.html.

Wilhelm, John. "A Short History of Unionization at Yale." In Nelson, *Will Teach for Food,* 35–43.

Williams, Jeffrey J. "Academic Bondage." In Carvalho and Downing, "Academic Freedom and Intellectual Activism in the Post-9/11 University," 421–36.

Wilson, Robin. "The AAUP, 92 and Ailing." *Chronicle of Higher Education,* June 8, 2007.

———. "Using New Policy, Students Complain about Classroom Bias on 2 Pa. Campuses." *Chronicle of Higher Education,* July 23, 2008.

Wood, Paul. "Documents Show Negotiations, Influence on UI Admissions." *News-Gazette,* June 26, 2009, 1, 8.

———. "Faculty Favor Restructuring Global Campus." *News-Gazette,* May 2, 2009, 1, 10.

Wood, Peter W., and Stephen H. Balch. "A Response to the AAUP's Report 'Freedom in the Classroom.'" NAS website, September 21, 2007. http://209.123.244.94/polArticles. cfm?Doc_Id=32.

Working, Russell. "Bogus Diploma Ring Busted with Help from UI Professor." *Chicago Tribune,* August 4, 2008.

Wright, David. "Creative Nonfiction and the Academy: A Cautionary Tale." *Qualitative Inquiry* 10:2 (2004): 202–6.

ABOUT THE AUTHOR

Cary Nelson is the national president of the American Association of University Professors (AAUP) and Jubilee Professor of Liberal Arts and Sciences at the University of Illinois at Urbana-Champaign. Among his twenty-five books are *Manifesto of a Tenured Radical,* also published by NYU Press, *and Revolutionary Memory: Recovering the Poetry of the American Left.* His work and career are the subject of *Cary Nelson and the Struggle for the University* (2009).